Essays on The Bhagavadgita

By Jayaram V

Published by
Pure Life Vision LLC
New Albany, Ohio

Essays on the Bhagavadgita

Copyright © 2012 by Jayaram V. All rights reserved.
Published and Distributed Worldwide by Pure Life Vision LLC., USA.
First edition 2012

This book is copyrighted under International and Pan American conventions. Printed in the USA. All rights reserved. No part of this publication may be reproduced stored in a retrieval system, or transmitted in any form or by any means, electronic, mechanical, photocopying, recording, scanning or otherwise, without the prior written permission of the publisher or the author. Requests to the publisher for permission or for bulk purchase of the book should be made online at http://www.PureLifeVision.com.

Limit of Liability/Disclaimer of Warranty: While the publisher and the author have used their best efforts in preparing this book, they make no representation or warranties with respect to the accuracy or completeness of the contents of this book and specifically disclaim any implied warranties of merchantability or fitness for particular purpose. No warranty may be created or extended by sales representatives or written sales materials. The advice and strategies contained herein may not be suitable for your situation. You should consult with a professional where appropriate. Neither the publisher nor author shall be liable for any loss of profit or any other commercial damages, including but not limited to special, incidental, consequential or other damages.

Pure Life Vision books and products are available through many bookstores and online websites. For Enquiries Please visit http://www.PureLifeVision.com.

Publisher Cataloging-in-Publication Data

V, Jayaram, (Vemulapalli)
Essays on the Bhagavadgita
       p. cm
       Includes bibliographical references
       ISBN- 13: 978-1-935760-09-2
       ISBN -10: 1935760092
       1. Bhagavadgītā--Criticism, interpretation, etc. 2. Bhagavadgita--Philosophy. 3. Bhagavadgita--Ethics. 4. Bhagavadgita--Study and teaching. I. Title

       BL1138.66.V15 2012
       294.5/924— dc22   2011913516

Printed in the United States of America
10 9 8 7 6 5 4 3 2 1
First Edition

Essays on the Bhagavadgita

By Jayaram V

ALSO BY JAYARAM V

1. Think Success: A Collection of Writings on Success and Achievement through Positive Thinking, Volume I
2. Think Success: A Collection of Writings on Success and Achievement through Positive Thinking, Volume II
3. Think Success: A Collection of Writings on Success and Achievement through Positive Thinking, Combined Volume
4. The Awakened Life: A Collection of Writings on Spiritual Life
5. Brahman
6. The Bhagavadgita Complete Translation
7. The Bhagavadgita: Simple Translation

FORTHCOMING

1. Introduction to Hinduism
2. The Yogasutras of Patanjali
3. Selected Upanishads: Translation and Notes

Contents

Introduction 1
The Status of the Bhagavadgita in the Sacred Literature 15
A Summary of the Bhagavadgita 22
The Meaning of Yoga in the Context of the Bhagavadgita 41
Five Lessons from the Bhagavadgita 46
Karma Yoga – the Path of Action 56
References to Karmayoga in the Bhagavadgita 64
Jnanayoga – The Path of Knowledge 70
Knowledge as the Means and the Goal 77
Buddhiyoga – The State of Wisdom and Discernment 81
Bhaktiyoga – The Yoga of Devotion 86
Maya – The Illusion of things 95
The True Meaning of Bhakti 107
Lessons from the Bhagavadgita for the Modern People 110
The Endearing Qualities of a Devotee 116
Atmayoga, Realizing the Self by the Self 121
Transforming the Physical Self 125
Stable Mind and Self-Realization 132
Purusha and Prakriti 141
Conquering the Ego, the False Self 147
The Divine Qualities of a Sattvic Person 154
Demonic Qualities of the Wicked 160
The Body as a Vehicle of Self-realization 169
Making Sense of the Senses 177
Descriptions of the Self 183
The Wisdom of the Bhagavadgita 191
The Triple Gunas 201
The Yoga of Sorrow 207
The Causes of Suffering 213
The Purpose of Sorrow 217
The Resolution of Sorrow 221
The Symbolism of Arjuna's Sorrow 225
The True Meaning of Renunciation 229
Symbolism in the Bhagavadgita 233

The Bhagavadgita in Daily Life 246
Bibliography 255

Vasudeva sutam devam
Kamsa-Chanoora mardanam
Devaki parama-anandam
Krishnam vande Jagatgurum

To Lord Krishna

Glorious God, son of *Vasudeva*
Slayer of *Kamsa* and *Charoona*
Source of great joy to Mother *Devaki*
Salutations to Lord Krishna, the World Teacher

Introduction

The Gita is not meant for any one person or creed or nation; it is meant for humanity. It speaks to a mind that has fought in life, a mind that is dissatisfied with constant want, a mind that is alert and thinking, and that has many conflicts. - - Swami Dayananda[1]

The *Bhagavadgita* is one of the most ancient religious scriptures of the world. It contains profound philosophical truths, representing "not any sect of Hinduism but Hinduism as a whole[2]." Disparate traditions and paths of the ancient world are finely integrated into a harmonious and meaningful philosophy in the form of a lengthy discourse and a divine revelation. In many ways, the scripture reflects the internal reform and revival that took place within the Vedic tradition, which contributed in no small measure to the survival and continuity of Hinduism later on. It is presented to us as a dialogue between Lord *Krishna*, the Supreme Self, and his dearest devotee in the person of *Arjuna*, a great warrior, and one of five the *Pandavas* of the epic *Mahabharata*. The discourse was composed originally in Sanskrit, but today its translations are available in almost every language. We do not know its exact antiquity. However, one of the popular opinions holds that its rendering in the current format was certainly pre-Christian and prior to the invasion of Alexander. Its religious and historical significance is intimately associated with the life and glory of Lord *Krishna*, who played a crucial role in the epic events of the *Mahabharata* and who is worshipped by millions of Hindus all over the world with love and devotion.

The historicity of Lord Krishna is uncertain. We have divergent opinions about His status as a divinity in our pantheon. In the *Vedas*, you do not find any hymns addressed to Him directly. Our *Puranas* affirm that Lord *Vishnu*, the *Isvara* of the manifested worlds, incarnated upon earth in the form of Lord *Krishna* to root out evil and establish dharma or righteousness upon earth. However, some ardent devotees of Lord Krishna do not consider

Him an incarnation of Lord *Vishnu*, but the Universal Self Himself who manifested upon earth to restore *dharma*. According to them, Lord Krishna represents Krishna consciousness, which is nothing but the universal consciousness from which emerge all the worlds and the entire creation. He is the universal Lord, with a universal form of infinite proportions. In His role as the preserver and upholder of *dharma*, He participated actively in the affairs of ancient India during the *Mahabharata* times and left behind a great legacy of His teachings in the form of the *Bhagavadgita* for the benefit of future generations. The scripture is truly an icon of the eternal religion (*Sanatanadharma*), with a universal appeal, showing the way to people to live righteously in a world that is characterized by ignorance, materialism, delusion and darkness, and resolve their existential suffering through self-transformation and the help of God.

The teachings

The *Bhagavadgita* portrays in many ways the core beliefs and practices of Hinduism. It reflects its universality and the ideal vision of God as the center and circumference of all creation. If Hinduism is a way of life, the *Bhagavadgita* suggests how to live it. Its principles and doctrines are not easy to practice. They challenge to the core your resolve and commitment to follow a disciplined and virtuous life that guarantees freedom and bliss. Its message simple, sacrifice your desires; but it is very difficult to practice because desires manifest numerously in our consciousness and we are not always aware of them. It exhorts those who are thirsty of knowledge to live selflessly and virtuously with faith, knowledge, wisdom, devotion, surrender, and detachment, and perform their duties dispassionately as an offering to God. This is in contrast to the egocentric worldly life, with which we are familiar and in which we pursue our desires rather selfishly as part of our conditioning and self-promotion. The *Bhagavadgita* tells us how to attain peace and stability, instead of strife and suffering, and live freely and fearlessly, without striving and without searching for happiness in worldly things and without suffering from the attraction or aversion to the pairs of opposites. The book is a discourse of immense spiritual value. It inspires those who are engaged in their daily battles and who want permanent solutions, like *Arjuna* himself, to resolve their problems and overcome their limitations, without ignoring their duties and responsibilities and without compromising their core values and beliefs.

The scripture is not difficult to understand; but it has some complexity, which can be overcome with effort. It has an infinite capacity to reveal itself to the extent you probe into its depths. With each reading, you learn more and develop newer insights. By studying it regularly, we can transcend our limitations and learn to live with humility, knowledge, wisdom and discernment. We can learn to live responsibly and dutifully, performing our obligatory duties, without losing our inner balance and without suffering from the consequences of our own actions. From its study, we realize how one can escape from the shackles of *karma* not by inaction, not by shunning one's responsibilities, not even by doing only the so-called good deeds, but by offering all actions to *Isvara*, as if one does not exist at all, attributing the doership and ownership to Him and renouncing the fruit of one's actions. In short, if you follow the scripture, you learn to live with real freedom as if your life is a great sacrifice with *Isvara* as the Sacrificer, the Sacrificed and the Witness.

The *Bhagavadgita* is a book of self-discovery and an inward journey towards liberation and the Abode of God. It deals with the essential truths regarding life and reality, the nature of our existence and our relationship with the God. It explains how our desire-ridden actions cause suffering and bondage and how one may escape from the hold of Nature through knowledge, devotion and selfless actions. It touches upon many subjects such as the importance of discernment and detachment, the perils of desire-ridden actions, the nature of our existence, the triple *gunas*, the practice of yoga, the meaning and importance of true devotion, the right attitude one should cultivate towards the dualities of life, the meaning and purpose of *maya* or delusion and so on. It explains the difference between the body and the Self, between action and inaction, between knowledge and ignorance, between heavenly life and immortal life, and between divine and demonic qualities.

The scripture provides guidance to those who want to control their desires and achieve liberation through renunciation and detachment. In eighteen chapters, it covers a wide spectrum of spiritual subjects. In the second chapter, Lord *Krishna* explains how contact between the senses and sense objects leads to attachment and how from attachment delusion arises, resulting in bondage and suffering. He reminds Arjuna that the body is like a garment, which is destructible and discarded by the soul from time to time during its existence upon earth under the control of Nature. He draws a clear distinction between the physical self (*jiva*) and the inner Self (*atma*) and reminds him that he should not worry about the destruction that was going to happen in the war because the Self could neither be killed nor destroyed.

From the *Gita* we learn that the source of *karma* lies not in actions but in the desire for the fruit of our actions. Therefore, one should not abandon actions but desire for their result. Renunciation is not an escape from duty and responsibility but a means to overcome attachment and egocentric actions. Since one cannot remain free from actions even for a moment, one needs to perform them always, offering their result to God who is the real Doer. When you do not live for yourself, God takes over your life and your responsibilities. When you live here as if you do not exist, your actions will not bind you. It is much better if you live here for the sake of others, as a service to God. It is part of a covenant between God and His devotees. It is a way out of the binding and deluding mechanism He Himself creates with His Nature. When people live for themselves, God remains in the background as a Witness, letting them live according to their likes and dislikes. When they themselves become passive witnesses and live for God sacrificing their desires and interests, He reciprocates with unconditional love and takes care of their welfare and liberation. This is not like a king bestowing his favors upon a few loyal subjects. The scripture states clearly that God has no particular interest in favoring a few who show Him loyalty. His mercy (*prasadam*) is part of a set of rules (*dharma*) that govern our lives. What bind men to this world are egoism, selfishness, desires, delusion, pride, lack of discernment, demonic qualities and the impurities of *rajas* and *tamas*. When they are gradually eliminated from one's character through austerities and the practice of yoga, one experiences peace, stability, equanimity, sameness and inner harmony.

According to the *Bhagavadgita* the external world is unreal not because it does not exist, but because it is unstable and ever changing. The reality that you perceive is set of independent circumstances that create in you the illusion of continuity and meaningful experience, where as in reality they are different perceptions and phenomena, which your mind joins to make sense of them just as it mentally connects distant dots on a paper to create the illusion of a meaningful form. Since it is not true except as an illusion and keeps changing from moment to moment, you cannot live in it with peace and stability unless you cultivate discernment and deal with it with detachment and sameness. Our knowledge arising from our perceptions and our interactions with the objective world is imperfect and incomplete. It is not true wisdom (jnanam), which leads to liberation. It is cleverness (*vijnanam*) that helps think for ourselves and adapt to the ever-changing circumstances according to our desires and preferences. What we consider knowledge is in truth ignorance because it does not take us beyond the illusion of appearances; rather it involves us with it deeply and makes our escape even more difficult. We cannot rely upon it truly to regulate our lives or find permanent solutions to the problems in our lives. We cannot also rely upon our perceptions or trust our senses fully because they are guided by our desires and inherent tendencies (*prvrittis*) rather than the reality of the world. They can only see the surface of things, instead of what is hidden and imperceptible. The knowledge that we accumulate through them is a mental construct, or an illusory formation, colored by our desires and predominant *gunas*. The world that we perceive through them is also essentially an illusion of our minds. It does not necessarily correspond to the truth or reality of the world itself. In many ways, it is a product of our delusion and ignorance, whereby we mistake truth for falsehood, the body for the Self, impermanence for permanence and bondage for freedom. The phenomenal world is subject to change and impermanence and our likes and dislikes. It is always in a state of flux just as our minds are. We cannot rely upon it to secure peace or happiness. We are bound to suffer if we cling to things that are impermanent and destructible. He who craves for material things in search of happiness suffers from the duality of gain and loss and rarely experiences peace.

Therefore, the *Bhagavadgita* suggests that we should seek permanent solutions to the transience of life, not by changing the world but by withdrawing from it and changing ourselves, overcoming our self-seeking attitude and our attachment to it. To escape from the illusion of your worldly experiences, you must take refuge in your inner Self, which is eternal, permanent and free from modifications. For that to happen, you must withdraw your mind and senses into your inner Self and escape from the illusions of the world. Through yoga, you have to remove the obstacles that stand between your physical Self and your spiritual Self and establish peace. Only when you silence your ego and your craving, you can see your real Self through the prism of your pure consciousness. The obstacles to peace and stability are ignorance, delusion, desires and egoism. They are the impurities arising from the *gunas* to which we all are subject. To overcome them or suppress them, a seeker has to practice self-discipline and restrain his mind and body until he develops *sattva*. He should free his mind from past life impressions and arrest the continuing cycle of karma. When they come to rest, a yogi rests in the peace of his own mind. In that stillness and self-absorption, he realizes that his life upon earth has all along been a mental construction and he was caught in an illusion of modifications and experiences.

The three secrets

In the eighteenth chapter of the scripture, Lord *Krishna* informs *Arjuna* that He taught him the most secret knowledge, which should not be imparted to those who were not austere, who lacked devotion, who had no interest to listen and who spoke ill of God. Hidden within the secret knowledge of the scripture are further secrets, discernible only to a few whose minds are pure and who are devoted to the knowledge of liberation. Among them, three are worth mentioning. They also constitute its core teachings.

Stick to your duty: The first one is you must do your duty according to your inherent nature as determined by your *gunas*, not what you find convenient, profitable or socially popular. Doing your duty is better than doing the duties of others (*para dharma*), however good they may be, because it is deeply connected to your past. Your duty is determined by your past actions and you cannot resolve the *karma* arising from them unless you fulfill your current obligations. Performing the duties that are expected of us and that have become part of our destinies, we resolve the accumulated consequences of our past actions and pay off our past debts. Through desireless actions, we also transcend the very *gunas* that induce desire-ridden actions and contribute to our bondage and suffering. According to the *Bhagavadgita* duty is neither a problem nor a burden but an opportunity to free ourselves from the hold of Nature and attain liberation. While it is true that *karma* arises from actions, it is not actions but the desires that are hidden in actions, which are responsible for one's *karma* and which lead to one's bondage and suffering. The desires are in turn induced by the *gunas*. Therefore, the scripture says that to resolve the problem of *karma*, the *gunas* should be neutralized and silenced first. The *gunas* will come to rest if we perform our actions with detachment and dispassion, giving up the desire for their fruit. When we perform our actions in this manner, we arrest the accumulation of *karma* and the possibilities of next birth. Free from attraction and aversion to things, we become equal to the dualities of life and experience peace and equanimity within ourselves.

You are an eternal Self: The second secret is about the presence of the inner Self. We are essentially spiritual beings. We have an eternal aspect beyond the physical aspect. This because the Self exists in all. There are no exceptions. All living beings contain an individual Self (*atman*) hidden behind names and forms. Since it exists deep within the core of each being, as either a small dot or flame, beyond the mind and the senses, incomprehensible and imperceptible, it cannot be known through ordinary means. It can be known through transcendence only, in a state of unity that is similar to the state of deep sleep, but in which one is self-aware without the distinction of the knower and the known. We experience it usually in advanced stages of yoga, when we practice *samyama* and combine the best techniques of concentration (*dharana*), meditation (*dhyana*) and self-absorption (*samadhi*). Because of ignorance, duality and delusion, worldly people cannot discern the Self within them. Under the influence of their egos, they identify themselves with their names and forms. This subjects them to the modifications of the mind and body such as aging, death and rebirth.

The Self is real, eternal, indestructible, immutable and absolute. In its essence and essential nature, it is the same as *Isvara*, the Lord of the Universe, but in its embodied state, it is held in check by the modifications of Nature. The *Gita* says that to cultivate true wisdom and overcome our attachments we must know the difference between our physical and spiritual selves. The Self is different from the physical being. It is distinct and different from the realities (*tattvas*) of Nature and entirely free from change and impermanence, even though it is held in bondage by it. Two opposite polarities exist in you, one pure and the impure. To experience peace and balance, you have to bridge the gap between the two and make them indistinguishable. The highest state of yoga is when these two are in perfect union and identical (*samatvam*). The *Bhagavadgita* declares that the physical self is a friend of the Self and its enemy. It means we achieve peace and liberation only when we subordinate the needs of the physical self to the liberation of the inner Self and subject it to necessary transformation so that it has divine qualities and reflects the purity of *sattva*. When you are in harmony with your inner Self, you achieve liberation; when you are in conflict with it you increase your suffering and your ignorance and delusion. To establish inner harmony, one must not only sacrifice the interests of the lower for the sake of the higher, but also integrate one's whole personality around the latter.

All this is for the habitation of God: The third secret is about the omnipresence of God. The world throbs with life because of the presence of God. Whatever that moves here, whatever that happens here is because of Him. The whole world is His manifestation. He is hidden in every aspect of it. He is both the cause and the effect. He is also the Creator and the created. He envelops all and pervades all. He inhabits the worlds He manifests, and He maintains them, even though He is complete in all respects and has no interest or desire whatsoever. Entirely free and independent and with no support for Himself, He supports everything. Timeless, there was no time when He was non-existent and there will never be a time when He would not exist. Ignorant people may not recognize His greatness or His manifestations, but His devotees know His diverse manifestations (*vibhutis*) and supreme perfections (*siddhis*). One may worship other divinities, but only by worshipping Him, one attains liberation. Therefore, says the *Bhagavadgita*, one should live in this world with the awareness that all that exists here is but *Vasudeva*. Since He is the real Doer and the Supreme Controller, one must perform one's duty with humility, surrender, devotion and detachment, offering Him the fruit of one's actions. By performing actions in this manner and cultivating devotion, one earns the right to enter His Abode and live there eternally.

Thus, knowing your purpose here upon earth, knowing your spiritual identity and knowing your inherent relationship with God, you should live upon earth with the spirit of sacrifice as a responsible human being in the service of God. Knowing these three secrets, you can work for your liberation, practicing yoga with stability, balance and sameness. The three secrets are known respectively as *guhya* (secret), *guhyatara* (more secret) and *guhyatma* (most secret). The first one frees us from the cycle of *karma*; the second one from delusion and ignorance; and the third one from death and impermanence. The second, third, fourth, fifth and eighteenth chapters of the *Bhagavadgita* deal with the first secret; the second, sixth, thirteenth to eighteenth chapters deal with the second secret; while the third, seventh, eighth, ninth, and tenth to eighteenth chapters deal with the third secret.

Prasthanatraya

The *Bhagavadgita* played a key role in shaping our philosophical thought and heralded the rise and popularity of several schools of *Vaishnavism* that emphasized the importance of devotion (*bhakti*) in achieving liberation (*mukti*). It played a very significant role in the rise of devotional theism in Hinduism and contributed to its survival and continuity during the medieval period. Its teachings are used by scholars and devotees alike to widen their knowledge and delve deep into the depths of their own consciousness through devotion and meditation to understand the relationship between the individual Self and the universal Self and between the Ultimate Reality and the empirical reality with which we are familiar. It is considered one of the three most important scriptures (*prasthanatraya*) of Hinduism (*sanatanadharma*), the other two being the *Upanishads* and the *Brahmasutras*. Followers of various schools of Vedic thought (*Vedanta*) have been relying upon these three since earliest times to explain and justify their respective philosophies. If *Shankaracharya* found in them undeniable evidence to justify monism (*advaita*), *Ramanujacharya* used the same scriptures to justify his philosophy of qualified monism (*vishitadvaita*), while *Madhava* found ample justification in them to support his view that duality was inherent in the numerous forms and aspects of *Isvara* and His creation. Apart from them, there were others such as *Nimbarka* (A.D.1162) the proponent of dual and non-dual doctrine (*dvaita-advaita*) and *Vallabha* (A.D.1479), the proponent of pure non-dualism (*suddha-advaita*). They too relied upon the same scriptures to interpret the nature of *Isvara* and reality to justify their respective beliefs. Thus, the *Bhagavadgita* is a text of standard knowledge, which is useful to ascertain standard truths (*sabda pramana*), even though officially it is not given the same status as the *Vedas*, which constitute the revelatory scriptures (*sruti*) of Hinduism and which are used for the same purpose.

Statistical data

Originally written in Sanskrit, the scripture has been translated into all the major languages and is now available to people all over the world. While it was composed long time ago in a language that is no more used in regular conversation, there is certain pragmatic directness and timeless relevance about its teachings, which make it profoundly appealing and inspiring. People can relate to it even today. Its teachings are relevant to present-day world as they were two thousand years ago. They can be practiced and tested by anyone having faith and devotion and willing to make some sacrifices and adhere to austere self-discipline. There is also certain plasticity and inclusiveness about its teachings and many expressions used in the verses. We can interpret them differently from different perspectives, just as we can do so with many universal truths. As a result, the more we read the *Bhagavadgita,* the greater is the insight we gain into its hidden secrets. With the *Bhagavadgita,* the learning never stops. Even after studying for years, we may not be sure whether we have mastered it. Despite our understanding, a verse or a chapter may still elude our intellect and challenge our notions of duty, devotion and sacrifice. The diverse philosophies and paths of liberation suggested in it are difficult to practice simultaneously. Hence, we may know part of it but seldom all of it.

According to the *Gitakaradinyas*, the presiding deity (devata) of the *Bhagavadgita* is Lord Krishna. Its seer is *Vedavyasa*. Its meter (*chanda*) is *anushtup*. Its seed (*bija*) mantra is 11th verse of the second chapter, which is as follows. It suggests that we should cultivate wisdom and not worry about things that are imperishable by nature.

The Supreme Lord said, "You are grieving for (those) who should not be grieved for. You have put forth wise arguments; but knowledgeable people do not grieve for the life that is gone or yet to be gone.

The 66th verse in the 18th chapter is its power (*shakti*) mantra, while the second part of the same verse serves as the axis or the center (*kilakam*) for it. It is as follows

"Renouncing all obligatory duties, take shelter in Me alone. I will liberate you from all sins. Do not grieve.

It contains 18 chapters and 700 (according to some versions 699) verses. It has four principal participants to whom the verses are attributed in the following manner.

1. *Dhritarashtra* - 1
2. *Sanjaya* - 41
3. Arjuna - 84
4. Lord Krishna - 574

Each verse is considered a *mantra*. Many verses contain specific phrases, alluding to major concepts and practices of Hinduism. They serve as useful mental hooks for contemplation and concentration.

In the *Bhagavadgita* Lord Krishna and Arjuna are addressed with several names. Lord Krishna is addressed with twenty-seven different names as: *Anantarupa, Achyuta, Arisudhana, Krishna, Kesava, Kesanishudana, Kamalapatraksha, Govinda, Jagadpatih, Jagannivasa, Janardhana, Devedeva, Devavarah, Purushottama, Bhagawan, Bhutabhavana, Bhutesah, Madhusudhana, Mahabahu, Madhavah, Yadava, Yogaviththama, Vasudeva, Varsheya, Vishnuh, Hrisikesa* and *Harih*. Arjuna is also addressed variously as *Gudakesa, Kaunteya, Partha, Paramtapa, Bharata, Dhananjaya, Mahabahu* and so on. These names have symbolic significance. They are used mostly to draw out a hidden purpose or meaning in the context of the intended teaching or to denote the mental state of the participants.

Historicity

It is difficult to determine the historicity and the antiquity of the *Bhagavadgita*. It is even more difficult to determine whether it was really delivered in the middle of the battlefield or the stage was chosen symbolically to signify the field or the body where the *gunas* wage a relentless war among themselves for supremacy. We are also not sure how it evolved into its present form. Its authorship is attributed to *Veda Vyasa*, who is also considered the author of the epic *Mahabharata* of which the *Gita* is a part. The scripture appears in the epic from chapter 23 to 40 in the section on *Bhishma (Bhishmaparva)*. The composition appears to be a work of later Vedic period. It was probably integrated into the epic in its current form after the emergence of many principal Upanishads as is evident from identical verses found in the *Upanishads* such as the *Katha* and the *Svetasvatara Upanishads*.

Connection with yoga

The *Bhagavadgita* is essentially a scripture on yoga (*yoga sastram*). It presents various types of yoga practices and their significance in attaining liberation. It is therefore rightly referred to as a yoga Upanishad. In fact, it treats yoga more comprehensively than the *Yogasutras* of *Patanjali* and broadens both its scope and purpose by integrating the various aspects of yoga into an integrated philosophy. Unlike the Yogasutras, it presents God in a dynamic role as the Creator and Sustainer. Each chapter in it deals with a specific type of yoga and bears the word yoga in its title.

The text might have been originally a later day Upanishad and undergone some modifications over time to acquire the status of an independent scripture of great spiritual value. We have many *gitas* (songs) in Hindu tradition, some long and some short; but the *Bhagavadgita* rules them all. Whatever may be its historicity or antiquity, it delivers a significant spiritual message to those who want to transcend themselves and achieve liberation.

Footnotes
1. *Swami Dayananda*, the Teaching of the *Bhagavadgita*.
2. S.Radhakrishnan, Introductory Essay, the *Bhagavadgita*, Harper Collins 1998.

The Status of the Bhagavadgita in the Sacred Literature

The *Bhagavadgita* occupies a unique position in Hindu religious literature. It is not a revelatory scripture (*sruti*) like the *Vedas*, but it is treated as one. It has popular appeal because of its association with the *Mahabharata*. Although Hinduism is not an organized religion, many regard it as the standard text of Hinduism and compare it with the principal texts of Christianity and Islam. Its title is variously defined, understood and interpreted by scholars according to their knowledge, wisdom and understanding. *Bhagavadgita* literally means the song of God. You may also interpret it as a divine song meant for the benefit of the *bhagavatas*, the servants of God. The scripture is a revelation by God about Himself and His numerous manifestations, in which He explains how we may find Him in creation, Nature, things, phenomena, beings, and within ourselves, and how we may relate to Him and worship Him for our liberation. We find a reference to the nature and status of the scripture in the scripture itself at the end of every chapter in the form of a chapter ending, which goes like this.

*"Thus ends the ... chapter named ... in the **Upanishad** of the sacred Bhagavadgita, the **knowledge of the Absolute Brahman**, the **scripture on yoga**, and the **debate between Lord Krishna and Arjuna**."*

This terse statement provides valuable information on the nature of the scripture and its status in our religion. It contains four important phrases, which are emphasized above in bold letters. Let us analyze them carefully to understand its meaning and significance.

The Bhagavadgita is an Upanishad

The *Bhagavadgita* is not just an ordinary religious text. It is prefixed with, "*srimad,*" meaning sacred and auspicious. Besides, it is an *Upanishad*. *Upanishad* means sitting near. As per tradition, the *Upanishads* are taught in person by a learned teacher to students who are well versed in the knowledge of the *Vedas* and related subjects. They constitute the end part of the *Vedas* (*Vedanta*). In other words, they are taught to those who have the essential knowledge the *Vedas* and related texts and advanced far in their study.

In the strictest sense of the word, the *Bhagavadgita* does not qualify as an *Upanishad* because it is part of an epic, not any *Veda*. However, the scripture has all the essential features of an *Upanishad* and serves the same purpose as the latter. Firstly, like in the *Upanishads*, it contains secret knowledge, which is not known to everyone. Lord Krishna Himself declared the knowledge the utmost secret or the secret of the secrets (*guhyatitam*). Secondly, like the *Upanishads*, its knowledge is not meant for everyone but for a qualified few who should be chosen carefully and taught in person. In the scripture, Lord Krishna specifies clearly four types of people to whom it should never be taught: those who do not practice austerities, who have no devotion, who cannot render selfless service and who dislike God. As you can see, a vast majority of the people falls into this category and does not qualify for the teaching. Thirdly, it should be taught in person and not revealed to everyone. Lord Krishna Himself taught this knowledge in person to Arjuna. At the other end, *Sanjaya* revealed it to *Dhritarashtra* again in person. In olden days, the scripture was recited before people in person with necessary explanation. Fourthly, the scripture is composed in the style of an *Upanishad* and contains a few themes and verses that are common to some of the oldest *Upanishads*. Like them, it deals with the knowledge and functions of Brahman, the individual Self, the nature of reality, divisions of Nature (*tattvas*), the means to attain salvation, descriptions of creation, time, manifestations of God, and so on. In many ways, it reflects the evolving vision of the Vedanta school and the unfolding of the bhakti movement. Finally, the scripture concurs with the *Vedas* in many respects and contains the same knowledge propounded by them. Technically, it is a synthesis of diverse Vedic traditions whose basis is the *Vedas* and inspiration the Upanishads. Thus, although strictly it is not an *Upanishad*, it qualifies in many ways as an *Upanishad*.

The Bhagavadgita is a study in Brahman

Fundamentally, the *Bhagavadgita* is a study in the knowledge of Brahman (*brahmavidya*). It opens our eyes to the knowledge of Brahman. It clears our confusion about the nature of our existence and the role of God in our lives. It presents the Supreme Self in the most personal terms as our Teacher and Benefactor. It increases our opportunities to secure His grace and live in His protection. Unlike the Upanishads, it brings Brahman into our lives and hearts as a personal God to whom we can relate and in whom we can seek refuge.

A lot of sacred knowledge is hidden in the scripture, which can be used for one's spiritual advancement as well as liberation. Its source is Brahman. Its goal is Brahman; its subject is Brahman and its purpose is Brahman. It describes the individual Self (Atman), the Supreme Self (Brahman) and the relationship between the two. It explains their transcendental nature, their role in creation, the obstacles to their union and the means to attain it. In every chapter, Brahman is its dominant theme and the fundamental goal. Those who study it sincerely find in it many opportunities to improve their knowledge of Him (*brahmavidya*) and overcome their ignorance and delusion. When we do not know Brahman, we suffer from ignorance and delusion and live our lives selfishly and egoistically performing our actions out of desires and suffering from their consequences. When we know who He is, we open our eyes to the truth concerning our existence and try to transcend ourselves and reach His Abode.

The concept of *brahmavidya* is well known to the scholars of the *Vedas*. The *Upanishads* refer to several types of *brahmavidyas*, numbering about 32, whose study and practice lead to knowledge and liberation, such as the science of breath (*pranavidya*), the science of fire (*pancagni vidya*), the science of space (*akasa vidya*) and so on. Just like them, the *Bhagavadgita* provides information on Brahman, the Supreme Self, His essential nature, His manifestations, His functions as the creator, preserver and destroyer, His universal form (*visvarupam*), His role in our liberation. Entire chapters in it are dedicated to the study and understanding of Him. For example, the eighth chapter deals with the Imperishable (*akshara*) Brahman, who resides in the body as the Witness, the Enjoyer and the imperishable Self (*adhyatma*). In the ninth chapter, He is described as the sacrifice, the sacrificer and the sacrificed, who is also Father, Mother, Sustainer and Grandfather of creation, Supreme Goal, the Final Abode, Friend, Origin and the End. The 10th chapter is dedicated to His manifestations while the next one to His universal form. In the 12th chapter, we realize that by fixing our minds upon Him and by devotion to Him, we can secure His mercy (*prasadam*) and attain liberation. Thus, the *Bhagavadgita* is rightly described as the science of Brahman (*brahmavidya*). It is a book on Brahman by Brahman Himself in the form of Lord Krishna.

The Bhagavadgita is a scripture on Yoga

The *Bhagavadgita* is rightly described as a scripture on yoga (*yoga sastram*). It deals with the subject of yoga more comprehensively than any other scripture, including the *Yogasutras*. It also expands its scope and purpose by adding many new elements to its theory and practice that are not found in other scriptures on yoga. In fact, we can even call it the *Yoga Gita* because its emphasis is on practicing various types of yoga and attaining sameness. It speaks about not one or two but a number yoga disciplines. Every chapter in it contains the word yoga and deals with some particular practice of yoga or state of yoga. For the *Bhagavadgita*, yoga is not just a discipline. It stands for both the state to be attained and the means to attain it. In other words, you practice different types of yoga to attain different yogas (states), which may be equanimity, detachment, sameness, discernment, devotion, purity and so on. The highest yoga is liberation or the state (*bhava*) of Brahman. The means are the yoga of action (*karmayoga*), the yoga of knowledge (*jnanayoga* or *samkhya yoga*), the yoga of renunciation (*sanyasayoga*), the yoga of discretion (*buddhiyoga*), the yoga of the Self (*atmayoga*), the yoga of devotion (*bhaktiyoga*), and the yoga of renunciation of the results (*karmaphalasanyasa yoga*).

The specific techniques to practice some of these yogas are the same as those mentioned in the *Yogasutras*, such as rules and restraints (*yamas* and *niyamas*), breathe control (*pranayama*), restraint of the senses (*pratyahara*), concentration (*dharana*), meditation (*dhyana*) and self-absorption (*samadhi*). The other similarities include description of the Self as the lord of the body (*Isvara*), meditation upon Him as *Aum*, arresting the modifications of the mind by cultivating purity (*sattva*), controlling desires, practicing detachment, stabilizing the mind, purifying the intelligence, practicing *samyama*, arresting the afflictions, cultivating sameness, transcending the senses, and so on. It also defines yoga (2.48) as sameness (*samatvam*) and declares that in the early stages of yoga, work is the means and in the later stages, equanimity. What it means is in the early stages one should focus upon performing one's obligatory duties and when one has progressed sufficiently on the path of desireless actions, one should aim to stabilize the mind and experience equanimity. The highest form of yoga is the yoga of devotion. Unlike the *Yogasutras*, the *Bhagavadgita* recommends a more personal and intense form of devotional worship (*Isvara paridhana*) in which not only the individual Self but also the Universal Self are revered as the objects of worship. Compared to the *Yogasutras* it also has more theistic elements and emotional appeal. It regards Brahman more personally as the source and creator of all, and His worship and grace as vital to achieving liberation.

The Bhagavadgita is a dialogue between God and man

The *Bhagavadgita* is a dialogue (*samvadam*) between Lord Krishna and Arjuna. Symbolically Lord Krishna represents the Supreme Self (Brahman) and Arjuna the embodied self (*jiva*) who is caught in the phenomenal world and subject to ignorance, duality and delusion. They are also referred to as *Narayana* and *Nara* respectively. *Nara* is the individual being made up of the waters of life (*naara*). *Narayana* is the one who pervades (*ayana*) all the individual beings (*naras*) and the entire waters (*naara*). The dialogue is a friendly conversation in which there is a mutual exchange of ideas and appreciation of each other's standpoints. It is not a dispute (*vivadam*) in which the participants contest their ideas to defend their egos or personal interests. It is also not a one-sided exposition (*vadam*) of a doctrine or philosophy, in which the other side is either suppressed or silenced with the threat of punishment or the fear of authority. It is a friendly debate or conversation (*samvadam*) between two open-minded individuals who have mutual love, respect and admiration for each other, who can understand and appreciate each other and share their thoughts and opinions without feeling dominated or oppressed.

The *Bhagavadgita* is an outstanding example of how faith and devotion can open the communication channels between God and man and bring transcendental knowledge from the highest heaven into the mortal world, without suppressing the human thought or ignoring our spiritual and material needs or our limitations in comprehending the transcendental truths. It represents a dialogue in which one has the freedom to ask questions, raise doubts and objections and seek clarifications. Throughout the discourse, Lord Krishna did not force His ideas upon Arjuna. He gave him ample time and opportunities to comprehend the truths He revealed to Him. He allowed him to absorb the knowledge and draw His own conclusions. He even helped Him understand it by bestowing His grace upon Him and showing him His universal form. In the last chapter (18.63), He even told him that He revealed him the secret of the secrets, upon which he should reflect and act according to his wish (*icchah*).

The purpose of this mutual conversation of extraordinary value is to resolve the problem of human suffering by providing spiritual solutions that do not add to our burdens further but only compliment our efforts without the need to abandon the world or our obligations. They address the root cause of our suffering, which is desire and how we may neutralize it. The scripture is not a conversation between Lord Krishna and Arjuna alone. Whoever reads it with sincerity and devotion can enter into a conversation with God and open His mind to the flow of His love and compassion. By reading the scripture, by assimilating the knowledge one can earn His grace and work for one's liberation. Most scriptures deliver the message of God indirectly in the second person; but in the *Bhagavadgita,* the entire discourse is delivered by God Himself directly in the first person.

A Summary of the Bhagavadgita

The *Bhagavadgita* teaches us how to live in this world, do our duties and yet remain like lotus leaves in the waters of life, untainted by the laws of *karma*. The world in which we live is a world of illusion. Out of ignorance and egoism and through desires and selfish actions, we cling to this world; and not knowing our true nature and purpose, we indulge in desire-ridden actions. In the process, we become bound to the cycle of births and deaths and to the forces of Nature until we wake up from our delusion and realize our mistake. The *Bhagavadgita* teaches us how to reach that austere goal, not by escaping from the burdens of the worldly life or avoiding our responsibilities, but by remaining amidst the distractions and afflictions of life and dealing with them squarely with dispassion, detachment and stability, accepting God as the Doer and doing our ordained duties as an offering and a sacrifice.

According to the *Bhagavadgita*, salvation is not possible if we shun our responsibilities and indulge in desire-ridden actions. True renunciation is renunciation of desires hidden in our thoughts and actions. Those who perform their obligatory duties without desire for their fruit are qualified for liberation. Those who live their lives with detachment in the contemplation of God earn His grace and qualify to enter His Abode. If liberation is the goal, first it must begin in the mind as an idea and resolve. Then it should be extended into our actions and relationships. The ideal state is freedom from the modification of the mind. When the senses move among the objects, the mind should be still and the perceiver should be indifferent. One must be free from delusion, ignorance, attraction and aversion, egoism, prejudices, opinions, dependencies and desires.

Actions do not bind us. Desires bind us. Desire for the fruit of our actions creates our *karma*. Expectations bind us to our future. Selfishness binds us to our names and forms. When we perform actions with expectation and seek things avidly, we become responsible for their consequences. Thus, largely the continuity of our existence upon earth is in our hands (*adhyatmikam*) while our liberation depends upon our effort as well as the grace of God (*adhidaivam*). With detachment, we can suppress the impure *gunas*, arrest the formation of latent impressions (*samskaras*) in our consciousness, and thereby stop the cycle of births and deaths. When the mind becomes still like a placid lake and the latent impressions are burnt away in the fire of selfless actions, we end the process of being and becoming.

The *Bhagavadgita* is for people like *Arjuna* and *Sanjaya*, who desire the company of God, who perform selfless service to the His devotees and who want to know answers to their suffering and perform their duties and obligations as an offering to God. If you want to know the perfect way to live upon earth, the scripture is the right choice for you. If you want to live in the company of God and make your life a great sacrifice, the scripture is the right one to guide you. If you want to know the truths concerning your existence and your essential nature, the scripture is the perfect source of knowledge for you.

The first chapter in the *Bhagavadgita* begins with the despondence of *Arjuna*, when he was suddenly overcome with profound sorrow in the middle of the battlefield at the thought of the bloodshed that was going to happen in his hands. Unable to bear the thought, he decided to renounce the world. His idea of renunciation was to abandon his duties as a warrior and live like an ascetic seeking alms. In that state of depression, he forgot that he had a responsibility to help his brothers in their righteous cause against their evil cousins. His predicament stemmed from his egoistic thinking, and mistaken belief that renunciation meant giving up actions to avoid their consequences. Lord *Krishna*, who agreed to act as his charioteer during the war, responded to his grief in a fitting manner and opened his eyes to profound metaphysical truths concerning himself, his duty and his equation with God. Out of extreme compassion and love, He taught him how to perform his ordained duties without incurring sin and how to work for his liberation by practicing renunciation and self-purification with the help of the yoga of action (*karma*), knowledge (*jnana*) and devotion (*bhakti*) without abandoning his duties or his obligations.

The following is a chapter wise summary of the sacred text, with special emphasis on certain topics that are central to the doctrine propounded by Lord *Krishna* about liberation and the means to achieve it. It provides you with an overview of the entire teachings. This summary is useful if you want to familiarize yourself with important points without going through the whole scripture. For a complete understanding of the scripture, please go through, "*The Bhagavadgita Complete Translation,*" or "*The Bhagavadgita a Simple Translation,*" both by this author.

Arjuna's Yoga of Sorrow

The chapter begins with a dialogue between *Dhritarashtra* and *Sanjaya* and introduces the principal characters involved in the war. Through the words of *Duryodhana*, we are introduced to the battle formations, the war strategy and the names of a few renowned warriors on both sides. The principal characters, Lord Krishna and Arjuna are introduced in the 14th verse. In the 21st verse, Arjuna asks Lord Krishna, who was acting as his charioteer, to take him into the middle of both the armies. Lord Krishna complies with his request. Upon seeing his kith and kin arrayed in the battlefield, ready to fight and sacrifice their lives, *Arjuna* suffers from great sorrow. He is overwhelmed with the thought of waging a destructive war and killing his own relations and great souls like *Bhishma* and *Drona*. He begins to worry that his actions would lead to the destruction of many people in his hands, which in turn might lead to other unhappy consequences for him and his family. In a fit of depression, he lays down his bow and arrow and decides to renounce fighting to avoid causing suffering and destruction to others. The first chapter is rightly titled as the yoga of Arjuna's sorrow since it describes the sorrow and anxiety experienced by Arjuna at the thought of war and its consequences. The scripture begins in right earnest with a chapter on sorrow because the teachings aim to resolve the problem of sorrow arising from our actions without us having to abandon them or escape from them. Arjuna's despondency also signifies the importance of sorrow in our lives. Sorrow is a rude awakener and a harsh teacher. It imparts valuable lessons by letting us know where we are wrong and what we should or should not do. It puts us on a pause and forces us to review our priorities, choices and actions. We usually turn to God in moments of crisis and great sorrow. As long as life goes on normally, we hardly pay attention to the larger issues of our lives such as our spiritual welfare or the need for our liberation. When things go wrong and life takes an unexpected turn for the worse, we veer towards God and look for His guidance and help. In moments of despair, we realize the futility of finding peace and fulfillment in the dualities of life and the pairs of opposites. In many ways, *Arjuna's* sorrow symbolizes our inability to comprehend truth or resolve the problems of our lives solely with our limited knowledge and intellect. It serves as a revelation for those who want to lead egocentric lives without acknowledging the role of God or His help in our spiritual transformation. It also reminds us of the need to work for our liberation and escape from the world of death and delusion.

The Yoga of Knowledge

Lord Krishna in his role as divine teacher responds to Arjuna's predicament with knowledge and wisdom, which He terms as *Samkhya yoga*. *Samkhya* is about the nature of existence and Yoga is about accomplishing inner transformation to become free from it and attain liberation. He reminds him that wise men do not grieve for the dead or living because they know that the Self which is hidden in all and which is our true identify cannot be slain or destroyed. The wise ones remain equal to both pleasure and pain because they know how the activity of the senses leads to attachment and duality towards the pairs of opposites. Those who remain equal to them become fit for immortality. One should also cultivate discernment to know what is perishable and what is imperishable. The body is perishable because it is like a garment worn by the Self, whereas the Self is imperishable and inexhaustible. It is unthinkable, invisible and unborn. Therefore, it is not appropriate to grieve about the death of any one. There is no sin in doing one's duty, especially when it is done for the sake of righteousness and without desire or expectation. Our right is to work only not for its fruit. We should perform our actions with even mindedness (*samatvam*), which means we should have sameness towards the pairs of opposites. Even mindedness is called yoga because its practice leads to liberation. When actions are performed with equanimity, we call it skill in action or *buddhiyoga*. He who has equanimity, who renounces the fruit of his actions is freed from the bonds of births and attains liberation.

Arjuna then wants to know the marks of a person whose mind is completely stable (*sthitaprajna*). Lord Krishna replies that he should be known as a stable person (*sthitadhi*) whose mind is stable, who is free from craving, contended in his mind, not perturbed by adversity or emotions, without affection everywhere, withdrawn and detached. He explains how we develop attachment because of the activity of the senses, how desires arise from attachment and how one perishes as desires lead to anger, delusion, confusion of memory and loss of discrimination. One should therefore control the senses and become free from likes and dislikes. When the mind is tranquil and steady, one becomes firmly established in *Isvara*. When desires are abandoned, one becomes free from attachment, egoism and attains the exalted state of Brahman (*brahma-sthiti*). He is no more deluded or subject to the cycle of births and deaths or the suffering caused by attraction and aversion to the sense objects.

The Yoga of Action

The second chapter is about the knowledge of the Self that leads to liberation and freedom from Nature. In the beginning of the third chapter, *Arjuna* wants to know if knowledge is so important why he is asked to perform actions. Lord *Krishna* answers by saying that the path of knowledge is for men of contemplation and the path of action is for those who are engaged in worldly actions. Liberation is not attained by abstaining from work, but by doing it selflessly without seeking its fruit. Action is superior to inaction because we cannot keep our bodies alive by remaining inactive. Besides, the worlds exist because both gods and beings perform their duties. Actions performed with desires bind the beings to *karma*. One should therefore perform actions with a sacrificial attitude, without attachment, taking delight in the Self alone. Men should perform actions to foster gods and gods should perform actions to foster men. Although He is free from desires, God Himself performs selfless actions to preserve the worlds and set an example to the people on earth. Actions are caused by the *gunas*, although people think they are doing them. We engage in actions because of desires induced by the *gunas* to seek objects in which they are present predominantly. Therefore, it is delusion to think that we are responsible for our actions and we are the doers. We should not take any credit for our actions because they stem from our inherent nature with which we should not identify ourselves. To be free from the consequences of desire-ridden actions, people should surrender their actions to God, with their minds fixed upon Him and perform them without attachment and hope. Attachment and aversion to objects are obstacles on the path of liberation since they keep the mind unsteady and distracted. One should not be swayed by them. A person becomes sinful when he acts under the influence of desires and passions caused by *rajas*. When wisdom is covered by the smoke of desires, one becomes deluded. To be free from it and conquer the enemy that exists in each of us in the form of desires, one should control one's senses with intellect and one's intellect with the knowledge of the Self.

The Yoga of Knowledge with Renunciation of Action

The fourth chapter begins with the assertion that the source of all knowledge is God and He imparted the ancient knowledge of

Yoga to the progenitors of the humankind. When Arjuna asks Him how it was possible for Him to teach the same knowledge to people of bygone eras, Krishna replies that although He was immortal, unborn, and the Lord of beings, He manifests Himself from time to time whenever there is a decline of *dharma* and ascendance of evil. He does it as a duty to protect the virtuous, destroy the evil and restore *dharma*. Those who have the knowledge of God become free from attachment and attain liberation. God is the source of creation and He is responsible for the order and regularity (*rta*) of the universe. He is not tainted by actions because He has no desire for their fruit. Those who are aware of this know how to perform their actions and remain free from their consequences.

Having explained how to perform actions with right knowledge and remain free from evil, He explains Arjuna the truth regarding action, inaction and prohibited action. A yogi sees inaction in action and action in inaction because his actions are burnt up by the fire of wisdom. Since he renounces attachment and does not depend upon anything, he does nothing and commits no sin even though he is engaged in actions. With no expectations, his mind under control, giving up all possessions, ever contended, free from envy, balanced in success and failure, he the *karmayogi* is not bound by his actions. Actions should therefore be performed with a sense of sacrifice.

There are many types of sacrifices, which lead to the dissolution of sin. However, the sacrifices made with knowledge (*jnana-yajna*) are superior to the sacrifices performed with materials (*dravya-yajna*) to attain peace and prosperity. One should attain such knowledge by seeking the guidance of wise people and serving them variously. When actions are performed with knowledge, they are reduced to ashes, which mean no sin incurs. Knowledge is the best purifier of all. Knowledge comes with faith, control of the senses and devoted service and having attained it one experiences supreme peace. When actions are performed with right knowledge and even mindedness, one is not bound by them.

The Yoga of Renunciation of Action

The fifth chapter begins with a question from *Arjuna* who wants to know of the two, the yoga of renunciation and the yoga of action, which one is better. Lord *Krishna* replies that both lead to supreme bliss, but the yoga of action is superior because he who performs actions without hatred and desires is a practitioner of true renunciation (*sanyasi*). Those who transcend the pairs of opposites attain liberation. Ignorant people think that the yoga of knowledge and yoga of action are different; but both lead to the same goal. One can achieve liberation by practicing either of them. However, without renunciation it is difficult to attain liberation even with the yoga of action.

Renunciation of action does not mean one should give up all actions. Renunciation of the desire for the fruit of one's action is true renunciation of action. A person who practices it does not incur sin even though he is engaged in actions. God determines neither doership nor actions of the beings nor their consequences. Nor he accepts the merits or sins of anyone. It is nature, which veils our knowledge and induces us to act in deluded ways so that we remain under its influence. Whoever possess the right knowledge and whose sins have been washed away, the Supreme Being reveals Himself to them. Such people view the world with equanimity and treat everyone with the same attitude. Unperturbed by the pairs of opposites they live firmly established in Brahman. Having renounced all worldly attachments, a person who is established in that state of perfection does nothing even when he is engaged in actions. He lives untouched by sin like a lotus leaf by water. Offering the fruit of his actions to God, remaining unattached, finding happiness within, balanced and self-absorbed, he attains supreme peace and great bliss. In contrast, those who perform actions with selfish motives incur sin and remain bound. One should therefore practice the yoga of actions, renouncing desires and attachments, establishing oneself firmly in the contemplation of Brahman and identifying oneself with Him. This is the yoga of renunciation of action.

The Yoga of Self-absorption

The sixth chapter begins with the assertion that he is a true *sanyasi* who performs his actions without depending upon their fruit, not the one who gives up work or the sacred fire when he enters into the last phase of his life (*sanyasashrama*). Renunciation and yoga are the same because one becomes a yogi only by renouncing attachment to the world. Perfection in yoga comes only when one renounces all worldly desires. For this, one should practice self-control and conquer the lower self or the ego-self. When the ego is disciplined, one abides in peace and remains equal to the pairs of opposites. He excels who remain dispassionate under all circumstances. A yogi should attain this state by practicing yoga, meditation and concentration in secluded places free from desire and possessions. He should practice yoga for self-purification, with his mind fixed upon God, practicing self-control and moderation.

In this chapter, Lord Krishna defines yoga as separation (*viyogam*) from union (*samyogam*) with suffering (*dukham*). In the mortal world, we are never free from suffering. Suffering is a constant factor in our lives, even when we are seemingly happy. We are separated from it only when we achieve perfection in performing actions with renunciation and detachment. By nature, the mind is very fickle. However, it can be controlled through practice and dispassion. Yoga becomes easier for one whose mind is subdued and who is established firmly in the thoughts of Brahman. Having heard the importance of subduing the mind, Arjuna then wants to know the fate of those who fail in their effort to control their minds and passions. Lord Krishna replies that there is no destruction for those who work for their spiritual wellbeing. Those who fall from yoga attain the ancestral world and after exhausting their good *karma* return to earth to take birth in a family of enlightened yogis. There he regains his knowledge and continues his practice. A yogi whose passions are subdued, whose mind is tranquil and who performs actions without attachment and desire for the fruit of his actions is superior to an ascetic, to men of knowledge and men of desire-ridden actions. Among them also, those who worship God and remain absorbed in Him are the best.

The Yoga of Knowledge and Wisdom

In this chapter, Lord Krishna turns his attention from the individual Self to the Universal Self. He explains how to achieve God-realization by practicing devotion and yoga of action together, with the mind established firmly in the contemplation of Brahman, the highest God. Among thousands of people, only a few know Him in essence and the reality (*tattvas*) concerning His materiality. The Supreme Lord has a twofold nature, the lower and the higher, from which arise all beings. He is both the material and efficient cause of creation; and in the end, everything becomes dissolved in Him only. He is the highest of all. Nothing is above Him or remains independent of Him. He is omniscient and omnipresent. He is hidden in all. Everything evolves from Him and dissolves into Him. Deluded by His divine *Maya* (illusion) induced by the *gunas*, ignorant people, under the influence of demonic nature, do not recognize Him as the Supreme and Imperishable. Therefore, they do not worship Him. The virtuous people who worship Him are of four types: the distressed, seekers knowledge, seekers of wealth and the wise. Of them the last type are extremely dearer to Him as He is to them. At the end of many births, people seek God, acknowledging Him as all. Others out of desires and bound by the *gunas* worship other gods and perform sacrificial rites to fulfill their desires. God does not interfere with their methods of worship or their object of worship. Whatever form they chose to worship, He stabilizes their faith in that. However limited is the fruit gained by those who worship gods. They go to them, while the devotees of Brahman go to Him only.

The Yoga of Imperishable Brahman

This chapter deals with afterlife and the fate of those die and depart from here. It begins with a question on the meaning and significance of Brahman, *adhyatma, karma, adhibhuta, adhidaivam* and *adhiyajna*. Lord Krishna answers that the supreme and imperishable Being is Brahman. One's own essence (*svabhavam*) is the individuality (*adhyatma*). Karma is the creative force that brings into existence all beings. All material things that are perishable constitute the material self (*adhibhuta*). *Purusha* is the individual Self, (*adhidaivam*) in the body, who acts as the inner witness; and *Isvara* or *Krishna* is *Adhiyajna*, the Supreme Self. Whoever remembers Him at the time of their death attain Him only without doubt. Whatever a person thinks at the time of death, he attains that. One should therefore remember God always, even while performing mundane actions, and live with one's mind absorbed in His contemplation. Those who attain Him in this manner and reach His abode never take birth again. All words, including the world of *Brahma*, are subject to rebirth, but not those who have attained Him. The time at which a person dies is important because it determines by which path the departed travels. Those who die during the first six months of summer solstice go to the world of Brahman by the path of sun, never to return to the earth. Those who die during the winter solstice travel by the path of moon and attain the world of ancestors. After exhausting their *karma* there, they return to the earth and take birth again. Knowing these two paths, a wise person cultivates devotion and becomes steadfast in the practice of yoga.

The Yoga of Sovereign Knowledge and Mystery

This chapter describes the supreme knowledge and supreme mystery concerning the Supreme Self. Knowing them, a person becomes free from impurities. God pervades the whole universe. All beings exist in Him and depend upon Him for their support; but He does not depend upon any. During each cycle of creation, He brings forth all beings and withdraws them into Himself at the end of it. Actions do not bind Him because He remains unattached and indifferent while performing them. Under His control, Nature (*Prakriti*) manifests the whole creation. Deluded people, who lack discrimination and who possess demonic nature, do not recognize Him as the Creator. However, the great souls take refuge in Him knowing that He is the prime cause of creation and worship Him with great devotion. God takes care of the welfare (*yogaksemam*) of such people personally. Those who worship gods instead of Brahman also worship Him; but it is not a proper form of worship. Those who worship gods or spirits or manes go to them; but those who worship Him, attain Him only. Whatever is offered to God with devotion He accepts it unconditionally, be it a fruit or a leaf, a flower or water. However, we should not be selective in what we offer to God. One should offer Him everything, whatever one does, whatever one eats, whatever one offers as an oblation, whatever gifts one gives and whatever penances one performs. Everything should be offered to Him without expectations. God is impartial. None is hateful or lovable to Him; but those who worship Him with devotion abide in him and Him in them. The devotees of God never perish. Even if a sinful person worships Him with pure devotion, He becomes saintly and righteous. One can therefore imagine how much merit will accrue if a pious person worships Him with devotion. Worship God with great devotion, with your mind fixed upon Him. Offer Him everything. Pay Him respects. If you do these, you will go to Him only.

The Yoga of Divine Manifestations

The tenth chapter is about the manifestations (*vibhutis*) and greatness (*mahimas*) of the Supreme Self. Knowledge of the Supreme Self is useful in liberation. No one knows the secrets of His origin because He is the First among the gods and seers, and the Source of all. Those who know Him as the unborn and without a beginning are freed from all sins. All the divine qualities and diverse feelings emanate from Him only. All are born out of Him only. Those who are free from delusion and know the reality worship Him with their minds fixed upon Him, surrendering to Him, speaking about His glory and taking delight in His thoughts. To those who worship Him thus, *Isvara* gives the yoga of wisdom (*buddhiyoga*) by which they attain liberation. Having heard these words, *Arjuna* wants to know how to know Him through meditation (*cintam*) and in what states (*bhavas*) one should contemplate upon Him. In reply, Lord Krishna tells him His prominent divine states (*yogam*) and manifestations (*vibhutis*). The Supreme Self abides in all and represents all known and unknown aspects of creation. Then, He concludes that there is no use knowing His glories because they are but a little fraction of Him.

The Yoga of the Vision of the Universal Form

In this chapter, *Arjuna* expresses his wish to see the Supreme Form of Lord Krishna. The Lord complies. He bestows upon Him special vision and shows him His resplendent Universal Form (*visvarupam*), containing all the worlds, planets, gods, beings, colors and shapes. In that Form, *Arjuna* sees everything, past, present and future and the fate of the war. He sees Him with countless arms, stomachs, faces and eyes, without a beginning, middle and end. He sees Him blazing as if thousands of suns are present in the sky at once. He sees His infinite vastness and His fierce and terrible form as Time (*kala*), the god of death and destruction. Showing him His fierce form, Lord *Krishna* asks him to slay his enemies, who are already slain by Him in His cosmic plan, and fulfill the duty and destiny for which he is born. The vision fills *Arjuna* with fear and trepidation. He praises Him profusely and, unable to see Him in that form, requests Him to revert to His peaceful and pleasant form. *Krishna* returns to his normal form and tells *Arjuna* that it is very difficult for anyone to see the universal form of God. Even the divinities do not see it. Then He adds that He cannot be seen in this form or known in essence through the study of the *Vedas*, charity or austerities, but only through single-minded devotion. He, who lives for Him, without enmity towards others, performing all his actions for Him and acknowledging Him as the Supreme, goes to Him only.

The Yoga of Devotion

The twelfth chapter is about the yoga of devotion. It begins with the question, which type of devotees is superior, those who worship Lord *Krishna* or those who worship the Imperishable.

Krishna says that those who worship Him are considered perfect in yoga. However, those who worship the Imperishable and Indefinable with their minds and senses under control also come to Him only. Painful is the path of those who want to worship the Unmanifested Brahman; but those whose minds are set upon Him, who is manifested, He rescues them promptly. Therefore, He urges *Arjuna* to worship Him with utmost devotion. If he is unable to fix his mind upon Him, he should practice (*abhyasam*) devotion. If it is also not possible, he should perform selfless actions for His sake. If he cannot do even that, he should take refuge in Him and renounce the fruit of his actions because renunciation of the fruit of actions is better than every other form of devotional service. Lord *Krishna* then states that a devotee who is steady, firmly resolved, undisturbed, full of devotion and equal to all is dear to Him.

The Yoga of the Field and the Knower of the Field

The thirteenth chapter describes the field, the Knower of the field and the meaning of true knowledge. The body is the field (*kshetra*), the Self is its Knower (*kshetrajna*) and the knowledge of both is considered real knowledge. The Self is the object of knowledge that leads to liberation. The field is subject to modifications arising from the *gunas*, where as the Self is imperishable and immutable. Beings manifest when the Self (*pursha*) seated in Nature (*Prakriti*) experiences *gunas* born of Nature. Attachment to the *gunas* leads to rebirth in good and bad wombs. The Self does not participate in the modifications of the field, but remain as Witness, the Support and Enjoyer. Those who know both the Self and Nature are not reborn. They attain liberation. The Self is attained by meditation, yoga of knowledge and yoga actions. Some realize Him through worship. They are also liberated. Every being in this world is born from the union of between the Self and the body. A man of knowledge knows that all actions arise from Nature, and thereby becomes a non-doer (*akarta*). When he sees that all beings exist in One, he attains Brahman. The Self illuminates the field just as the Sun illuminates the whole world. Although it resides in the body, it remains pure, untouched by Nature. Those who know the distinction between the Self and the field and the liberation of the beings from the hold of Nature attain the Supreme Brahman.

The Yoga of the Division of the Triple Gunas

This chapter deals with the division of the *gunas* and their essential features. *Isvara* is the seed giving Father. Nature is the womb. From their union are born all beings. They manifest because of the *gunas*, which are three in number, namely *sattva*, *rajas* and *tamas*. *Sattva* is pure and luminous. It manifests in us as divine qualities and binds us through attachment to pleasure, happiness and knowledge. *Rajas* is born of passions and egoism. It binds us through attachment to actions. *Tamas* is born of ignorance and it binds us through negligence, laziness and sleep. The *gunas* try to dominate the field (body) suppressing each other. Thus, *sattva* dominates by suppressing *rajas* and *tamas*. *Rajas* dominates by suppressing *sattva* and *tamas*; and *tamas* dominates by suppressing *sattva* and *rajas*. When the mind is illuminated with knowledge, *sattva* predominates. When *rajas* predominates one indulges in selfish actions. When *tamas* prevails, one suffers from ignorance, inactivity, delusion and carelessness. When a purely sattvic person dies, he attains the highest world and never returns. When a rajasic person dies, he attains the ancestral world. Upon his return to earth, he is born in a family of hardworking people. When a tamasic person dies, he too goes to the ancestral world, but upon his return to earth, he is born to deluded parents. The fruit of *sattva* is purity while the fruit of *rajas* is sorrow and that of *tamas* is ignorance. From *sattva* arises knowledge, from *rajas* selfishness and from *tamas* ignorance. When a seer perceives *guna*s as the real doer, he transcends them and reaches the Supreme. When an embodied self transcends the *gunas*, he becomes free from births and deaths. He who transcends them remains free from delusion and attachment. Knowing that only *gunas* are responsible for actions, he remains indifferent and equal to the pairs of opposites. He attains Brahman, who is eternal and who upholds *dharma* for the welfare of all.

The Yoga of the Supreme Person

This chapter is about the Supreme *Purusha*, the Cosmic Self. It begins with a description of the Tree of Creation (*asvattha* tree) whose roots are in heaven and branches down below. A projection of Brahma, one can escape from it only through non-attachment. With liberation as goal, one should seek refuge in Brahman from whom creation ensues and reach the Supreme Abode from where men do not return and where neither the sun nor the moon shine. The embodied self is an aspect (*amsah*) of Brahman only. When he leaves the body, he goes taking along with him the mind and the senses. Those who are ignorant, deluded and impure do not perceive the Self in their bodies. Only those who have the eyes of wisdom (*jnana-caksu*) see Him. The Universal Self who inhabits the whole creation is the highest of all. The sun and the moon shine because of Him. He pervades the earth and supports all beings by His vigor (*ojas*). He remains seated in the body as the digestive fire and digests the fourfold food (solids, liquids etc.). He alone resides in the hearts of beings and is responsible for their knowledge, memory and wisdom. The transcendental Self is imperishable, while the lower Self is perishable. The Supreme *Purusha* (*purushottama*) is distinct from both and superior to both. Those who know Him as such and worship Him with devotion become accomplished in duty.

The Division of the Divine and Demonic Properties

In this chapter, Lord *Krishna* enumerates the distinction between the divine and demonic qualities. The divine qualities lead to liberation while the demonic ones lead to bondage and delusion. Based upon them the beings in the world are divided into divine and demonic. Because of their cruel, sinful and demonic behavior, God casts them into worlds of darkness from where redemption is difficult to attain. One should therefore cultivate divine qualities abandoning the three gates of hell, namely passion, anger and greed and attain the Supreme State. Those who defy the scripture and the word of God attain neither happiness nor Supreme Abode. Therefore, one should follow the scriptures to determine what should be done and what should be avoided and act according to guidelines prescribed in them.

The Yoga of the Threefold Division of Qualities

In this chapter, Lord Krishna describes the threefold division of faith according to the predominant nature of beings. A person's faith is determined by his nature. Sattvic people worship gods, rajasic people worship celestial beings (*yakshas* and *rakshsas*) and tamasic people worship ghosts and elemental spirits. Those who are deluded and filled with vanity and egoism and induced by lust and passions perform severe penances not approved by the scripture and subject their bodies to senseless torture. The food we eat is also of three types based on the *gunas* they represent. Sattvic people like sattvic food, which promotes purity and brilliance. Rajasic people prefer rajasic food, which promotes lust and passions; while tamasic people choose tamasic food, which promotes sloth and ignorance. Based upon the *gunas*, sacrifices are also of three types. The sacrifices, which are performed according to the scriptures, without seeking their fruit, as a duty, are sattvic in nature. Those, which are performed with desire for their fruit, for the sake of vanity, are rajasic in nature. Tamasic sacrifices are performed, without faith and in total disregard to the scriptures and established traditions. Just as faith is of three types, the austerities (*tapas*) are also of three types. Sattvic austerities are performed in a gentle and selfless manner; rajasic austerities are practiced in a selfish and egoistic manner; and tamasic austerities are performed in a painful and destructive manner. The rest of the chapter is devoted to describe the three types of gifts and the reason to commence sacrifices, charity and penance always by uttering the sacred mantra, *"Aum Tat Sat"*

The Yoga of Liberation by Renunciation

The last chapter begins with a question on renunciation (*sanyasa*) and sacrifice (*tyaga*). Lord *Krishna* explains that *sanyasa* means renunciation of desires hidden in actions and *tyaga* means renunciation of the fruit of one's action. Actions such as sacrifice, charity and austerities should not be given up. They should be performed by renouncing attachment for their fruit. Abandoning obligatory duties owing to delusion is declared tamasic. Abandoning them because they are troublesome or difficult to practice is declared rajasic; but performing them as duty with detachment and sacrificial attitude is called sattvic. A man of true renunciation has neither aversion to disagreeable work nor attraction towards agreeable work. Free from doubt, he attains purity. It is not possible for embodied beings to give up work completely; but they can renounce their desire for their fruit. All actions, whether they are right or wrong arise from five causes, namely the body, the doer, the sense organs, the organs of action and divine providence. He who has no ego, whose intelligence is free from attachment, is not bound by his actions. He remains free even though he performs them. Every action is induced by knowledge, knower and the object of knowledge; and every action involves one or more causes, the mechanism of action and the doer. These three are again of three types according to the *gunas*. By sattvic knowledge, we see everything as part of Brahman. By rajasic knowledge, we see everything as separate and distinct. By tamasic knowledge, one sees nothing beyond oneself or one's actions. Sattvic actions are performed, without desire and attachment, as obligatory duties. Rajasic actions are performed strenuously with desire and egoism. Tamasic actions are performed delusionally without consideration for truth or reality. Similarly, we can classify the doers (*kartas*) into sattvic, rajasic and tamasic based upon their attitude and conduct. Based upon the triple *gunas*, intelligence (*buddhi*), firmness (*dhriti*) and happiness (*sukham*) are also of three types. Thus, the *gunas* pervade everything. There is nothing in the manifested worlds, which is free from them. Based upon them, the scripture prescribes different duties for different categories of people. By performing them according to one's nature, with detachment and devotion, one attains peace and perfection in action. Having attained perfection in the yoga of action, he attains Brahman. Attaining Brahman, he neither grieves nor desires. Equal to all beings, He experiences supreme devotion to God. Through devotion, he realizes the truths about him and finds a place in the Supreme Abode.

Having explained the division of the *gunas* and their manifestations, Lord *Krishna* advises *Arjuna* to perform actions with his mind fixed upon Him, without egoism, mentally renouncing all actions to Him. Even if he decides to act otherwise, the *gunas* in him propel him to perform actions. Finally in the end, having explained the importance of duty, actions, renunciation and detachment, Lord *Krishna* tells *Arjuna* that He revealed to him most secretive teaching because he was dear to Him. He advises Him that it should be taught only to those who are qualified and who have faith and devotion. He who teaches the knowledge of the *Bhagavadgita* is the dearest to Lord Krishna. Next are those who study it and then come those who listen to the discourse through others. Having heard the discourse, Arjuna experiences great joy and declares that his delusion is gone and he is now to ready to fight. Hearing their conversation from far, *Sanjaya*, who has been narrating the discourse to *Dhritarashtra* expresses great joy and thanks sage *Vyasa* for giving him an opportunity to act as a messenger to the king.

Thus ends the *Bhagavadgita*, the divine teaching of Lord *Krishna*, the great *Upanishad*, and the scripture of Yoga, containing the knowledge of the Absolute and the debate between *Arjuna* and Lord *Krishna*.

The Meaning of Yoga in the Context of the Bhagavadgita

It is difficult to understand the meaning and significance of yoga from the teachings of the *Bhagavadgita*, if you are accustomed to the traditional definition of yoga as a union, practice, type of knowledge, discipline, or collection of techniques. The scripture uses the word in a broader sense to denote not only these but also state or mode. The latter definition carries greater significance in the *Bhagavadgita*, and unless we understand this clearly, we cannot grasp its teachings correctly.

For many people, yoga means practicing some highly formalized and even commercialized techniques of breathing, postures, meditation and concentration. In truth, they represent but one aspect of yoga only. They are the means to attain the state of wellbeing (*yogakshema*) or a pristine state of mind that is completely free from modifications (*vrittis*) and impurities. Even *Patanjali* declares yoga as a state that is free from modifications (*yoga cittavritti nirodhah*). Some scholars interpret it as its purpose too. The *Bhagavadgita* uses the word yoga to denote a state and the means. One may also use a specific mental or physical state to practice yoga to reach another state or mode. Thus, yoga (practice) leads to yoga (state). Everything in the world exists in some state. Literally speaking, everything is in some yoga. However, these are relative and imperfect states and they subject us to modifications.

Yoga means state

The scripture interprets yoga in terms of techniques and practices such as selfless service, self-study, practice of rules and restraints, restraint of the senses, breath control, meditation, concentration, and devotion. It also uses it to denote any state or condition. Its purpose is self-transformation or purification that eventually leads to the highest yoga (state), which is variously described as the state of self-absorption (*samadhi*), union with the Self (*atmasamyam*), union with the Supreme Self (*brahmasparsa*), aloneness (*kaivalyam*) and supreme bliss. In this journey, whatever mental or physical states one cultivates or the actions one performs to attain the transcendental states are also considered yogas. Hence, we have different yogas such as the yoga of action, the yoga of knowledge, the yoga of devotion and so on.

This concept is not peculiar to the *Bhagavadgita* alone. We find references to it in other scriptures also. They use yoga to refer to both material and spiritual states found in creation. For example, *brahmayogam* means the state of Brahman. One may attain it by the grace of God or by effort. *Mahayogam*, means the supreme state, which may be any extraordinary situation in which one experiences greatness or abundance of something. *Vishadayogam* means the state of sorrow, which Arjuna experienced in the beginning of the discourse. All human beings experience it whenever they are overwhelmed with difficulties or adversity. *Subhayogam* means the state of auspiciousness, which arises from good works, sacrificial actions or the blessings of gods. *Vivahayogam* is obtained by marriage. *Putrayogam* arises from the birth of a son. *Rajayogam* arises from gaining a kingdom. *Dhanayogam* arises from attaining wealth. These yogas refer to different states of attainment and have little relevance to the discipline of yoga or the philosophy of yoga. The opposite of *yogam* is *viyogam*, which means separation or loss. When you attain something, it is *yoga* and when you lose something, it is *viyoga*. Even inanimate objects have a state, the state of inertia (*jadayogam*).

Today many people practice yoga for health reasons, as some form of exercise. No doubt, it is an auspicious goal. However, one should aim for spiritual well being through yoga to experience not only good health but also peace, balance and equanimity. In a general sense, we go through various yogas as we experience union and separation from things. Every experience (*anubhava*) and state of being (*bhava*) through which we pass or with which we become involved mentally or physically is a kind of yoga only.

Some of them are ordinary yogas, even impure ones, which arise naturally in the field (*kshetra*) of experience, while some are very extraordinary ones experienced rarely. At some point, these experiences eventually culminate in the highest yoga, which is the state of liberation or bliss.

The whole universe exists in a state of union (*yoga*) between the Supreme Self and the Primal Nature. It has many intermediary states some of which are eternal and some temporary. Creation is yoga. Divinity is yoga. Existence is yoga. Ignorance is yoga. Knowledge is yoga. Wisdom is yoga. In the course of our lives, we go through many different states (yogas), both positive and negative. Some of them arise in us naturally and some through effort.

The *Bhagavadgita* mentions various types of yoga as both states and means, such as *karmayoga, jnanayoga, sanyasayoga, buddhiyoga, karmaphalasanyasayoga, atmasamyamayoga*, and *bhaktiyoga*. They are complimentary yogas. You practice them by cultivating specific states of purity, thinking and attitude. At the same time, it also recommends some techniques of the classical yoga such as the practice of rules and restraints (*yamas* and *niyamas*), breathing (*pranayama*), restraint of the senses (*pratyahara*), concentration (*dharana*), meditation (*dhyana*) and self-absorption (*samadhi*). These techniques help us purify our minds and bodies so that they can sustain and experience higher states (*yogas*) of awareness and intelligence.

Cultivating states

You practice yoga either by cultivating a state or by following certain techniques. Such practices may lead to either temporal states or transcendental states. The ultimate purpose of all these yogas is to attain the highest state of union with Brahman. Since one cannot reach it directly, one has to practice different means and cultivate the required purity to qualify for it. The scripture recommends *karmayoga* as the most basic yoga to perform actions with a state of detachment and selflessness. In this state (yoga) you do not shun your obligations. You appreciate your obligatory duties as the means to overcome desires and express your devotion to God by offering them to Him. You enter into this state by cultivating detachment, acknowledging God as the real Doer. *Jnanayoga* is another important state the scripture recommends. You practice this yoga by cultivating the state of knowledge and awareness whereby you realize that you are an eternal soul rather than a mere physical being. The practice of *jnanayoga* leads to the knowledge of the Self and Brahman whereby you experience oneness with them. In *buddhiyoga,* you enter into a state of wisdom whereby you know the right from wrong and the good from evil. You learn to use your discretion, choose wisely and avoid negative consequences. In *sanyasayoga,* you resort to a state of renunciation, whereby you renounce desires and the fruit of your actions. You do not renounce work but the desire hidden in it.

You may interpret the other yogas mentioned in the scripture similarly as states that that are essential for one's transformation. You cultivate these states with resolve until they become part of your awareness. You focus upon them and cultivate the required attitudes and thinking modes until they become firmly established in you. These states are the means to your transformation and liberation. They lead you from the state of sorrow (*vishadayoga*) to the state of final liberation (*moksha*). With their help, you bring God into your life and stabilize your mind in Him. Eventually, you reach the state of God and experience peace, equanimity, stability, sameness, devotion and oneness with Him.

Reaching the highest state

If you want to pursue liberation, you have to integrate you whole personality into a harmonious whole. You have to bring your lower nature into harmony with your higher one and align them both so that they work for the same goal, while your consciousness stabilizes in sameness (*samatvam*) in which nothing can disturb you or distract you. This knowledge has great practical value. If you understand yoga as a state and know that certain states (yogas) lead to bondage and suffering and certain states lead to peace and equanimity, you can use such knowledge to your advantage. With practice, you can cultivates certain modes of thinking and remain in particular states to stay free from desires and passions. By entering into certain mental states that facilitate desireless actions, knowledge, wisdom, renunciation, devotion, purity and sameness, you can gradually move towards the highest Yoga, which is union with God Himself.

Five Lessons from the Bhagavadgita

The *Bhagavadgita* is a book of learning, knowledge and guidance. A practical philosophy studded with gems of ancient wisdom, it has the ability to sharpen our intelligence and refine our character. It has a purifying effect upon all those who read it and assimilate its teachings. It leaves a strong impression upon all those who are pure in their hearts and who contemplate upon its wisdom and integrate its philosophy into their daily living. To be exposed to its light and brilliance is a blessing and to practice its wisdom is to change your destiny forever. Every living being upon earth ekes out an existence; but living responsibly and dutifully with knowledge and intelligence is what sets us apart as human beings. Many people live in the darkness of their minds, unmindful of their spiritual obligations, surrounded by ignorance and delusion, and prefer to live that way even if it causes them pain and suffering. From the *Bhagavadgita* we learn that we do not have to live in darkness and there are ways and means to break the inertia that consumes our minds and achieve liberation.

Lord Krishna also leaves a stern warning to those who succumb to dark passions and demonic qualities, stating that they will descend to the darkest hells from where redemption will be very difficult. The God of the *Bhagavadgita* is not a vengeful God. He is indifferent and dispassionate. However, He insists upon austere discipline and commitment to virtuous living. He sets in motion several laws to regulate the worlds and beings of His creation. To break them means inviting punishment and destruction, not from God but from your own actions. Thus, according to the scripture, your life and your destiny are mostly in your hands, although the hand of God shapes them every moment. You are safe if you live with humility and spirit of surrender, claiming neither the doership nor the ownership of your actions and transfer the responsibility and the consequences of your actions to the One who is the source of all. Your liberation from this world is ensured if you follow His immutable laws dutifully and sincerely and do your part in ensuring the order and regularity of the world and society, without developing attachment to the things with which you may come into contact in the course of your existence. If you hanker after them or strive to make them your own, you will attract punishment and cast yourself into the deepest and darkest hells. In other words, if you ignore the warnings found in the scriptures either as revelations or otherwise and jump willfully into the turbulent waters of life against all wisdom, you have to blame yourself and accept responsibility for the mindless actions you perform and the consequences you reap from them.

The *Bhagavadgita* contains transformative wisdom. If you are serious about liberation, you do not need any guru. Just accept Lord Krishna as your teacher and follow His teachings. You will be rescued from the world of impermanence. Many verses in the scripture contain seed thoughts, fragments of profound wisdom, flashes of immense brilliance, which you can use for concentration and contemplation and find great comfort in the possibility of securing liberation and divine grace. With the *Bhagavadgita* in your hands, you are in the company of Lord Krishna Himself. By thinking about it, you invite Him into your life. By practicing it, you open yourself to the secret knowledge that shows you the way to the Abode of Brahman. In the eighteenth chapter, Lord Krishna identifies three types of people who are dearest to Him. First are those who preach the scripture to others and take the message of the *Bhagavadgita* to His devotees. Next are those who study the scripture with devotion and sincerity. In the third category are those who hear the knowledge from others and assimilate it. Thus, having even a little interest in the divine teaching has its own beneficial effect.

The book is not meant to proselytize people or thirst its wisdom upon unwilling minds. Lord Krishna makes it amply cleat that His teachings constitute secret knowledge, which should be imparted only to qualified few who deserve it and who are ready for it. Under no circumstances, He says one should teach it to those who are not austere, who do not have devotion, who envy

God and who have no desire to listen to it. The following are a few important concepts we find in the scripture, which we can use to transform ourselves.

1. Know that you are an eternal Self

One of the important lessons we learn from the *Bhagavadgita* is having right awareness about oneself and becoming centered in the eternal Self. Ordinary people identify themselves with their individualities as distinguished by their names and forms; but the *Gita* teaches us that we are immortal selves. We are different from the minds and bodies that we think we are. If you think carefully, you will realize that the problems we face in our lives arise mostly because we regard ourselves as mortal beings and fail to acknowledge our eternal existence. Fear, anxiety, worry and insecurity arise when you think you have but one life and you are vulnerable to death and destruction.

The *Bhagavadgita* states clearly that the body is unreal. It is like a garment worn by the Self. It is a temporary construct, subject to modifications. If are attached to it, you will experience sorrow and suffering as it happened in case of Arjuna. If you think that you are an eternal being, you will take things in your stride and look at your problems and your existence from a broader perspective. Such awareness makes you more responsible and dutiful in your thinking and actions since you know that your actions may leave impressions that may last for several lives and seriously hamper your chances of liberation.

We should therefore learn to look at ourselves as spiritual entities and bring a paradigm shift in our thinking and attitude. We should identify ourselves with our real Selves and consider ourselves eternal, immutable, indestructible and real. The inner Self is an aspect of the Supreme Self. It is beyond the grasp of the mind and the senses. We are free only when we liberate our true Selves from the hold of Nature by overcoming our ignorance and delusion.

2. Learn to control your desires

Our minds are the storehouses of memories, thoughts, desires, impulses, habitual thought patterns and latent impressions (*samskaras*), which ensure our continuity as embodied selves in a world of change and impermanence. They act as the reservoir of our perceptions and the seat of our ignorance, delusion and duality. Our wandering senses keep them in a state of turmoil, as they are constantly flooded with wave upon wave of information, demanding our attention and provoking our responses. By constantly interacting with the world outside, our sense organs, (*jnanendriyas*) and the organs of action (*karmendriyas*) create in us desire for the sense objects and our attachment to them. In turn, they subject our minds to various modifications (*vrittis*) and conflicting emotions. Thereby we experience attraction and aversion to the pairs of opposites.

An unstable mind that is subject to duality and delusion is not conducive to peace or stability. It is subject to suffering and afflictions arising from egoism and desire-ridden actions. Those who are bound to things are never free. They are enslaved by Nature and held in its control for the purpose of creation. As long as their minds are unstable, they are not fit for salvation. Their senses keeps wandering among sense objects while they remain entangled in the impermanence of the phenomenal world. Instability of the mind is therefore a serious problem yoga tries to address to establish a solid foundation for practicing various disciplines that lead to liberation such as austerities (*tapas*), duty (*dharma*), renunciation (*sanyasa*), firmness (*dhriti*), rules and restraints (*yamas* and *niyamas*), breath control (*pranayama*), withdrawal of the senses, concentration, contemplation and self-absorption (*samadhi*).

By nature, the mind is fickle. It is very difficult to control its movements even after years of practicing yoga. We need intense and sustained effort, with complete resolve, to experience balance and stability in our thinking and attitude. The *Bhagavadgita* suggests that through selfless actions, knowledge of the Self and devotion to God, a devotee should control his senses, develop detachment from the sense objects and achieve tranquility and sameness (*samatvam*). When the mind is tranquil and the senses are resting, we remain the same to both pleasures and pain and we stop reacting to the situations arising in our lives. With peace ruling our minds, we experience love and devotion to God. When our desires rest in the silence of our minds, we rest in the bliss of the Self. We become free from the delusion and ignorance to which we are subject. We journey to the world of immortals travelling by the sunlit path.

3. Know what true renunciation means

One may achieve mental stability by living in secluded places, renouncing all duties and responsibilities and avoiding public contact. This was the tradition of renunciation practiced in ancient India at one time. After certain age, people gave up their worldly possessions and retired to forests to practice asceticism and achieve true loneliness. To silence their cravings, they stopped the use of fire and even cooking food and subsisted on meager food rations until their bodies wasted away. The *Ajivakas*, an ancient Indian sect that thrived in 6th century B.C.E., believed in fatalism. They shunned their duties and responsibilities, and led passive lives, as they believed that everything was predetermined and they had no control over their lives or destinies.

The doctrine of *karma* suggested on the other hand that human beings had the ability to change their lives and destinies by indulging in righteous actions and avoiding evil actions. The *Bhagavadgita* added another layer of complexity to the practice of renunciation suggesting that *karma* was determined not by actions but by the desires hidden in them. Therefore, the focus should be not on actions but upon the desires hidden in them and one should practice renunciation of desires rather than actions. It is better accomplished when one engages in actions without desire for their fruit. This approach would ensure the preservation and orderliness of the world and at the same time our liberation from the world of births and deaths.

According to the *Bhagavadgita,* inaction is also not a solution to the problem of *karma* because firstly, inaction is impractical and secondly, inaction has consequences, which may lead to bondage and delusion. Actions are imperative for our survival and the continuity of the world. Even God engages in them for the sake of order and regularity of His creation. None can ever remain free from engaging action. The *gunas* make sure that we remain helplessly active performing actions and pursuing our desires. The wise ones know this and therefore they renounce the desire for the fruit of their actions and offer them to God. An ignorant person acts with attachment thinking, "I am the doer," whereas the wise one acts without attachment, desiring the welfare of the world-order. For him there is no interest in what is done and what is not to be done, nor has he to depend upon anyone for anything. In this respect, says the Gita, God Himself is a great example. Actions do not taint Him, even though He is engaged in actions, because He has no desire for their fruit. A wise man follows His example upon earth and becomes free. He acquires the knowledge of actions and the various ways in which sacrifices are performed. Knowing thus, through knowledge, he becomes free from the bondage of action. His actions are burnt up in the fire of wisdom. Thus through knowledge, he attains peace by performing actions with discernment, without desire and doership.

The *Gita* says that better than renunciation of action is renouncing the sense of doership and the desire for its fruit. The knower of truth while performing actions knows that he does nothing at all because he is not bound by their consequences. He acts offering his actions to God, without desire and attachment. Detached and unbound, he remains untouched by sin as the lotus-leaf by water. A man of action (*karmayogi*) performs actions only with his senses, mind, intellect and body, giving up all attachments for his inner purification, offering the fruit of his actions to God. Mentally renouncing actions and self-controlled, he lives in his body happily, neither acting nor making others act. Offering the fruit of his actions to God, he attains peace in the form of Self-realization. He becomes one with God and attains liberation.

The *Gita* further declares that he is a true *sanyasi* who ceased to have any attachment either to the sense-objects or to actions and who has renounced all thoughts of the world. He conquers his ego-self by his real Self. He becomes established in God and remains the same to heat and cold, pleasure and pain, honor and dishonor. For him a piece of earth or a piece of gold is the same. He is equal-minded among friends and foes, among the partial and impartial, and among saints and sinners alike.

4. Make your life a devotional offering to God

The Supreme Brahman is universal, eternal, imperishable, and immutable. At the beginning of every cycle of creation, He creates the multitude of beings with His divine *Maya* (*yogamaya*) and keeps them under its influence. Therefore, according to the *Bhagavadgita*, He is both the material and efficient causes of creation. Actions do not bind Him because He is unattached and indifferent to them. In the body, He dwells as the divine Self (*adhidaivam*) and the inner Witness (*sakshi*). While He is untouched by the activities and modifications of Nature, the Self is bound to the world until it is liberated.

The *Bhagavadgita* states that all knowledge emanates from God and He is the original teacher. Those who know the truths about Him become absorbed in steadfast yoga. Since He is the source of everything, we must look to Him only for our liberation. To achieve that auspicious goal we must consecrate our lives and actions to Him, remaining contended and happy, with the spirit of surrender and humility, acknowledging Him as the Supreme. To them who are absorbed in devotional service with love, He gives them knowledge and wisdom by which they come to Him only. Out of mercy for them, He removes their darkness, residing in them as their own Self, and shines upon them the lamp of knowledge. One should therefore take refuge in that Primal Being

(*Adi Purusha*), who is seated in the heart of all and who is responsible for memory, knowledge and even their loss. By practicing the yoga of action, with their minds fixed upon Him, giving up all attachments, the yogis attain the Supreme Self. His very thoughts are so purifying that whoever remembers Him only at the time of death, attains immortality.

In the *Gita* we find the assurance that those who surrender to God in devotion and offer their lives to Him, He takes care of their lives and responsibilities. Fools do not recognize His greatness and disregard Him; but the wise ones know His true nature and worship Him with unwavering devotion. Thus says the scripture, those devotees who worship Him only, always thinking of Him, and ever united, God takes care of their wants and needs and looks after their welfare. Even those who worship other gods also in a way worship Him because He is the Lord of all offerings. In whatever way people worship Him, He strengthens their faith in that. Those who worship the gods go to them; but those who worship Him attain Him only. Therefore, while one may worship any divinity, it is always better to worship the Supreme Self because He alone ensures our liberation and a place in His eternal Abode.

The Gita says that God accepts whatever that is offered to Him by those who have faith and devotion. He accepts our offerings unconditionally because He has no expectations and nothing that would complete Him or compliment Him. However, He is merciful. Although He is complete and perfect and does not require anything, out of mercy He is always willing to help His devotees. He bestows His grace upon them who approach Him with faith and devotion. Therefore, offer Him whatever you have, whatever you do and whatever you sacrifice. Give Him all keeping nothing for you. When you give Him selflessly with a pure heart, you earn His grace and His infinite love. Through pure devotion, by constantly thinking of Him and worshipping him, doing actions for His sake, taking refuge in him and renouncing the fruits of your actions, with your desires subdued, with no expectations, steady of mind, you can easily attain God.

5. Self-purification is self-transformation

The body is the field of activity and God dwells in the body as the Knower of the Field. The body is made up of five great elements, the intellect, the unmanifest nature, the ten senses, the mind and the five objects of the senses. It is also the seat of all desires, feelings, emotions and mental energy. The body is an aspect of *Prakriti*. It is subject to modifications, which are caused by the *gunas* (modes or qualities), namely *sattva*, *rajas* and *tamas*. The *gunas* have a tendency to suppress the other ones and promote themselves. Our actions arise from this internal strife waged by the *gunas*. By pervading the body and mind, and promoting desires and attachment through the senses for objects of similar nature, they bind the imperishable soul to the body and keep it in bondage. *Sattva* is pure and luminous and it binds the soul through attachment to happiness and knowledge. *Rajas* is born of passion. It binds the soul through selfish actions and attachment to the fruits of actions. *Tamas* is the quality born of ignorance, delusion and indolence. It binds the soul through negligence, inertia, sloth and sleep. We cannot escape from the influence of the *gunas* altogether. However, we can practice virtues, austerities and yoga to remove the impurities of *rajas* and *tamas* from our minds and bodies and at the same time increase *sattva*, which leads to purity, illumination and liberation.

Conclusion

According to the *Bhagavadgita*, true renunciation means renunciation of desire and attachment. One may live in secluded places to practice *yoga*, but one should not abandon one's obligatory duties or indulge in inaction to avoid the consequences of *karma*. Instead, one should perform one's obligatory duties with devotion and as a sacrifice, without attachment, ownership, doership and egoism. Restraining his mind and senses, controlling his desires, practicing self-purification, he should keep his mind focused upon God with faith and devotion, offering Him the fruit of his actions and accepting life as it happens. Actions performed in this manner or life lived selflessly do not bind us. They lead to knowledge, equanimity, illumination devotion and liberation. We can learn many lessons from the *Bhagavadgita*. We can interpret its teachings in various ways and apply them to various disciplines, professions and pursuits. The ones, which we have discussed above, are some important ones and by following them, we can experience peace and balance in our lives.

Karma Yoga – the Path of Action

In a very broad sense, *karmayoga* means performing actions sacrificially to attain liberation. It is a state of mind, in which you engage in selfless actions, without desires and attachments, as an offering to God. In a very narrow sense, it is performing obligatory duties as an offering to God. The state of mind (yoga) or the means required to practice this yoga is detachment, dispassion, absence of desires and an attitude of duty and sincerity. Truly speaking, every other of yoga can be regarded as a type of *karmayoga* only because activities such as pursuing knowledge, practicing meditation, worshipping God also count as actions only. However, in the context of the *Bhagavadgita*, *karmayoga* means performing obligatory duties as an offering to God. *Karmayoga* is appropriate for all classes and ages of people, more so, for those who lead worldly lives as householders. In the world of God, every living being participates in actions in one form or another. The highest of all *karmayogis* is God Himself. Although He is complete and perfect in all respects and has no desires, He engages in actions to set an example and ensure that the worlds are preserved until the end of the time cycle. He performs His obligatory duties of creation, preservation and destruction. He helps His devotees and protects them from evil. He imparts knowledge and uplifts those who want to escape from the hold of Nature. He enforces *dharma* to maintain the order and regularity of the worlds. Whenever the worlds fall into confusion and chaos, He incarnates upon earth to restore order, protect the weak and promote orderliness. He also rescues from the phenomenal world, those who worship Him and surrender to Him with faith and devotion.

Our actions are responsible for our bondage and suffering. The *karma* arising from our actions in the form of consequences bind us to the world of death and rebirth. *Karmayoga* is an antidote to the problem of sin as well as merit arising from our actions. In *karmayoga*, we use the very actions, which bind us normally, to liberate ourselves. In other words, we convert the chief cause of our suffering into the main source of our liberation. We convert the problem into a solution by performing actions in such a manner that they do not bind us. *Karmayoga* is a perfect solution for those who want to lead active lives and do not want to escape from the material world and their obligations.

Actions are of various types and produce different types of consequences. Since we live in a world of duality, we can divide actions into pairs of opposites such as good and bad, divine and demonic, moral and immoral etc. The *Bhagavadgita* says that actions by themselves are neither good nor bad. What gives them these characteristics is the desire hidden in them. Good actions may be performed with bad intentions, while bad actions may be performed with good intentions. When this happens, the consequences arising from them will also be different from what society expects. A yogi on the path of liberation should be interested in neither good nor bad consequences because they both prolong our liberation. He must aim to be free from all consequences arising from his actions. He can accomplish it only when he performs actions without desire and without expecting any result. His practice of *karmayoga* becomes more effective when he offers all his actions to God as a sacrificial offering without seeking their fruit.

Karmayoga is thus a way of sanctifying our lives and actions and consecrating them to God as the means to self-purification and inner transformation. It is bringing God into the center of our lives and making Him the owner and doer of our lives and actions. It is transferring our responsibilities to Him and making Him the caretaker of our destinies. When actions are performed sincerely and dutifully as an offering to God, He assumes responsibility for our lives and takes care of our needs. In the *Bhagavadgita*, we find this assurance from Lord Krishna clearly and loudly. Continued and regular practice of *karmayoga* leads to self-realization. Even a little practice has its own rewards. Those who fail do not lose anything. Upon their death, they go to the ancestral world. Once their *karmas* are exhausted they return to the earth and take birth in a good family to continue their journey further.

In the context of the *Bhagavadgita*, "*sanyasa*" means renunciation of actions that are prompted by desire, and "*tyaga*" means giving up the fruit of such actions. Both are necessary for a *karmayogi* to achieve peace and perfection on the path. One should not renounce actions but only desire for their fruit. According to the scripture, a true *sanyasi* does not hanker after results while performing actions. He worships God. He serves others, especially those who are devotees of God. He performs sacrifices for the welfare of others and fulfills his obligations towards his family, ancestors, gods, spirit beings and other living beings. He does them as duty. Lord Krishna says a person of such merit is a true *sanyasi*, not the one who gives up activity or the sacred fire (6.1).

Significance of karmayoga

Karmayoga is the most simple and straightforward approach to resolve the problem of suffering and bondage. Anyone and everyone can practice it by injecting into their actions certain spirituality and selflessness. Knowledge, discretion and renunciation make it a very powerful means to stabilize the mind and body. Knowledge is essential to understand the underlying causes in any action and the way they bind us to the world. Discretion enables us to discern things correctly and remain centered in the divine rather than the demonic nature. Renunciation helps us cleanse our minds of the latent impressions and burn away the seeds of our future through selfless actions.

While desires are the root cause of our suffering, desires are in turn caused by the triple *gunas*. The *gunas* have a tendency to compete with one another for their supremacy and in the process induce us to indulge in actions and seek things. They are responsible for our experience of attraction and aversion to things and the pairs of opposites. Since they are inherent in us, none can escape from performing actions. They drive the all ceaselessly into performing actions of one kind or the other since through actions alone they acquire strength and become predominant. Therefore, the *Bhagavadgita* rightly states that freedom from action cannot be achieved by avoiding actions or by renouncing them. He, who indulges in mere meditative practices, restraining his organs of actions, neglecting his obligations, is but a deluded soul and a hypocrite. By refraining from action, it is not possible to maintain even one's own body. Dynamism (*chaitanyam*) is the fundamental characteristic of life. Even in the inanimate objects, unseen activity happens at the atomic and subatomic levels. Therefore, it is delusion to believe that one can escape from the consequences of actions by not doing anything. Even the Imperishable Supreme Brahman does His work dutifully although He has no desire either to perform them or seek their fruit. There is nothing in the three worlds for Him to do or yet to attain. Still He engages in actions, because, says Lord *Krishna*, if He does not perform His duties men would follow His example and neglect their own.

Therefore, those who want to attain liberation should follow His example and do their obligatory work, without attachment and without any interest whatsoever in what is being done or not done, knowing that their right is to work only, but not to the fruit thereof. They must live dutifully, even minded in both success and failure, surrendering to God, offering the fruit of their actions to Him, and partaking of only that, which has been offered to Him.

Actions bind people when they are performed with egoism, thinking that one is the doer, with a desire to enjoy their fruit. Whoever thinks that he is the doer of his actions is but a deluded soul who does not know the truth about the influence of the *gunas* and how they are responsible for all binding actions. Performing actions out of desires and attachment, with an intention to enjoy their fruit, a deluded soul becomes bound to their consequences, whether they are good or bad. Depending upon the nature of his activities, he may gain either sorrow or happiness in this world or other worlds.

An enlightened *karmayogi* on the other hand, knows action in inaction and inaction in action (Ch.4.17). He knows who the real doer is, how the *gunas* drive men to perform actions and how they bind them to sorrow and suffering. When he performs his actions, he remains unconcerned because he is aware that it is only the senses that are occupied with the object of his senses. Thus, he actually becomes inactive even while performing actions and remains untouched by the fruit of his actions like a lotus leaf by water.

A *karmayogi* ought to be aware of the nature of the *gunas* and their influence upon his behavior. All actions arise from *gunas* only and whether they are sattvic, rajasic or tamasic, they all bind people and beings. One should not therefore aim to perform particular types of actions. The aim should be to perform actions that are part of one's obligatory duties without expectations. While *sattva* is the preferable quality, there is no cause for concern if the other two qualities predominate. The qualities cannot be wished away or suppressed easily. They persist in us despite our best efforts and intentions, since we accumulate them over several lifetimes. A *karmayogi* should focus upon performing his actions selflessly in harmony with his *gunas* rather than against them. He should adhere to his essential nature (*dharma*), however inferior it may be, rather than adopt the nature (*dharma*) of another. When actions are performed with the spirit of renunciation in accordance with one's *gunas* it will eventually lead to the predominance of *sattva* and strengthening of divine qualities.

Karmayoga is the highest form of sacrificial action (*yajna*). It disciplines the mind and purifies the body, establishing a firm foundation for one's liberation. It is the simplest form of physical austerity, although not everyone can practice it with utmost perfection. Even the animals and lower life forms practice *karmayoga* of some sort. No special knowledge is required to practice this yoga. However, sincerity and attitude are very important to control one's desires and expectations in performing actions. Persistent practice of *karmayoga* leads to knowledge, wisdom and devotion, stabilizing the mind and leading to equanimity and sameness.

Karmayoga in daily life

Karmayoga is the most suitable form of spiritual activity for people who are householders and who are particularly devoted to worldly actions because of either desires or duty. Ascetic people also perform *karmayoga*, but their actions are meant for performing bodily functions and keeping their minds and bodies alive. A householder on the other hand has to fulfill many obligations and responsibilities, which keep changing as he progresses from one phase of life (*ashrama*) to another. He has therefore many opportunities to practice *karmayoga*, following the principles and techniques suggested in the *Bhagavadgita*, and test its real value in self-transformation. He can rely upon *karmayoga*, as true servant of God to overcome his desires, selfishness, impurities or rajas and tamas and experience dispassion, detachment, equanimity and sameness. With its help, he can bring God into the center of his life and sanctify his actions with His presence.

A devotee can practice *karmayoga* in many different ways, according to his duties and obligations. He can perform actions holding the thought that he does nothing, but every action is performed by God only with him as the instrument. He can remember him constantly while engaged in actions, holding Him as the real Doer and their true owner, acknowledging the energy and the inspiration as the blessings from the heaven. While performing his actions, he may even step into the role of God and identify himself fully with Him or believe that he is doing them for the sake of God and with His help and guidance. Knowing the omnipresence and omniscience of God, he can acknowledge that the actor, the action and the result of the action are God only. Most importantly, he should consecrate his actions to Him and take no credit whatsoever for them. A *karmayogi* makes himself invisible. It is as if he does not exist. He replaces himself with God. He lets Him rule his mind and body. He lets Him control his life and shape his destiny. He does not take credit for his actions. He does not call attention to himself. He neither projects himself nor defends himself. He keeps his ego under check and refuses to participate in egocentric clashes. He may fight the battles of life or even fight with others, not for himself but for the sake of God to fulfill his obligations towards society or religion.

One simple and direct method to practice *karmayoga* is to remember God in everything you do and make Him the real Doer without claiming credit or discredit for your actions. If you remember God constantly, you are already on the path of *karmayoga*. If you keep God always in the back of your mind, your life becomes one continuous *karmayoga*. If you focus your mind upon the result, your performance will suffer. If you focus your attention upon your performance, most likely you will become skilful in actions. It makes senses to focus on the action or the technique rather than the result and perform your tasks with due diligence. When you concentrate on actions rather than their outcome, results will take care of themselves. Planning is essential. A *karmayogi* may have a plan for his actions, but he would offer the plan as well as the result to God.

Karmayoga is a very practical and suitable solution to bring God directly into the center of our lives and use every available opportunity in our lives to remember Him and express our love and devotion to Him. In today's competitive world, you can use it to raise your efficiency and skill in action without suffering from stress and anxiety. You can face the challenges of your life, with God on your side rather than against you. By saturating your mind with the thoughts of God, you can elevate your own consciousness and discern things clearly. You can use your actions to transform and elevate you mentally and spiritually rather than bind you to egoism, ignorance and delusion.

With *karmayoga*, you can experience peace and stability and become free from the modifications and afflictions of your mind. A *karmayogi* accepts responsibility for his life and actions but he would not take pride in his achievements. With great humility, he attributes his successes and failure to fate or God. He is troubled by neither his past nor his future. He feels no anxiety. He does not suffer from insecurity. He does not feel the compulsion to outsmart others or belittle them to feel important. He does not use aggression or anger to intimidate others or coerce them into submission. He does not lie or cheat to impress others or mislead them. He is not ashamed of his failures or his weaknesses. He reposes complete trust in God and lets Him rule his life and dictate his actions, reactions and responses. He lives in the present and performs his actions with detachment and dispassion. He plans his work with precision and executes it with utmost sincerity, but he would not be consumed by the fear of failure or passion for success. Keeping his emotions firmly under control and accepting God as the real Doer, he takes things in his stride without being disturbed by their consequences. Since he is duty bound, he would not hesitate to take unpleasant decisions or express his opinions frankly. At the same time, he would treat others with dignity and respect, acknowledging their divine nature and their identity as immortal souls.

References to Karmayoga in the Bhagavadgita

The yoga of action (*karmayoga*) suggested in the *Bhagavadgita* teaches an individual how to perform obligatory duties, without being tainted by them, and qualify for liberation. It is the first discipline to be practiced on the path of liberation. With perfection in it, one can practice the yoga of knowledge (*jnanayoga*) and the yoga of devotion (*bhaktiyoga*) more skillfully and experience profound peace and joy. *Karmayoga* encompasses one's whole life. The worlds exist because of the actions (*karmayoga*) performed by God and the various divinities, who are duty bound to their roles and act according to the Will of God to keep the worlds in good order. Human beings can practice it in all the four phases (*ashramas*) of their lives as part of their essential duties (*ashrama dharmas*), even when they renounce worldly things, and retire to secluded places to perform austerities and practice the yoga of renunciation (*sanyasa*).

Karmayoga is a state of mind (*yoga*), in which you perform actions with sameness, indifference and disinterest. It is characterized by dispassion, detachment and commitment to selfless and desireless works. According to the *Bhagavadgita*, actions arising from desires bind men to their consequences and subject them to their karmic consequences. However, this does not mean you can resolve the problem of *karma* by inaction or selective action. Both are troublesome and binding, because they have consequences too. As the *Bhagavadgita* declares, none can attain freedom by abstaining from work or renouncing it (Ch.3.4). It is delusion to believe that if *karma* arises from actions, we can prevent it by doing nothing. None can remain inactive even for a moment. The *gunas* drive every one hopelessly to perform actions (Ch.3.5). Actions keep us alive. Actions are necessary to keep ourselves alive, sane and healthy. Without actions, we cannot maintain our bodies or keep them in good health (Ch.3.8). The autonomous functions of our bodies such as breathing and digestion that are not under our control. Whatever we may resolve, those actions we cannot stop or renounce. Therefore, the *Bhagavadgita* concludes that actions are superior to inaction and they should not be renounced under any circumstances.

In life, we receive many things from the universe and incur many debts. We have to repay them in some form. Whatever we receive from God as a blessing should be returned to Him as an offering. The offering may be a simple acknowledgement or a dedication. It does not matter; what matters most is the attitude with which you receive and return. Of the many blessings we receive from God, food is the most important one because the universe is sustained by it. Our bodies need food for survival. The gods need food for their survival. The universe needs food (energy) to sustain creation. The nourishment for all comes from *Isvara* only. He is the ultimate nourisher. He created food before He created beings because He knew that the beings would need food to remain alive and perform sacrificial duties to keep others alive. Thus says the scriptures, the virtuous ones who know this show humility and gratitude by eating only that which has been offered to God as a sacrifice, and they do it for the sake of nourishing their bodies alone. In this manner, they do not incur any sin (Ch.3.13).

On the path of action (*karmayoga*), there is no loss, nor any adverse consequence. Even a little practice safeguards one from the fear of birth and death (Ch.2.40). Man's right is to work only, but not to the fruit of his actions or to inaction (Ch.2.47). True *karmayoga* consists of performing ones duty without attachment and remaining even minded in both success and failure (Ch.2.48). This can be accomplished by controlling the senses (Ch.2.64-65) and desires (Ch.2.71). A true *karmayogi* knows that controlling the senses is important (Ch.3.6) because desires and attachments stem from them. He therefore engages in actions by restraining his mind and senses, unattached, directing his organs (*karmendriyas*) to work. (Ch.3.7). He overcomes in this way his desires and remains contended, taking delight in his Self alone (Ch.3.17). For him there is no interest whatsoever in performing actions or in not performing them, nor does he depend upon anyone for anything (Ch.3.18). He performs his duty without attachment, with his mind and body under firm control. He lives his life as a sacrifice and an offering. He lives his life as if he guided by God every step of the way. He lives by the word of God as revealed by Him in the scriptures.

Even the Lord Supreme is a true *Karmayogi*. He also engages in actions, although there is nothing in the three worlds for Him to do or attain (Ch.3.22). He performs actions so that men would follow His example (Ch.3.23) and worlds could be saved from disorder and confusion (Ch.3.24). The ignorant ones act with selfish motives, with attachment, while the wise ones act without attachment, for the greater good of the world (Ch.3.25). They follow the footstep of God and exemplify His attitude towards duty.

The sense of doership is another area of personal reform. A knower of the triple *gunas* knows that all actions are caused by them (Ch.3.27) and therefore remains detached (Ch.3.28). He surrenders his actions to *Isvara*, with his mind fixed upon Him, free from expectations, attachment and mental agitations (Ch.3.29). In performing selfless actions, restraint of the senses is more important than restraint of actions (Ch.3.34). The merit lies not in performing right or wrong actions, but performing them with right mental attitude, in a spirit of surrender and devotion. The *Bhagavadgita* declares that desire is an eternal enemy of the wise upon earth, the insatiable fire (Ch.3.39), which deludes the soul by over powering the senses, the mind and the intellect (Ch.3.40). A true *karmayogi* therefore controls his senses and desires, with wisdom and discipline, and performs desireless actions. He performs his duty and never abandons it even if it is imperfect, because as the *Bhagavadgita* declares, real fulfillment arises from performing one's duty rather than that of another, however perfect it may be.

Renunciation of actions with knowledge is described in the fourth chapter. Lord Krishna affirms that he taught the supreme knowledge of renouncing actions through knowledge to many great people in the past, but in course of time it was forgotten (Ch.4.2). Therefore, He revealed the secret once again to *Arjuna*, his beloved devotee, to revive the tradition and redeem the world.

Renunciation of action through knowledge means becoming free from the bondage of actions by renouncing the desire hidden in them and by knowing the truth concerning action, inaction and prohibited action (Ch.4.17). By knowing them and by cultivating detachment, a *karmayogi* learns to see inaction in action and action in inaction. God Himself follows this ideal in His actions concerning creation, preservation and dissolution of the worlds. Although He is unborn and everlasting, He incarnates upon earth from time to time to restore order, to protect the pious and destroy the wicked (Ch.4.8).

For a man of action, the knowledge of *Isvara* is in itself liberating and uplifting. The *Bhagavadgita* gives us the assurance that those who know the divine birth and actions of God are freed from the cycle of birth and deaths (Ch.4.9). By the fire of knowledge of the Divine, they attain His being (Ch.4.10). The fourfold order was created by Him (Ch.4.13), with no particular desire, but with a view to establish order and regularity in the world. The ancient seers knew that actions would not taint Him, as He had no desire for the fruits of His actions. By that knowledge alone, they attained perfection. No wonder, our sacrificial ceremonies are modeled on the Great Sacrifice performed by Brahman in the beginning of creation to create the worlds and beings using Himself as the sacrificer and the sacrificed.

The scripture suggests that after knowing the truth about actions, and using that knowledge, a man of wisdom engages himself in actions that do not bind him. How does he achieve this? The answer is provided in the fourth chapter. He does it by renouncing attachment to actions, and remains ever contented, without any shelter (Ch.4.20) and without expectations, with his mind and body under his firm control, giving up all possessions, performing only body related functions (Ch.4.21). He remains contended in that state with whatever that comes to him on its own, free from jealousy, beyond dualities, and equal in success and failure (Ch.4.22). With his attachments gone and his mind purified and established in wisdom, his actions become elevated as sacrificial actions and he is completely liberated from the bondage of actions.

The *Bhagavadgita* also makes it clear that renunciation of actions through knowledge alone is very difficult to achieve; but it can be achieved easily in conjunction with the yoga of action by performing one's actions dutifully and selflessly (Ch.4.6). However, one should know how to renounce actions by performing them, rather than avoiding them. A true *sanyasi* is one who does his work without depending upon the fruit of his actions, not the one who gives up actions and the sacred fire (Ch.6.1).

According to the *Bhagavadgita*, true renunciation is renunciation of doership, ownership and desire for its fruit, not action itself. A *karmayogi* accomplishes this by offering his actions to God, shaking off his attachments (Ch.4.10. He performs them with his body only, for the sake of self-transformation and inner purification (Ch.4.11). He offers the fruit of his actions to God only, since all actions arise from Him, and there by attains Supreme Peace (Ch.4.12). The qualities of a true *sanyasi* described in the fifth chapter are listed below.

- A true practitioner of renunciation (*sanyasi*) renounces all actions mentally and rests happily in the city of nine gates (Ch.5.13).
- He looks with the same eye upon everything, remaining intelligent, humble and unassuming (Ch.5.18) in his approach.
- He does not rejoice upon getting what is pleasant, nor does he feel depressed when he gets what is unpleasant (Ch.5.19).

- He is unattached to the external world, always engaged in the contemplation of Brahman, identifying himself with Him (Ch.4.21).
- He is self-disciplined, having the ability and discernment to control his desires and anger whilst still in the body (Ch.4.23).
- He is delighted in himself and is illuminated within (Ch.4.24).
- He does not engage in selfish actions, but in such actions, which promote the welfare of the world (Ch.4.25).

How should one attain such an exalted and perfect state? The *Bhagavadgita* says that it can be done by withdrawing the senses from the external world, with the gaze fixed firmly between the eyebrows and by regulating the flow of *prana* and *apana*. Controlling his senses, mind and intellect, and overcoming his desires and anger, he attains the highest freedom. This is the path of action as suggested by Lord *Krishna* in the *Bhagavadgita*.

Jnanayoga – The Path of Knowledge

'*Jnana*' means knowledge. Yoga means state or union. In *jnanayoga* you enter into a state of knowledge through knowledge. You use knowledge as the means to reach the highest knowledge, which is the knowledge of the individual Self and the Supreme Self, and become one with it. In this quest for knowledge, you may resort to many practices and approaches. Initially, you may study the scriptures to understand the truths concerning the world and yourself. You may serve a master to know the transcendental truths that are imperceptible and incomprehensible to ordinary minds. Knowing them, you overcome your delusion and enter into advanced states (*yogas*) of balance, harmony, stability and sameness. Knowledge (*jnana*) opens our eyes to the truths beyond the apparent reality and dispels our mental darkness and inner chaos. It serves as a bridge that rests on the pillars of faith, devotion, sacrifice and resolve, by which a devotee can safely cross the river of delusion and ignorance and connect with *Isvara* in a transcendental state.

In Hinduism, the word "*jnana*" has many meanings. Knowledge is viewed as both liberating and binding, depending upon which knowledge you pursue and for what purpose you use it. In life, we use knowledge as a means to achieve certain ends. We may use it to fulfill our desires or liberate ourselves. We may use it to know the truth or to cover it up. Nature conceals knowledge. Using the senses, the mind and the elements, it deludes us. We can use knowledge to overcome these obstacles and see the truth hidden behind the perceptible reality. We can also use it to know how to perform actions with right attitude to overcome the problems of *karma* and rebirth.

Hindu scriptures identify two forms of knowledge, the lower and the higher. Both are essential for material and spiritual progress upon earth; but at some stage, one must know the difference and choose between the two. The knowledge that leads to the fulfillment of obligatory duties (*dharma*), material wealth (*artha*) and physical enjoyments (*kama*) is considered lower knowledge. Sometimes it is also termed as *avidya* or ignorance because it perpetuates ignorance of the Self rather than reveal it. This knowledge is good, but it does not liberate people. The knowledge that leads to the truths about Self and liberation is considered higher knowledge or the real knowledge (*vidya*). Real knowledge liberates us from the three delusions of our existence, namely the delusion that the ego is the real self, the delusion that through desire-ridden actions we can experience happiness and fulfillment and the delusion that we are distinct and different from the rest of creation. It also liberates us from the three impurities of Nature, namely *sattva*, *rajas* and *tamas*. Right knowledge also frees us from the afflictions created by the disturbances in the mind, from the dualities of life and from the pairs of opposites.

Jnanayoga is the pursuit of true knowledge on the path of self-realization. It is ideal for those who are driven by curiosity to know themselves, the world and God. With its help, we can understand our true nature, the nature of the Self, the distinction between knowledge and ignorance and the essentials of self-transformation that eventually leads to sameness, equanimity and self-absorption.

Types of knowledge

In the practice of *jnanayoga*, a yogi relies upon different types of knowledge in his progress to achieve self-realization. These are listed below.

1. **Knowledge of the field (*kshetrajnanam*)**: This knowledge helps us understand the truths concerning our minds and bodies, how modifications arise and how we become bound to the world through our desires and actions.
2. **Knowledge of divisions (*tattvajnanam*)**: This knowledge helps us understand how constituent aspects of Nature contribute to our bondage and delusion. From this knowledge we realize how the activity of the senses leads to attachment,

how the *gunas* induce desire-ridden actions, how the elements cause modification and how the internal organ (*antahkarana*) creates mental fluctuations (*vrittis*) and prevent us from knowing the truth concerning ourselves.

3. **Knowledge of the scriptures (*sastra jnanam*)**: This is acquired through study or listening to others. By studying the scriptures, we open our eyes to the reality concerning our existence. Scriptural knowledge may not help us directly in achieving self-realization; but it helps us sharpen our intellect and discern things rightly. The widely recommended method to obtain scriptural knowledge is self-study (*svadhyaya*).

4. **Knowledge of sacrifices and other obligatory duties**: This knowledge helps us to perform our duties selflessly and achieve perfection in the practice of karmayoga. We acquire this knowledge from others, teachers, scriptures and our elders.

5. **Knowledge of the Self (*atma jnanam*)**: This is the knowledge concerning the individual Self and its essential eternal nature as an aspect (*amsa*) of God and its bondage to Nature in the mortal body. This knowledge helps us stabilize our minds in the contemplation of the Self and experience equanimity, stability and sameness.

6. Knowledge of God (*brahmajnanam*): This is the knowledge concerning the Supreme Self and our relationship with Him. This knowledge helps us know about Him and the means to secure His mercy (*prasadam*) through, sacrifices, desireless actions, devotion and surrender.

7. **Knowledge of gods, divinities and other beings (*divya jnanam*)**: This knowledge helps us perform sacrifices and nourish the gods, ancestors, spirit beings and other creatures. With this knowledge, we can practice religious duties (*dharma*) and contribute to the order and regularity of the worlds and beings.

8. **Knowledge of the means to liberation (*moksha jnanam*)**: This knowledge helps us understand the significance of liberation,

the various means that are available to us to achieve it and the path that may be most suitable for our specific needs.

Knowledge vs. ignorance

True knowledge is the knowledge concerning the inner Self and ignorance is the absence of it. Knowledge is knowing that you are an eternal and indestructible Self and ignorance is identifying yourself with your mind and body and accepting your individuality or ego as your true Self. When the Self is enveloped by the impurities of darkness and delusion you will consider the phenomenal world as real and fail to discern the truth hidden beyond the surface reality. Knowledge is becoming aware of your hidden Self in a state of self-absorption and ignorance is experiencing the distinction between the knower and the known in a state of duality. Knowledge is overcoming our desires and attachment and treating everything with an equal eye and ignorance is pursuing our desires and suffering from attraction and aversion to the pairs of opposites. With knowledge, we know what binds us to the world and make necessary effort to liberate ourselves from the mortal world. With ignorance, we acknowledge truth as falsehood and falsehood as truth and allow demonic nature to take root in our consciousness. Knowledge liberates us while ignorance binds us. We come to know about the distinction between the two with the help of intelligence (*buddhi*), which is considered the highest faculty of Nature. The various limbs of yoga and types of yoga help us to cleanse our minds and intelligence and develop right knowledge and awareness about God, our existence and our essential nature.

Worldly knowledge vs. spiritual knowledge

Knowledge is also classified in our scriptures as worldly knowledge (*vijnanam*) and spiritual knowledge (*jnanam*). Some people also classify this as knowledge and wisdom. In a much broader sense, worldly knowledge (*vijnanam*) is the knowledge of the material universe, things and beings. It is the immediate and direct knowledge of the world, which we experience regularly in our wakeful state (*jagrt*). It helps us in pursuing our material interests and performing our duties. We acquire it through study, observation, perceptions, analysis, intellectual deliberation, direct experience and learning. In a narrow sense, worldly knowledge is the knowledge of sacrificial ceremonies, scriptural knowledge, which helps us perform our obligatory duties and nourish the gods, ancestors and other beings whereby we earn good merit and seek peace and happiness in our lives. True knowledge (*jnanam*) is the knowledge concerning the individual Self and the Supreme Self and their relationship. It is the transcendental knowledge, which cannot be acquired through the senses or the intellect, but only through direct contact with the inner Self or the Supreme Self (*brahmasparsah*). True knowledge is beyond the mind and the senses. However, in a state of purity, true knowledge is reflected in the brilliance of the intellect (*buddhi*). True knowledge is neither lost nor gained. It is always present in our consciousness. Because of ignorance and delusion, we cannot discern it. When delusion is removed, it reveals itself as the knowledge of the Self. Ignorant people do not have transcendental knowledge. Therefore, what is knowledge to them is ignorance for the wise ones. For them true knowledge is that which is eternal, unchanging, independent, liberating and enlightening. Through the practice of *jnanayoga*, they receive this knowledge and remain centered in it.

The importance of Jnanayoga

In *jnanayoga*, we advance from one state of knowledge to another. We progress from ignorance to knowledge, from delusion to wisdom through a gradual enfoldment of consciousness arising from the purity of our intention and clarity of thought and purpose. In this yoga, knowledge is the means and knowledge is the goal. The purer the knowledge, the greater the progress. From the practice of *jnanayoga*, we come to know how desire-ridden actions bind us to the cycle of births and deaths and how we may find freedom from it. We learn to control our minds and senses and remain focused on the inner Self so that we can gradually distance ourselves from the phenomenal world and our attachment with it. *Jnanayoga* also helps us draw the distinction between the field (*ksehtra*) and the knower of the field, and know the cause of rebirth, the means to liberation and the interplay of the triple *gunas*.

The *Bhagavadgita* identifies *jnanayoga* as one of the important paths to liberation, which may directly lead to liberation or advanced states of self-absorption and devotion. It is superior to the path of action, and complimentary to the path of devotion. Its practice eventually leads to inner perfection and pure devotion. The practice of *jnanayoga* may take years to yield positive results. In the first stage, you become aware of the truths concerning your existence and the means to escape from it. In the second phase, you put into practice the knowledge you gain from your study and observation and with its help, you achieve perfection on the path of yoga. As your mind and body are filled with the brilliance of sattvic knowledge, your devotion to God increases and your mind becomes stabilized in His contemplation. While the path of devotion is described as superior to the other two, one cannot practice pure devotion right away. *Jnanayoga* sets the stage for the cultivation of devotion. It is especially suitable for those who are deeply intellectual and who are not easily satisfied with the outer aspects religious observances.

Jnanayoga is rooted in the knowledge of the individual Self, the Universal Self and Nature. Its source is the traditional *Samkhya* philosophy, but the *Samkhyayoga* expounded in the *Bhagavadgita* is purely of theistic nature and different in many respects from the original. However, the concepts and practice of yoga proposed in the *Bhagavadgita* bear close resemblance to those of the *Yogasutras* of *Patanjali*. In many ways, the scripture elaborates the themes presented in the *Yogasutras*, with special emphasis not just on the essential practices of yoga, but its practical value in active life. Rightly, the *Bhagavadgita* is described as a scripture on yoga (*yogasastram*).

The second chapter of the *Bhagavadgita* is known as *Jnanayoga* or *Samkhyayoga*. It is one of the most comprehensive chapters in the scripture. In terms of its importance, perhaps it is the most important one because it contains a summary of all the teachings and covers all important concepts and ideas presented by Him. In this chapter, Lord Krishna explains how beings become deluded and come under the influence of Natures. Following are some of the important points covered in this chapter.

- The Self is eternal and distinct from the physical self, which is destructible and regularly discarded by the Self like a garment.
- Desire is the root cause of our suffering and binds us to the consequences of our actions.
- Renunciation of desire is more important than renunciation of actions because it alone saves us from *karma*.
- Attachment, anger and delusion arise from the activity of the senses and lead to delusion and bondage.
- Actions should be performed as an offering to God with a sacrificial attitude to attain liberation.
- The *gunas* are three. They contribute to our suffering by inducing in us desire-ridden actions.
- One may cultivate equanimity and sameness by controlling the senses, stabilizing the mind, and restraining both of them from the sense objects.
- An awakened person (*muni*) differs from the rest by abandoning his desires and remaining free from craving, attachment and egoism.

Knowledge as the Means and the Goal

The mind is an obstacle. It is also the doorway to knowledge and liberation. You are unique, because with your mind you can perform many tasks and manage your life and actions according to your life's essential purpose. You can think, reason, feel, know, remember and discern things from one another to navigate your way through the labyrinth of life. The course of your life depends largely upon how creatively and intelligently you use your mind and determine your priorities and your life's central purpose. Your life offers you many choices. You may not acknowledge them, limited by your fears and circumstances. You may fill your mind with knowledge or ignorance; you may fill it with the light of the Self or the darkness of evil; and you may use it to serve God or fulfill your our own selfish desires. They are your fundamental choices, which decide the direction of your life. He who does not know how to use his mind is ignorant; he who does not know how to use his mind correctly delays his liberation; but he who uses it for evil purposes falls down into the darkest hell. We learn this from the *Bhagavadgita*.

You can transform your mind. You can elevate your character and bring light and wisdom into it with your actions, knowledge, sense-restraint, intelligence, purity, renunciation, devotion, concentration, meditation and self-absorption. These purificatory processes transform a churning mind into a resting mind, a seeking mind into a self-absorbed mind, and an ignorant mind into an enlightened mind. They lead you to stability, sameness, detachment, equanimity, balance, harmony, surrender, knowledge, wisdom, compassion, devotion, contentment and discernment. Knowledge plays an important role in this process. With knowledge, you transform your mind, and experience peace and equanimity even if you are actively engaged with the external world. With knowledge, we overcome our ignorance and delusion and become aware of the causes of our suffering and the means to overcome it. As we lit up the dark corners of our minds, in that illumination we see the hidden presence of the Self and realize that as eternal souls we have a destiny beyond the mortal life to which we are presently bound. The purpose of *jnanayoga* is to lead us on this path of self-discovery from untruth (*asat*) to truth (*sat*), darkness (*tamas*) to light (*jyotih*) and death (*mrtyu*) to immortality (*amrit*) by learning to control the very forces that prevent us from knowing the truth about our existence.

Knowledge is of different kinds. We can pursue any of them, but we have to pay the price if the knowledge that we acquire does not lead to liberation but to delusion and bondage. The highest knowledge is the knowledge of the individual Self and the Supreme Self. This supreme knowledge arises in us at the end of a great journey stretching over several lives. Material knowledge leads to bondage and suffering, while spiritual knowledge leads to enlightenment and liberation. You cannot gain spiritual knowledge, unless you purify yourself with *sattva* and keep your mind and senses under firm control. To accomplish it, you have to practice detachment, stability and self-control. You have to recognize the factors that disturb you and you have to deal with them firmly.

From the *Bhagavadgita* we learn that self-transformation is a comprehensive process. You cannot focus on just one aspect of your life and expect liberation. You have to deal with all your vulnerabilities through a detailed set of yogic practices and use your daily experiences and obligatory duties to practice the highest ideals of yoga. Your liberation has to happen here and now, in the midst of life facing the ordinary and the mundane challenges where your faith and beliefs are tested severely and where you are vulnerable to the forces of Nature and the temptations of life.

On the path of liberation, ignorance is a major problem for everyone. We are not only ignorant, but also ignorant of our ignorance, which makes our transformation even more difficult. The knowledge that we acquire through self-study (*svadhyaya*) is helpful, but it does not take us far unless we awaken the knowledge that is inherent in us. Mental knowledge puts us on the path of liberation, but at some stage in our progress, we have to silence our minds to experience equanimity and sameness, which arise only when we are silent in every sense of the word. To see your hidden Self, you have to step aside, withdrawing your senses and silencing your mind. In other words, we may rely upon our minds and senses to cultivate certain attitudes and states of mind that are essential for our transformation, but later on we have to keep them under control to transcend ourselves and see the truth hidden deep within ourselves.

Right knowledge leads to liberation. *Jnanayoga* is the use and pursuit of right knowledge for a right cause. If liberation is your aim, you must know what right knowledge means and how it manifests in your consciousness. The scripture says there is no failure on this path. Even a little practice in its pursuit has beneficial effect. Even if you fail in securing right knowledge, you will have opportunities in future to redeem yourself. It is not easy to suppress the *gunas* or shut down the mind completely. However, in moments of deep meditation you will experience the cessation of all mental activity for a very brief time. You will also enter this state when you land into the silence that is hidden in your mind between one thought and another. In those moments, you will experience great awakening. Such moments may not last long or recur frequently; but if you keep your resolve and persist in your practice, they begin to linger and take roots in your consciousness.

In today's world, we have access to a lot of information on spiritual subjects, which was hitherto unavailable to people except through a *guru*. Today, we can also reach out to many gurus directly by visiting them or indirectly by reading their writings and discourses. With the knowledge thus gained and with firm resolve of sattvic type, we can bring transformation within ourselves by becoming God-centric and by cultivating virtues and divine qualities. With faith and perseverance, we can perfect our practice of various yogas, applying the principles we learn from the *Bhagavadgita*, and experience peace and stability. The practice of *jnanayoga* and the transformation of the mind and the body lead to the following.

- Self-knowledge
- Freedom from ignorance and delusion
- Knowledge concerning the phenomenal world
- Detachment
- Divine qualities
- Devotional services
- Sacrificial attitude
- Discerning wisdom
- Predominance of sattva
- Suppression of rajas and tamas
- Devotion
- Grace of God
- Strengthening of faith and devotion
- Peace and equanimity
- Freedom duality
- Sameness
- Skill in yoga

On the path of knowledge, to stabilize the mind one may pursue knowledge by various means. The important ones are self-study (*svadhyaya*), listening to others (*sravanam*), recollecting the name of God or the knowledge already gained (*smaranam*), and contemplation (*dhyanam*) upon the inner Self and the Supreme Self. Repeated practice (*abhyasam*) and the grace of a *guru* or God (*Isvara prasadam*) also lead to enlightenment. For the knowledge to be effective, one should have detachment even towards the knowledge one acquires through these means.

Buddhiyoga – The State of Wisdom and Discernment

Buddhiyoga is the ability to find direction in the darkness of earthly life with the help of awakened intelligence. It is a state of intense awareness marked by discretion and discernment. When you enter this state, you are no more deluded by the duality of your perceptual experience. *Buddhi* means intellect or discerning wisdom. Because of it, we are able to think and act rationally and make sense of things. Intuition, insight, common sense, reasoning and analytical ability arise from *buddhi* only. It is the highest aspect of Nature present in us. When it is pure, it reflects the brilliance of the Self and reveals to us the transcendental nature of our existence. It is responsible for our discernment, and our ability to make wise decisions and perform self-willed actions. When it is pure and filled with *sattva*, we discern things clearly without being judgmental.

In *buddhiyoga*, you sharpen your intelligence to the point where you know clearly the right from wrong and the truth from falsehood. You also learn to avoid actions that lead to suffering, bondage, ignorance, delusion and demonic nature. According to our scriptures, the mind (*manas*) and the intelligence (*buddhi*) are separate entities. Intelligence is not considered an aspect of the mind but an aspect above the mind. You may even refer to it as the higher mind. The mind is a repository of mental knowledge (*avidya*), while intelligence is that which dissects it and uses it to make sense of the world. Both are aspects (*tattvas*) of Nature and form part of the internal organ (*antahkarana*). Awareness that arises from the perception of the Self is called knowledge (*jnanam*), while understanding arising from the intellect is called wisdom (*vijnanam*).

In Buddhiyoga, you remain undisturbed by external events as you learn to remain equal to all situations. According to the *Bhagavadgita*, even mindedness is called *Buddhiyoga* (2.48). It arises from staying free from both attraction and aversion to things, which is difficult to achieve because of the conditions in which we live. Our minds remain disturbed and preoccupied mostly with some problem or the other because of desires and our attitude towards the pairs of opposites. The *Bhagavadgita* says that equanimity, detachment and sameness towards all should be cultivated by controlling the mind, the body and the senses, practicing inner discipline and renunciation of desires. Even mindedness culminates in the state of self-absorption (*samadhi*), as one transcends the mind, the senses, and the duality and becomes completely immersed in oneself, unaware of the world outside and detached from it. Thus, through yoga, one finally accomplishes its supreme purpose, disconnection from the union with pain and suffering, *dukha samyoga viyogam*, (6.23).

"Buddhi" is pure intelligence in contrast to "citta," which is pure consciousness. From the *Bhagavadgita* we learn that *buddhi* gives us the discriminating power to make wise choices and stay on course in the pursuit of our liberation. It is the source of our discerning wisdom and analytical knowledge. A man of lesser *buddhi* does not discriminate well and does not make right decisions. Most likely, he remains deluded and even perverted, with increased *tamas*, in this thinking and actions. He is constantly driven by his senses and the desire for sense objects, whereby he remains disturbed or distressed as he experiences union and separation from sense objects and attraction and aversion to them.

Buddhiyoga is the use of intelligence and wisdom to overcome the weaknesses of our minds and achieve a state of equanimity so that we remain alike in pleasure and pain, gain and loss, victory and defeat (2.38). When we make right decisions and know the truth concerning our existence, we achieve freedom from the bondage caused by our desire-ridden actions (2.39). The *Bhagavadgita* declares that performing disinterested actions through cultivated intelligence (*vyavasayatmika buddhi*) is the aim of *buddhiyoga*. It gives us the ability to see through things and phenomena and remain indifferent to them.

The scripture affirms that the practice of *Buddhiyoga* leads to many rewards. In this yoga, there is said to be no loss of effort. Even a little practice protects one from the fear of birth and death (2.40). However, sincere effort is required to achieve correct results. Perfection in this yoga cannot be achieved by the mere study of the *Vedas* or by engaging oneself in flowery speeches and intellectual discussions (2.42). There should be sincere effort to control one's desires and detach oneself from the things of the world including one's thoughts, beliefs and opinions. The three *gunas* or qualities have to be balanced and the senses have to be withdrawn and turned inward. It is by overcoming the three *gunas* enumerated in the *Vedas*, by conquering the sense of duality and by establishing oneself in *sattva*, one can obtain enlightenment (2.45). By developing even mindedness in success and failure, renouncing the fruit of actions, detached, says the *Bhagavadgita*, a *buddhiyogi* becomes free from the bondage of mortal life. (2.48-51).

However, how to know whether we have achieved perfection on this path? What are the marks of the one who truly excels in mental stability (*sthithapragna*)? The scripture provides the answers. A yogi of stable mind gives up all the cravings of his mind and remains withdrawn and satisfied (2.55). He is not afraid of adversity, nor does he crave for happiness. He is a stabilized sage (*sthithadhir muni*), who is free from passion, fear and anger (2.56). Without friends or relations (*anabhisneha*), equal to auspicious and inauspicious events and situations, he remains detached, unconcerned and absorbed in himself (2.57).

The senses are responsible for the delusion and the disturbances of the mind. They make us restless and keep us ignorant of the truths they cannot grasp. By establishing contact with the outside world, by constantly dwelling upon the sense objects, they subject the mind to experience attraction and aversion to them. This is attachment. When we are attached, we are not free. Out of this attachment, desire for the sense objects is born. From desire, arise passions, delusion, anger, loss of memory, confusion and finally loss of *buddhi* or intelligence (2.62&63). This leads to karma, births and rebirths.

Knowing this truth, a *Buddhiyogi* tires to achieve mental stability by withdrawing his mind form the sense objects, the way a tortoise withdraws its limbs (2.58). He stops enjoying the sense objects and thereby ends his sorrows. Controlling his senses, devoting himself, heart and soul to *Isvara*, he becomes firmly established in Him (2.65). He becomes an awakened Yogi, who is fully awake with wisdom and discernment when all beings are asleep with ignorance and delusion. He is asleep to ignorance and delusion when all being are awake to them in the world of desires (2.69) and impermanence. He becomes the ocean itself, undisturbed by the rivers of knowledge that keep flowing into him from all sides (2.70).

To achieve such a Supreme State of pure consciousness through *buddhiyoga* and remain detached from Nature, one has to practice the yoga of self-discipline (*atmasamyama-yoga*), which is described in the sixth chapter (10-19). *Atma* means the Self. *Samyama* means the simultaneous practice of concentration, meditation and self-absorption. When you practice it upon the Self, it becomes *atmasamyama-yoga*. It leads to the highest state of self-absorption and oneness with the Self.

The scripture says that a yogi should concentrate his mind constantly upon his Self, leading a solitary life, controlling his mind, free from desires and possessiveness. Placing his seat firmly in a clean place, neither too low nor too high, covering it with a soft cloth, deer skin and kusa grass, he should practice yoga for his purification, keeping his mind, senses and activities under firm control. Holding his body, neck and head erect in a straight line, concentrating his gaze on the tip of his nose, undistracted, with peaceful and fearless mind, practicing celibacy, subdued in passions, he should become established in *Isvara* and attain the highest peace and *nirvana* (6.10-15).

The scripture cautions us not to resort to extreme measures to sharpen our intellect. Discretion is the hallmark of *buddhiyoga*. There is no place for extremities in it (6.16-18). This yoga is neither for the voracious eater nor for the non-eater. It is neither for the constant sleeper nor for the one who does not sleep well. A *buddhi-yogi*, who is regulated in eating and relaxation, in sleeping and waking, becomes impervious to the dualities of life, resting in the Self only. Freed from all desires, he becomes established in the yoga of equanimity. In that state, he realizes his essential nature, becomes satisfied in the Self (6.20), finds unlimited happiness, develops an understanding of the transcendental state through his intellect and remains unmoved by all sorrows. He enjoys extreme bliss from his union with Brahman. Envisioning Him in his own heart, he experiences the Self in all and all in the Self (6.21-29).

Buddhiyoga is the foundation for success and perfection in all wakes of life and in the practice of other yogas. It is an adjunct to the practice of both *jnanayoga* and *karmayoga* and means to perfect the practice of *bhaktiyoga*. Without discernment and right knowledge, it is difficult to attain perfection in other yogas. A true *karmayogi* has to subdue his mind, restrain his senses, control his desires and develop detachment from the world to practice true renunciation, offering the fruit of his actions to God with a sacrificial attitude (3.7&5.3). A true devotee of God must control his mind and his desires, by detaching himself from all the objects with which he develops attachment and remain devoted to God only, so that he can concentrate his mind upon Him and become fully absorbed in Him (Chapter 9&12). *Buddhiyoga* makes a human being a truly rational and intelligent being. It brings out his humanity, frees him from the clutches of his social conditioning and elevates him mentally and intellectually to think freely and fearlessly with a clear mind, clear goal, wisdom and discernment.

Bhaktiyoga – The Yoga of Devotion

In terms of both the intensity and the object of one's veneration, we may classify devotion into many types. Of them, devotion to God, a deity or some supreme power through direct worship is considered the highest form of devotion. It is sustained by purity, faith, conviction, and, according to our scriptures, the grace of God Himself. Devotion may be sattvic, rajasic or tamasic in nature. Rajasic devotion is passionate and demanding. Tamasic devotion is deluded and even perverted. Sattvic devotion is pure and free from delusion and attachment. When we are not free from desires, we seek fulfillment of our desires through devotion. When we are not pure, we cling to the objects of our devotion. In their lives, people become devoted to many things, depending upon their knowledge, awareness and predominant qualities.

If we do not have discernment, we may mistake passion for devotion. In its purer aspect, devotion is a form of spiritual love, the longing of the individual Self for the Supreme Self. Sometimes it may also degrade into a kind of attachment, especially when it is induced by desires and worldly concerns. Devotion may also manifest in us in various ways. Some become devoted to their work, some to a cause, and some to material things, concepts, ideas, relationships and institutions. Some people worship wealth and some power. In these cases, devotion arises from the activity of the senses, in a state of duality between the knower and the known. In these instances, one can physically grasp the object of one's devotion. It is difficult to experience the same in case of devotion to God, who is invisible and transcendental. Hindu tradition recognizes this problem and permits the worship of idols so that people may see God in them and express their devotion to Him physically. The idols are deemed living symbols or direct manifestations (*arcas*) of God so that we can treat them as His living embodiment in image form. Idol worship may not be the ideal practice for the spiritually advanced souls, who are inclined to worship God in other ways. However, it has its place and value in one's spiritual progress and inner transformation.

The *Bhagavadgita* lays great emphasis on devotion and its importance in liberation. It advises people to cultivate devotion to God, fixing their minds upon Him constantly, cultivating virtues and knowledge, and offering their actions to Him with an attitude of sacrifice without seeking their fruit. Lord Krishna promises to deliver those who are devoted to Him and who worship Him wholeheartedly. He also declares that worshipping other deities is also worthy, but worshipping Him directly alone delivers one from the mortal world. We learn from the scripture that single-minded devotion to *Vasudeva* is the surest path to self-realization. Perfection in this practice leads to union with Brahman (*brahmasparsha*) and a sure place in the Highest Abode.

However, *bhaktiyoga* is not easy to practice. Going to temples, praying to God, performing occasionally ceremonial worships (*poojas*) and temple rituals (*archanas*) are considered obligatory duties (*dharma*) rather than acts of true devotion unless they are performed with exceptional purity and without expectations. Such devotional services may strengthen your faith and earn you a place in heaven, but they do not lead to liberation. In true devotion, the object of worship alone remains and the devotee disappears. Such self-effacement is not possible unless one's mind is completely absorbed in the contemplation of God and one's own identity is lost in His thoughts. True devotion arises after years of practice, after one has achieved perfection in the yoga of action, renunciation and knowledge. When the mind and body are purified and filled with *sattva*, feelings of selflessness and surrender intensify and true devotion arises. True devotion, is free from attachment and selfishness. It is characterized by intense aspiration to be with God and experience oneness with Him with no ulterior motive. True devotion is not practiced for personal gains or worldly benefits. A true devotee does not look to God in times of distress only when there are difficult problems. The *Bhagavadgita* affirms clearly that closeness to *Isvara* is achieved through love and devotion. In whatever way a devotee approaches Him, says Lord Krishna, He accepts them, because men approach Him from all directions (4.11) and what draws them closer to Him is not the path they choose, but their love for Him.

People who are completely devoted to God and who devote their lives to Him unconditionally are difficult to find in today's world. Such people are born only after earning great merit in their previous lives. Great souls (*mahatmas*), who are born thus, know how to worship God with undivided mind. They know Him to be Imperishable and the true cause of all beings (9.13). Always singing His glories, says the *Gita*, striving to attain Him, with firm determination, prostrating fully before Him, ever established in Him, they worship Him (9.14). A true devotee is never lost to God. He lives in His constant gaze and under His continuous protection. The Lord always takes care of the needs of a pure devotee who is totally lost in his devotion to him (9.22). Pure devotion is the highest form of love to which God responds with unconditional love and immediate attention. The *Vishstadvaita* (qualified monism) school holds the view said that when a devotee departs from here, God eagerly awaits his arrival. He sends many messengers and close attendants in advance to make sure that he receives a grand reception. When he finally arrives at His Doors, He personally comes forward to meet him. The essence of this is God is as eager to meet His devotee as the devotee is. He is as fond of the company of His devotees as they are. The Abode of God (*Vaikuntha*) is a happy place because everyone from Supreme Self to the last of His devotees is filled with unlimited love and rapturous bliss.

The *Gita* gives us the assurance that those who worship *Vasudeva Krishna* with single-minded devotion are speedily rescued from the ocean of mortal existence (12.7). Upon their death, they travel by the sunlit path of immortality and reach Him directly. The *Bhagavadgita* says that a person should live in God, with his or her mind and intelligence fixed upon Him to attain Him (12.8). If devotion with concentration of mind is not possible, then one should practice concentration (12.9). If that is also not possible then one should take refuge in Him and renounce one's desire for the fruit of one's actions (12.11).

God is omniscient, omnipresent and omnipotent. All living beings are created by Him and they exist in Him. He is their source and support; but deluded by the threefold modes of nature, many do not recognize Him, nor do they acknowledge His supremacy and greatness. The deluded persons of illusory hopes and actions follow the way of the demons (*asuras*) and do not give Him their due respects (9.12. However, the noble and the virtuous, who are pure and who possess divine nature, knowing Him as the prime cause of creation and imperishable, by worshipping Him and identifying themselves with Him, in a complete state of surrender and egolessness, become extremely dearer to Him.

In the scripture, Lord Krishna gives the assurance that His devotees would never perish. Even if a sinful person worships Him with complete devotion, he should be regarded as a saint because he made the right decision to work for his liberation. By the grace of the Supreme Lord, he speedily becomes a righteous soul (*dharmatma*) (9.31). Redemption is therefore possible for those who have a change of heart and surrender to God with faith and humility; but those who act with hatred and envy towards Him and give themselves to demonic behavior will perish having fallen into the lowest hells.

There are however some conditions to obtain the grace of God. One should worship the Supreme Self only, who is Highest and the Lord (*Isvara*) of the Universe. Devotees of the Supreme Self stand well above all those who worship lesser divinities. Those who perform sacrifices (9.20) and those who worship other gods (9.23) worship in a way Brahman only; but they do not attain Him, because their surrender is not direct. Only those who worship Him qualify for liberation. You may however worship other divinities as the Highest. It would be deemed worship of the Supreme Self only.

Death and destruction are not for those who reach the Supreme Abode (*parandhamam*). According to some traditions, devotees of God who are liberated (*muktas*) will not perish even during the dissolution of the worlds, while everything else around them perishes. The knowers of the *Vedas* who worship Him through sacrifices, ascend to the heaven upon their death and after enjoying the celestial pleasures and exhausting their merits return to the earth to take birth again (9.20 & 21).

Those, whose wisdom is carried away by desires, worship other gods in order to fulfill their desires (9.20). They do not attain liberation. This does not mean that God is partial to those who are not directly devoted to Him. He does not punish people if they do not worship Him or if they worship lesser divinities. He does not envy those who worship other gods nor does He want to punish them individually for their ignorance. Rewards and punishments arise from one's *karma*. The lives and destinies of beings are shaped by the universal laws (*dharma*) He establishes in the manifested worlds. He does not condemn the sinners particularly into a torture chambers nor does he direct the pious towards Himself against their will. He does not confuse the deluded ones with the wisdom they cannot understand. He gives them the freedom to live according to their individual wills and pursue their own paths. He allows people to grow in the direction of their thoughts and desires. He does the same in case of devotion. In the *Bhagavadgita* He gives us the assurance that in whatever form a devotee worships Him with faith, He stabilizes the faith of that devotee in that particular form and helps him obtain through that form his desired enjoyment (9.21 & 22). However, the scripture warns that finite is the fruit gained by such men of lesser wisdom. The worshippers of gods go to them, but the devotees of Supreme Lord go to Him only (9.23).

Types of devotees

Even among these who worship God, there are categories. The scripture identifies four types of worshippers: those in distress (*arta*), the inquisitive types (*jignasu*), seekers of material wealth (*artharhti*) and the wise beings (7.16). Of them, declares Lord Krishna, a wise person who is established in single-minded and uninterrupted devotion is extremely dearer to Him (7.17). According to Lord Krishna, all devotees are noble, but He regards a man of wisdom as His own self who is in perfect union with Him (7.18). It is only at the end of many births that a person is able to achieve such a supreme state of devotion (7.19). We find an irrevocable assurance in the scripture that those who are fully absorbed in Him (8.14 &10.10) with utmost devotion are assured of immortality and a permanent place in the world of God. Lord Krishna declares that to a constantly busy devotee who remembers Him always without diverting his attention elsewhere, He is very easy to attain. He further adds that those who worship Him always with loving devotion, to them He gives real wisdom.

Purity of heart and devotion are supremely important in practicing the yoga of devotion. It does not matter what you offer, but with what attitude you do it. The *Gita* says that whatever that is offered to *Isvara* with pure devotion, be it a leaf, a flower, a fruit, or water, He readily accepts that sacred offering of the pure soul with unconditional love (9.26). One can even make an offering of one's whole life and actions. A true devotee offers everything to God, without conditions and expectations. He lays before Him selflessly whatever he does, whatever he eats, whatever he accepts or gives away and whatever penances he observes. He does it with a clean heart, out of love and without expectations. He does it with the awareness that everything here is for the habitation of the Lord and nothing belongs to us. Relinquishing the ownership and doership, he performs his works selflessly. Living and with such sacrificial attitude, He earns His love and attention (9.27).

God is impartial. He has no desires. He has no particular agenda to do or not to do any action. We may quarrel among ourselves about the names and forms of God, but for Him everything is part of Him and inhabited by Him. The individual souls are his aspects (*amsah*) only. For Him none is hateful or dearer. He is equal to all and is present in all. However, He does respond to devotion. He listens to our prayers and helps those whom He may deem fit for help. The scripture states clearly that those who worship Him with devotion are forever closer to Him and earn His grace. They are in Him and He is in them (9.29). The power of devotion is such that by remembering God at the time death a devotee would easily attain the Highest Goal (8.13). However, remembering God at the time of death is not easy, especially for those who spend their lives pursuing material goals and craving for worldly pleasures. In order to remember Him all the time and even at the time of death, a devotee must be steadfast in yoga (*nityauktaysa yoginah*), with his heart and mind filled with devotion, remembering Him always and thinking of him alone (8.14).

While no restrictions are imposed on what deity we should worship or how we should worship, Lord Krishna advises people against worshipping the Unmanifested Brahman. He states that worshipping formless and Unmanifested Being is not only difficult but painful (12.5) for the embodied beings. However, by worshipping the Manifested Brahman in the form of *Isvara* or Lord Krishna, with single-minded devotion, one can easily attain the Highest Abode never to return to the mortal world.

Types of devotion

Based on the *gunas* we can classify devotion also into three types, namely sattvic, rajasic and tamasic types of devotion. Sattvic devotion is practiced by those who have the predominance of *sattva* and who are inclined to the pursuit of liberation. They practice austerities, sacrifices, charity and penances as obligatory duties to promote *dharma* and establish peace and harmony. They seek oneness with God through devotion, practicing virtue, adhering to righteousness (*dharma*) and offering their actions to Him, without egoism and attachment. Rajasic people practice devotion to increase their power and wealth and fulfill their material desires. They approach God with expectations to overcome their problems or fulfill their desires. Their devotion is induced by egoism and selfish desires. Tamasic people practice devotion for all the wrong reasons for destructive and evil purposes. Ignoring traditions and established practices, they resort to perverted methods of worship. They practice devotion out of vanity or ego to show off their power and prestige or to increase their destructive power or control over others.

Sattvic devotion arises from knowledge and purity; rajasic devotion from greed; and tamasic devotion from delusion and ignorance. Of the three, sattvic devotion is the best. Sattvic devotion results in inner purification and transformation, which hastens one's progress on the path of liberation; rajasic devotion leads to sorrow and bondage; and tamasic devotion to ignorance, self-destruction and spiritual downfall. However, for a yogi on the path of liberation, sattvic devotion is not an end but only a means. Higher than all these is the devotion of the one who transcends the *guans*. When devotion arises from the soul's aspiration rather than from the *gunas*, it is the highest and purest form of devotion. The soul is always in love with God. One cannot feel it unless one is free from the influence of the *gunas*. For God also the love of the soul is irresistible. He speedily rescues those who let the devotion of their souls express through them without any interference from their *gunas*. For the human beings, this state is not easy to attain, unless they become adept in their practice yoga.

Those who transcend the *gunas* seek the company of God and derive their happiness solely from their thoughts of Him. They spend their lives in His contemplation, seeing Him in all and all in Him, offering Him whatever they have and expecting nothing in return. They remain unconcerned, unmoved by the *gunas*, staying alike in pleasure and pain, censure and praise, honor and dishonor, and treat everything with stability and sameness. They remain contended with what is obtained by the will of God and live freely and fearlessly with detachment, dispassion, sameness and equanimity. One reaches this supreme state of devotion after reaching perfection in their practice of the yoga of action, the yoga of knowledge and the yoga of renunciation and after removing the impurities of *rajas* and *tamas* from their minds and bodies. Devotion is soul's intense yearning for oneness with God or its longing to return to its original state as the free Self. It arises in a person whose mind and body are pure and whose heart is clean. True devotion is possible only when the mind is free from cravings and the ego is completely in submission to God. It is the highest and most sublime form of emotion.

Maya – The Illusion of things

In the great epic *Mahabharata*, when *Duryodhana* enters the hall of illusion (*maya sabha*), he loses his way, becomes confused, angry and envious. Seeing his predicament when *Draupadi*, laughs at him, he becomes uncontrollably angry, feels insulted, and vows to take revenge against the *Pandavas* for their display of power and wealth and the insult he suffered in the presence of a woman. It is in the hall of illusions that the seeds of the great *Mahabharata* war were actually sown which germinated and ultimately consumed the whole *Kuru* clan bringing them untold misery and great destruction. The epic *Mahabharata* shows in many ways how human beings can bring misery and destruction to themselves and others through their actions cased by their delusion, ignorance, egoism, desires, attachments, selfishness, pride, envy and such other weaknesses.

The world in which we live is not very different from the hall of illusions described in the *Mahabharata*. It is a world of transient phenomena and ever-changing vistas. We are not sure what it is and we cannot take it for granted. Although we live in it, we do not know whether it is an entity by itself or an illusion created by the association of diverse things and phenomena it contains. We also find it difficult as mortal beings to know ourselves and be ourselves. Deluded by the *gunas* and clouded by our desires and attachments, we fail to discriminate between truth and false hood, and engage in actions that draw us out and involve us deeply with the world and its attractions. Seeking things that seem to enhance us through attraction and aversion, we develop attachment to them and ignore the truths hidden within our consciousness. If someone reminds you that you are a divine soul, you may not believe in it. Centered in your physical identify you may find it hard to accept your spiritual nature and your subtle bodies. Inherently we want to live forever, free from aging, sickness and death but find it difficult to accept the assurances given by our religious scriptures or self-realized masters about the possibilities of achieving immortality through spiritual effort. We need proof, which we cannot have, unless we are willing to make sacrifices and spend considerable time and energy to purify ourselves and discipline our minds and bodies.

One of the unique concepts of Hinduism is *maya* or illusion. Usually, it is used in reference to our current state of existence and that of the world. It signifies how truth is concealed and distorted in a world of transient phenomena behind a cloak of appearances and deceptive formations. It helps us to understand how we become entangled with the objects of our desires and weave in the process a web of deception around ourselves, forgetting who we are and what the true purpose of our existence is. *Maya* is a state as well as a condition, in which each being considers itself separate and distinct from the rest of creation and God Himself. Our scriptures suggest that our world is a trap and *maya* is the trapping mechanism. Nature employs it to entice the individual souls into an embodied state and then holds them bound to the world through desires and attachment. Once we are bound, we forget our essential nature and become involved with the process of becoming and being, imprisoned by our own thoughts and desires, suffering from births and deaths, and binding ourselves to the consequences of our own actions.

Who unleashes this potent force? Our scriptures say that God unleashes it. He is the grand master of illusion, the supreme Conjurer (*Mayavi*). He casts His net of illusion and ensnares the individual souls to remain deluded and bound to the world. *Maya* thus becomes a very potent force in the continuity of creation. The *gunas* aid in the process by inciting desire-ridden actions and subjecting beings to the twin modes of attraction and aversion to things. According to our scriptures, God is not only a Conjurer but also a Concealer. He conceals truth. He conceals truth and knowledge so that beings remain deluded until they practice yoga and overcome their delusion. He hides Himself from His creation and there by perpetuates the belief that He is not what He is or He is different from what He seems to be. *Maya* is thus not only a deluding mechanism but also a concealing mechanism. The first one leads to indiscretion and the latter to ignorance.

The *Bhagavadgita* explains how delusion arises and how we may overcome it. Lord Krishna states that deluded people bind themselves to the cycle of births and deaths through desire-ridden actions because they lack discrimination (*buddhi*). They assume ownership and doership and fail to discern the presence of God amidst them. They indulge in actions that bring them misery and suffering. However, there is a ray of hope for everyone. With effort and through practice of yoga, everyone can overcome their delusion and work for their liberation. To achieve a correct understanding of the mechanism of *maya* is vital. The following account is based on the concepts presented in the teachings of Lord Krishna.

1. The Senses

The senses are ten in number, five organs of action and five organs of perception. The mind is the eleventh. Apart from these, we can also mention, the five subtle sensory experiences (*tanmatras*), which are responsible for our feelings of attraction and aversion to the things we perceive. They are the experiences of hearing, touching, seeing, tasting and smelling. The ten sense organs together with the mind and the subtle senses are the main instruments through which Nature deludes the beings by subjecting them to the desire for sense objects and the attachment arising from them. According to the *Bhagavadgita*, out of desire comes attachment and out of attachment a person becomes deluded by seeking things in order to satisfy his or her craving.

Even from our daily experiences, we know that the senses are not reliable instruments of truth. The world is not what it appears to be. The truths hidden beneath the surface of things provide a different picture of the world in which we live. Things appear differently when we view them from different perspectives and consider them as aggregate of things. The *Bhagavadgita* therefore urges people to look beyond the appearance of things into the essential reality that pervades them and envelops them as their source and support. The same power manifests differently in different things. We have to understand That (*Tat*) which has this power and we have to experience it within ourselves to become free from the world of illusion and duality. That manifesting power is God, the Supreme Lord of the universe. His manifestation is what we perceive with our senses and mistakenly consider it as the sum total of all. This is the delusion, which we need to overcome. When we shift our attention from His manifestation to Himself and from the projections and modifications of own minds to our essential nature, we become aware of the transcendental truths that exist beyond our senses.

2. Loss of buddhi (discrimination)

When we pursue sense objects, we become deluded by the activity of our senses. We ignore the profound truths that are not immediately perceptible, thereby missing the central purpose of our lives, which is achieving liberation with righteous conduct. When we are deluded, we do not know truth from falsehood. We accept the visible world as true, ignoring the source that is responsible for it or the transcendental reality that exists beyond it. When we do not know who we really are, we accept our physical identities as the sum total of our existence and make decisions from a very narrow perspective, ignoring the possibilities of our existence beyond life and death and the consequences of our actions upon our future lives. The senses, as we have discussed before, contribute to these deluded notions that we entertain in our minds about our existence and ourselves. Those who depend upon them solely for direction and guidance cannot go beyond the visible and perceptible world and experience the reality that exists in the stillness of their own minds. Our delusion results in ignorance and the loss of wisdom to know the reality from unreality, truth from untruth, the divine from demonic and the right actions from the wrong ones. Out of the ignorance thus born, an individual soul indulges in wrong actions and becomes bound to the mortal world. When we do not have right knowledge, we make wrong choices and suffer from the consequences. When we do not know that we suffer from the consequences of our actions because of our desires and attachment, we indulge in desire-ridden in actions and become bound to them. However, through the practice of yoga when we cleanse our consciousness and open ourselves to the transcendental truths, we become aware of the need for self-transformation to establish within ourselves equanimity, stability and sameness towards all. We realize the true meaning of renunciation and learn to perform actions without seeking their fruit. The study of the *Bhagavadgita* helps us greatly to overcome our delusion and know our identities. It study will help us discern truths concerning God and ourselves. With our intellect refined by its knowledge, we will overcome our delusion and work for our liberation.

3. Desires and attachment

Whoever is under the influence of *Maya* is always attached to the world and its objects. He is attracted not only to worldly things but also to his own egoistic personality, his memories, thoughts, opinions and relations. Memories pursue him, time haunts him and thoughts possess him. Having become attached to the world, and conditioned by memory and accumulated knowledge, he develops envy, selfishness and many negative qualities such as pride, fear, greed, anger, malice, caprice, cruelty, callousness, lust and intense desire for success and personal advancement. He views life as a battleground in which he has to win at any cost. For him failure and weakness are not options. Attracted to pleasures, averse to pain, fearful of loss and hopeful of gain, unable to go beyond the lures and temptations of the world, although aware that all is vain in the end, he plods on, striving and struggling, as if death would never touch him

4. Sense of duality and multiplicity

Both the individual Self and the Supreme Self are eternally independent, whereas beings (*jivas*) are dependent entities. Even when the individual Self is in association with Nature, it remains independent. The beings exist in relationship with things and beings whereas the Self exists by itself. The relationships they form result in the delusion of duality and the experience of union and separation from things, which in its turn leads to conflicting emotions and mental afflictions. We are drawn to objects because we consider them separate and distinct. We seek them because we develop attachment to them through our *gunas* and senses. This duality leads to desire-ridden actions and our bondage to earthly life. When we depend upon our senses, we perceive duality and diversity, and experience attraction and aversion to the pairs of opposites. This leads to the delusion of ownership and doership and the compulsion to perform desire-ridden actions and perpetuate our individuality and beingness.

5. Transience, Instability and Destructibility

The phenomenal world in which we live and which we call *samsara* is subject to modifications, impermanence and destruction. It is driven by cause and effect, induced primarily by the *gunas*. Our physical personalities are part of this world and subject to the same qualities. We accept them as true because we cannot see the real Self that is hidden within us, which is eternal, immutable and indestructible. Arjuna suffered from sorrow because he had the same delusion. He thought that he was a destructible being and his actions would lead to the death and destruction of others. He did not consider death and destruction the modifications of Nature that are put in place to facilitate the soul's journey upon earth. In the phenomenal world, because of the *gunas*, our physical selves overshadow our true selves and when we are centered in them, we accept ourselves as limited beings subject to death and destruction. When we purify our minds and bodies, we realize our immortality and experience peace and stability. Our existence is not impermanent. The modifications are. Our impermanence is an outer aspect, a mere phenomenon, like a dream, which will vanish when we realize our true nature and become absorbed in it.

6. Ego and False identification

Just as Nature manifests an alternate reality in the universe of God, it manifests an alternate reality in microcosm of each individual in the form of ego consciousness, whereby each being identifies itself with its name and form rather than its inner Self. The ego is an illusion, but we perpetuate it because we spend our lives protecting it and promoting it. It is the false center of our consciousness. It acts as the knower of the field (*kshetrajna*) where as the Self is true Knower. It acts as the enjoyer of the perceptions arising in the field of consciousness, whereas the true enjoyer is again the Self. It also assumes ownership and doership, whereas the true of owner and doer is God Himself. These misconceptions induced by the ego of an individual lead to its attachment, delusion and karma.

The ego is responsible for our self-preservation instinct and our inclination to further our interests and fulfill our desires even at the expense of our own spiritual welfare. If it is left to itself, it will promote and perpetuate demonic qualities, whereby its possessor does not know how to perform actions selflessly or what right conduct means (16.7). As the *Bhagavadgita* states, under its influence, each *jiva* or individual develops a false sense of identity and thinks he is the lord, the enjoyer and the perfect one (16.14). Thinking thus, he engages in desire-ridden actions and, in extreme cases, destructive and terrible actions that lead to his downfall. The ego is both the cause and effect of delusion. It is responsible for ownership, doership, duality, corporeality, materiality, and bondage. It keeps the mind in a state of flux and prevents it from experiencing stability, equanimity and self-absorption. Under its influence, the deluded ones offer sacrifices for their name, wealth or pride, whereby they are cast into sinful and demonic wombs.

7. Incorrect Relationship with God

Because of ignorance and delusion, mortal beings cannot perceive God even though He is omnipresent and hidden in every aspect of creation. Therefore, their knowledge of God remains largely incomplete and incorrect. This ignorance interferes with their ability to form meaningful relationships with God and worship Him with right attitude. In the *Bhagavadgita* Lord Krishna mentions four types of devotees who worship Him, namely men in distress, seekers of knowledge, seekers of material wealth and men of wisdom. Of these four, He declares the last one the best. Apart from these, He also mentions others whose wisdom is carried away by desires and who worship other gods through sacrifices for the fulfillment of their desires. He also mentions those who worship Him as the Unmanifested or who consider Him as the unmanifest having manifestations (*avyaktam vyaktam*). He further adds that people develop these wrong notions about Him because of His divine power (*yogamaya*) and fail to recognize Him as unborn and imperishable Supreme Self (7.24-25).

The knowledge we gain from the study of scriptures does not help us to experience the absolute reality, unless we develop corresponding inner purity that can bring us into direct contact with our inner Selves. Thus, most people, even after years of study and devotional services, remain largely ignorant of God and His manifestations. Even Arjuna with his direct vision saw but one aspect of God as Time (*Kala*). None can therefore comprehend God truthfully even after transcending their senses. They may understand Him but in parts. They may enter His consciousness, but cannot recollect the full extent of their experience since the distinction between the knower and the known is absent in transcendental states. As a result, our relationship with God remains largely personal. Ignorant people cannot truly realize the greatness of God. Even if they do, they cannot contain that experience in their limited consciousness. Only a few know Him, even at the time of their death that He is the Lord of all gods (adhidaivam), Lord of the material universe (*adhibhutam*) and the Lord hidden in each living being (*adhyatma*).

8. Mortality and the Cycle of birth and death

The purpose of divine *maya* is to keep the beings ignorant and bound to the world. It perpetuates ignorance by overshadowing their knowledge and discernment, whereby they pursue sense objects through selfish and desire-ridden actions and develop attachment to them. The dependence leads to karma and bondage. The *Bhagavadgita* portrays all beings living under delusion and subject to attraction and aversion to the pairs of opposites. They are born repeatedly until their achieve liberation or until the worlds are dissolved. Those who die and travel by the southern path (*dakshinayana*) to the world of gods or ancestors return to the earth eventually after exhausting their *karmas* and take birth again, while those who go to the highest Abode of Brahman never return. Beings return to the earth because of unfulfilled desires and unfinished tasks arising from their latent attachments, unexhausted *karmas*. Depending upon their previous actions, they take birth in different wombs and live under different circumstances to repay their past debts and continue their mortal existence. This process goes on repeatedly until they overcome their ignorance and delusion, performing selfless actions with the right knowledge, and achieve liberation.

9. Deliverance from Maya

Mortal existence is temporary. Maya works so long as the beings choose to remain ignorant and perform desire-ridden actions under the influence of their egos. Their delusion manifests in several ways, most importantly as duality and as attraction and aversion to things. Fortunately, it does not last forever and it remains only as long as the beings choose to pursue their desires. It means we do not have to wait until the end of the worlds for our deliverance. We have an opportunity to escape from the hold of Nature and return to eternal life. We can escape from this illusory existence by overcoming our ignorance with right knowledge and the grace (*prasada*) of God Himself. We can follow the teachings of the *Bhagavadgita* or any other scripture of spiritual value to cultivate purity and stabilize our minds in the contemplation of God. Whoever practices yoga and experiences the advanced states of concentration, meditation and self-absorption, reaches the Abode of God quickly. One may also achieve the same goal by remembering God at the time of one's death. Even evil people have a chance to redeem themselves, if they change their ways and worship God with devotion. They become righteous quickly and attain everlasting peace (9.31).

10. Overcoming the field

We are conditioned to live and act according to our perceptions and experiences. Since we cannot look beyond the visible and apparent reality of the world, this is the only way, as far as we know, to survive upon earth and ensure our continuity. We seek peace and happiness by living within the laws of Nature and doing what is naturally possible and permissible to deal with the dualities of life. From experience, we learn that whenever we transgress Nature, we have to endure pain and suffering. Alternating between the contrasting realities of life, we try to stay within the circle of our experience to maintain our sanity and security. Ignorance and delusion are the means Nature employs to keep us bound to the phenomenal world and its objects. We live under the illusion that the knowledge we gain from our interactions with it is true and reliable. It is true, but in a limited sense. In truth, our empirical knowledge arises from the delusion of duality and diversity. It does not help us much in knowing the transcendental truths that are hidden from the intellect or the senses. It does not also help us much in our liberation. It may suggest some solutions and the possibilities, but cannot remove our delusion or ignorance. For that, we need more reliable and substantive reality that is permanent, indestructible, absolute and self-existing.

The truths that we know through our empirical experience are not absolute truths. They are standpoints or perspectives to which we become attached emotionally or egoistically, and defend them as if we are defending ourselves. They are relative truths that do not stand the test of time. We can justify them or refute them according to our convenience, worldviews, beliefs, prejudices and preferences. Our knowledge, memory and intellect are shaped by our desires and therefore, as instruments of truth, are unreliable. A mind that is free delusion assimilates truth without being oppressed or limited by it. It can harmonize and integrate the conflicting facts of life as diverse aspects of the self-same reality. It can hold the various facets of life as complimentary aspects of one holistic truth.

Truth is such. It is everything. It is eternal, multidimensional, indefinable and all encompassing. It reconciles everything into itself and resolves every duality into one harmonious whole, what our human minds are not habituated to do, accustomed as they are to relative thinking and limited perceptivity. This limitation of the human intelligence arises from the divine play of *maya*. It is what happens to your intelligence and knowledge when you come under its influence and do not even know that what you experience is an illusion. The world that you see is an illusion not because it does not exist but because you see it from a limited perspective, through the narrow prism of your desires, fears and egoistic consideration. The duality you experience is in itself a delusion that arises from your experience of attraction and aversion to things.

The world in which you live is an illusion because it is largely a creation of your mind. It is bound to your desires and expectations. You relate to it according to your knowledge, understanding and attachments. You build it inside your mind and project it outwardly upon the world you perceive. You do not see as it is but as per your dominant desires and mental modifications. You mix your past impressions with your current perceptions to create in your mind the illusion of seeing and experiencing. Thus, what you experience may not be the truth but a concoction of your mind and senses. What you know may not be true knowledge, but part of your deluded belief. Our existence is such that we do not know when we are truly awake and when we asleep; why we are here and to what end all this leads.

The True Meaning of Bhakti

It may be surprising to many to know that the concept of *bhakti* came to us from Vedic sacrifices and is deeply associated with the ritual terminology of the Vedic period. As time passed by the idea became more refined and sublimated as the highest expression of love and self-sacrifice to God. The *bhakti* movement emerged in India in the later Vedic times with the internalization of Vedic rituals and its elevation as a yogic practice. Symbolically it is deeply associated with Vedic rituals and may be even animal and human sacrifices and the ascetic practice of self-mortification as the means to escape from the bonds of Nature.

*Bhakt*a means food, the sacrificed; *bhakt*i is the act of sacrifice; and *bhokta* is the recipient of the sacrifice. In a ritual sense, a bhakta is one who offers himself or who is offered as a sacrifice in a sacrificial ritual. *Bhakta* (devotee) also means he who offers sacrificial food (*bhakta*) as an offering to God, who is the final recipient and the Enjoyer (*bhokta*) of all material things. He is also the devourer.

Bhakti (*devotion*) is thus a sacrificial offering to God. God's mercy or grace (*prasadam*) is the leftover or the outcome of this sacrifice or offering. It is customary to redistribute the remains of the sacrifice or the food that is left over from a sacrifice among the worshippers. It is known as *prasadam* or God's mercy, food that is touched and purified by the effulgence of God. Whoever eats it is purified of sins. Thus, devotion is a sacrificial act of offering in which you earn the grace of God by offering either yourself or what you have as the sacrificial material or food.

In a general sense, *bhakti* means having devotion, attachment or loyalty to God. Every Hindu who participates in a ritual worship receives *prasadam* and knows that it signals the end of the ritual. However, few people know what it means and what it signifies. The ideal represented in a ritual worship is one should live by sacrifices, making offerings to God, who is the source of all, rather than accumulating things for oneself. What you accumulate becomes your burden. In end, you have to account for it because you have taken what does not actually belong to you. You cannot wash it away with a few temple rituals or dropping a part of your wealth in the temple coffers (*hundis*). You must take the sacrifice or the ritual everywhere. You must make your whole life a ritual offering, a continuous worship. In truth, we do not accumulate wealth, name or fame through our selfish and egoistic actions. We accumulate sin. When you take what does not belong to you, it is called stealing (*aparigraha*). You should therefore return what does not belong to you to the One to whom it actually belongs.

An offering is therefore an important act of liberation and a right solution to the problem of *karma*. Every offering that you make to God is returned to you in the form of God's mercy. As the *Bhagavadgita* declares, when you eat food for yourself without offering it to God you eat sin. It means it binds you through your selfish actions (*karma*); but when you offer it to God and eat it as His mercy, no sin will incur to you. A devotee worships God with single-minded devotion as if nothing else matters. Out of unconditional love, he offers Him reverence, homage and service. His offerings lead to his liberation, as he remains untouched by his actions.

Bhakti is a sattvic feeling whose location is in the heart region, the seat of the Self. True devotion of the purest kind, which leads to liberation, arises in those who have discerning wisdom (*buddhi vikasam*), and disinterest (*virakti*) in material things, and who are free from attachments arising from the impurities of *rajas* and *tamas*. The gross body does not experience devotion as much as the subtle ones. It arises in those whose minds and bodies are filled with the radiance of *sattva*. Therefore, the practice of devotion is considered an advance practice of yoga not possible for everyone. *Bhakti* leads to freedom (*vimukti*) or liberation (*mukti*). If you are attached to Nature and have passion for material things, you cannot attain liberation (*mukti*).

How such devotion arises in people? According to the Bhagavadgita, true devotion arises after one achieves perfection in the yoga of action (*karmayoga*) and knowledge (*jnanayoga*).

A devotee exemplifies divine qualities. He surrenders to God and remains ever absorbed in His thoughts and contemplation. His devotion is free from the impurities of egoism, vanity, desires and expectations. It is characterized by an attitude of reverence rather than craving. It is devoid of attachment and demonic passions. It is free from the impurities of egoism and delusion. It liberates rather than binds. It is not sustained by fulfillment but by sacrifice.

You should not worship God with selfish attitude. Deluded people may worship Him for material gains; but it does not qualify as true devotion. Sacrifice is the basis of true worship. Devotion is an act of offering, not receiving. A true devotee makes an offering to God without expectations. When you worship God, you give Him whatever you have. You surrender to Him unconditionally and make your life an offering; and you do it selflessly out of profound love, reverence and gratitude. You do not eat the fruit of your labor. You offer it to God and live freely.

Lessons from the Bhagavadgita for the Modern People

Many timeless lessons are hidden in the sacred text of the *Bhagavadgita*. They reveal themselves to the extent you probe into it. To practice them effectively, you require discipline, purity, faith and devotion. The following are a few important ones.

1. **You are transcendental and immortal**. Birth, death and aging are not for you but for your mind and body. They wither and fall away, while you remain eternally as an individual Self. The Self is immortal, untouched by the impurities of life or its limitations. Bliss is its essential nature. Acknowledge this and identify yourself with it completely. Keep your consciousness centered in that notion. Hold on to the belief that you are an immortal Self and someday you are going to be free from this world. When you are centered in yourself, you experience peace and stability. Your consciousness, freed from attachment to the mind and body, experiences oneness with the Supreme Self. You realize that the whole world is a play of God filled with His numerous forms and manifestations.
2. **What attracts you holds you in its grip**. The world is a beautiful place to live, but it is also a big trap. Your freedom is an illusion. When you seek things, know that you are not free. When you depend upon things for your happiness, know that you are not free. When you suffer from fear and anxiety, know that you are bound to your own expectations. Your free will is actually not free. It is bound to your desires, expectations and the consequences of your past actions. It is bound to the *gunas* and their interplay. You are a prisoner of your desires and attachments. You are held in their grip by Nature. The world holds you in its bondage through them. Your relationship with it is your undoing. It is the cause of your suffering. If you extend yourself and become involved with things and people, you will be caught in it and lose your freedom like an insect

that is stuck in the web of a spider. Your goal should be to become desire-proof and live like a lotus plant in the waters of life, without being tainted.

3. **There is a lot you can do in your life by yourself.** There is also a lot more you cannot do because your life is not entirely within your control. While your abilities are limited, your knowledge of what guides you and controls you here is also limited. Some causes propel you into action despite your best intentions. They are clearly outside your control. Although some of them are part of you and your essential nature, you cannot control them enough or their functioning. Therefore, cultivate humility and tolerance, as wise people do, to accept your limitations and that you cannot control. Know what dominant tendencies drive you and compel you into seeking things and holding on to them, even when you want to be free from them. Resolve them to stay free from the negative and binding influences of life. Unburden your mind of the burdens that you carry in you as painful vestiges of your past rooted in your inherent nature that so powerfully controls your every thought and action as if it has a life of its own.

4. **You do not know why you are here.** You are a mystery. Your existence is a mystery. You do not know why you are here and what dreams you have left unfinished in the past that you want to fulfill them now. Apart from what you read in the scriptures, you do not know about your existence prior to your birth. You may never know what happens to you or your individuality when you leave this world. There is a mysterious quality about life, which we cannot comprehend easily with our minds or reason. However, you can be sure of what is happening now and what you experience in the present moment. It is life as it unfolds before you with each breath of fresh air you inhale. It has been given to you in consequence of your own actions. You can experience it consciously with each moment as long as you live. Make the best use of it, living it consciously, conscientiously and mindfully, doing your duty, meeting your obligations, helping others, living virtuously,

with knowledge and wisdom lighting up your consciousness, without unduly worrying about what may happen in future and how your actions may turn out eventually

5. **Do not give up life; do not give up living.** Whether you live in a democracy or dictatorship, whether you are rich or poor, high or low, you are bound to this world and not free. This is unequivocally validated by our scriptures. If you struggle unwisely for your liberation, Nature will tighten its hold upon you and make your escape even more difficult. If you give up completely, you will remain trapped forever until the end of times. You must therefore find the right way and employ the right means, using discretion and moderation, giving up whatever is necessary, and strengthening whatever that lightens you up and sets you free. You must know what binds you here and stay away from it. You must sacrifice that which increases your involvement with the world and leads to your suffering. Life is a means to perfect yourself through your actions and overcome your entrapment. It provides you with an opportunity to cultivate closeness to God through the very means that otherwise bind you and trap you in the darkness of your desires.

6. **Stay clean.** One lifetime is sufficient to know that this world will never be free from good and evil. Both are here to stay. Both are inherent in us. The earth is a battleground for these two opposing forces represented by gods and demons. Both live inside us and fight their battles with or without our cooperation. In this battle, you have to decide on whose side you are and whom you should strengthen. It is difficult to be a good person and practice virtues when the world seems to be falling increasingly under the sway of evil; but this choice is important because it will decide your fate. If you grow the divine in you, you will move towards truth (*sat*), light (*jyoti*) and immortality (*amritam*). Otherwise, you will enter the sunless worlds of utter darkness (*asurya lokas*) and perish.

7. **Have faith.** For a human being, the greatest challenge is to live by faith and not suffer from doubt and despair. It is a test how

you hold yourself when your faith is tested by adversity or acts of God. To believe in God is not easy, especially when He does not communicate with us perceptually and does not answer our prayers promptly. You cannot believe in God by your feelings alone, especially when your mind is not yet settled in the thoughts of God and it has not yet advanced into deeper states of meditation. However, faith is the only means to escape from this world. It is the raft, by which you can cross the phenomenal world. You can sustain it with the help of the scriptures, the words of wise men and the practice of yoga.

8. **Acknowledge the contribution of others in your life**. Many events happen in our lives without our active participation. We have control over some but not all. We may control some aspects of our lives, but we cannot shape our destinies all by ourselves. We need the help and cooperation of others and the world in general. Others do play an important role. So is the case with acts of God. For all practical purposes, your birth itself is a fortuitous event. You might choose your parents, but you parents are not born for your sake only. What does this mean? It means forces greater than you are at work and controlling this world. It means others have a role in your life. You must acknowledge this fact and the role others play in shaping your life and destiny. You must show your gratitude by letting go of the things you cannot control. You must forgive others and help them , practicing charity, meeting your obligations and performing your duties selflessly.

9. **See the hidden presence of God in this world**. We see the universal form of God every day. We do not acknowledge it because we are conditioned to see God as a person. Everything here is permeated with the sacred presence of God. With a quiet mind, you can discern the silence hidden in creation. You can see space permeating everything. You can see with your own eyes how big, complex and beautiful this universe is. You may not see the infinity or the vastness of God, but you can understand the infinity of the material universe in which we live. We are part of this universe. We live in it. We are

made up of it. Our knowledge is about it and arises from it. Our relationship with it is common to all. We are its dependent realities, united by our relationship with it. Our bodies are made up of the same material as the universe. We share the same elements with the stars, planets and galaxies. The same energy that is in us pervades this universe. We live in its womb, as its numerous forms and aspects. We are its numerous hands, eyes and ears. You must acknowledge this connection between you and the universe, transcending your traditional view of God as a father figure or a benign person having a form of His own.

10. **The world is not what it appears to be**. Do not trust or rely upon your mind and senses alone to comprehend the reality of the world and its secrets. They can hide things, deceive, distract, ignore, mislead or misrepresent. You may rely upon them, but not blindly. Your senses are the windows to the world, but they are also trap doors. They present to you a world of contradictions and duality. A vast part of the reality about this world and ourselves is hidden from us because of them. We should therefore keep our minds open, cultivate wisdom and learn to discern things clearly, so that we will not be trapped in the illusions of our own making. Most importantly, we must control our senses rather than following them blindly in pursuit of our desires.

11. **You become what you think**. Your essential nature drives your thoughts and actions. In turn, they strengthen your essential nature. Thus, you are drawn into a vortex in which you become the cause as well as the effect. This is *karma* at the most basic level. You are a sum total of your thoughts and actions. They sow the seeds of your suffering. Through your own thoughts and actions, arising from your desires and expectations, you create your suffering and victimize yourself in the process. Your suffering continues as long as you remain ignorant of their underlying causes and do not find the means to escape from them. Know that your mind is the source. It creates your life and your future out of your own thoughts

and actions. Therefore, your mind is where you should begin your transformation and purification to break free from your habitual thought patterns and create a new beginning for yourself. The best way to do it is saturate your mind with knowledge and wisdom. Alternatively, you can stop feeding the demons of your consciousness with negative and destructive thoughts and focus your mind solely upon the thoughts of God and your inner Self.

12. **Discipline your mind and body**. Your mind and body are instruments of Nature. If you want to take control of them and prevent Nature from taking control of your life, you need to bring them both under your control. Yoga helps you greatly in this regard. You must learn how to hold on to your resolutions, keep your promises, practice self-discipline and honor your obligation even under the most testing conditions. If you can restrain your senses, discipline your body and practice concentration and meditation, you will win this battle.

13. **Consecrate your actions**. Habitually we take credit for our actions and try to shift the blame elsewhere for our failures. If you think carefully, you realize that apart from your own efforts, numerous factors contribute to your life and achievements. The world in which we live is in its current form because of the efforts of countless people, both living and dead. If we are able to use the modern amenities, devices, programs, applications, inventions and discoveries, it is because of contributions made by other people. We should therefore not take credit for our actions. Instead, we should offer them to God who manifests in this universe in diverse forms and helps us in numerous ways.

The Endearing Qualities of a Devotee

Who is a true devotee? What are his endearing qualities? Who earns the grace (*prasada*) of God? Does the practice of devotion require prior preparation? What qualities lead to devotion of the highest kind that ensures our union with Him? How should we worship Him to secure our liberation? In the *Bhagavadgita*, we find answers to these and others questions about devotion and its importance in our liberation. It declares that ritualistic devotion and halfhearted measures, without purity and perfection in one's thinking and attitude do not lead to salvation. Devotion is an act of offering, not receiving. It is a sacrifice, in which you surrender to God and put your life at His disposal.

Devotion and renunciation go together. You cannot practice true devotion without renouncing worldly life. One may earn good merit from devotional services performed out of desire and go to heaven or attain a good birth in a family of pious people in the next life, but they do not lead to salvation. In the heart and mind of a true devotee, there is no place for desire or desire-ridden devotional service. A true devotee gives up everything and worships God with wisdom, knowledge, detachment and dispassion. He does not seek God because He has other aims. He worships Him without desires and expectations and offers Him unconditionally whatever he has. He is established in purity (*sattva samavistah*). He neither detests disagreeable actions nor favors agreeable ones (18.10). He gives up attachment to his actions and even to their fruit. He sees God in all and considers them His numerous manifestations. If you see a devotee craving for money and worldly pleasures in front of God, know that he is a long way to go on the path of devotion.

A true devotee does not use his devotion to show off his power or wealth. Demonic people do it. They perform sacrifices out of vanity (*dambham*) and for namesake. A true devotee worships God because he loves Him truly and cannot bear separation from Him.

His mind remains absorbed in Him. His life revolves around Him. He remembers nothing but the name and form of God. In his heart, you find nothing but the light of God. If you probe into his mind, you hear nothing but the silent reverberation of his reverential prayers and the chanting of His names and forms. His surrender is so pure and complete that he does nothing at the prompting of his own ego or his desires. His devotion expresses itself in his sacrificial actions and expressions. His identifies himself with God so completely that he does everything for the sake of God and nothing for himself.

The lives of *Hanuman*, the *Alvars* and *Nayanars* of southern India, great saints like *Chaitanya, Vallabhacharya, Meerabai, Kabir, Tulsidas, Tukaram, Sri Ramakrishna* are a few examples of perfect devotion. Their lives are a proof that with effort, faith and discipline, human beings can reach out to God through intense devotion, overcoming mental and emotional barriers induced by their egos and desire for self-preservation. A devotee of God never perishes. However, those who trouble them may. Outwardly, he may not be impressive enough. He may even appear withdrawn, delusional and depressed; but his devotion distinguishes him from others. A devotee is dearer to God. His devotion draws Him closer to God and earns him His grace and love. The *Bhagavadgita* portrays God as the merciful and generous Being who readily responds to the calls of His devotees and attends to their daily needs as if they are His own. At the same time, He does not hesitate to punish the wicked and evil souls by casting them into demonic wombs and darkest hells.

Pure devotion arises from the predominance of *sattva*. It means you cannot experience devotion until you reach perfection in the practice of yoga and your self-transformation. It is experienced when the mind is empty and free from passions and emotions. It is experienced when the ego is silent and subdued in the silence of the senses. Devotion and distraction do not exist in the same space. They cancel each other. If you are distracted, you will have passions and emotions, but not devotion. A distracted mind may be devoted to the things of the world, but it cannot experience pure devotion. To experience true devotion, a devotee must lay down his life at the feet of God. He should become an offering himself. He should become the oblation or the sacrificial food in the sacrifice of his life. His actions should be burnt in the fire of detachment and dispassion. When he achieves perfection in *karmayoga* and *jnanayoga* and when he practices renunciation and detachment with complete sincerity, his heart is ready for the flutter of devotion and the dawn of wisdom. Devotion arises with the predominance of *sattva*. When *rajas* and *tamas* are suppressed and *sattva* predominates certain rare qualifies manifests themselves in a devotee, which are described as divine qualities in the *Bhagavadgita*. They facilitate the practice of devotion and bring a devotee closer to *Isvara*. Some of them are listed below.

- Pure, intelligent, and stable
- Skillful, impartial and undisturbed
- Renounces the feeling of doership
- Solely devoted to God and meditates upon Him always
- Worships only the Highest with supreme faith
- Steadfast in devotion
- Seeker of truth and knowledge
- Remains focused upon God or His thoughts always
- Knows that *Isvara* is the eternal Seed of all beings
- Identifies himself with God completely
- Is born at the end of many births
- Practices devotion with sattvic resolve
- Works for his liberation
- Always singing His glories, prostrating before Him with firm vows, worships God with single minded devotion out of love but not desire or expectation
- Practices detachment and renunciation
- Free from desires, envy, hatred or ill will
- Friendly, compassionate, and forgiving
- Free from egoism

- Whatever he does, whatever he eats, what oblation he pours in the sacred fire, he offers that to God
- Practices non-violence, non-covetousness, truthfulness and cleanliness
- Is without ownership, doership, cruelty, and egoism
- Self-restrained and virtuous
- Practices sameness and remain equal to friend and foe, honor and dishonor, heat and cold, pleasure and pain
- Equal to being criticized or praised
- Silent in both honor and dishonor
- Contended with whatever he has
- Is without a fixed abode
- Remains contended, self-controlled, and selfless
- Free from joy, envy, fear, anger and excitement
- Neither disturbs nor feels disturbed
- Remains free from the consequences of his actions, by renouncing doership and striving in both auspicious and inauspicious works
- Pure and impartial

A true devotee follows the immortal dharma faithfully as ordained, holding God as the Supreme and accepts life as willed by Him. Krishna declares firmly in the scripture (Ch.18) that among His devotees those who teach the knowledge of the *Bhagavadgita*, those who study it and those who hear it from others are dearer to him in the same order than the rest. A true devotee, therefore not only practices devotion, but also enlightens others about His greatness speaking about Him and sharing his knowledge with them.

Stages in devotional worship

In the 12th Chapter of the *Bhagavadgita*, Lord Krishna explains the alternative ways in which He can be worshipped. He states categorically that one should not worship Unmanifested (*avyakta*) Brahman because it is difficult and painful. Then He proceeds to explain how to worship the Manifested Brahman. The best way to do it is through surrender, meditation and single-minded devotion. Worshipping Him with devotion and concentration is the highest form of devotion once can practice in an embodied state. Those who are capable of practicing it are sure of being rescued from the ocean of mortal existence. God lives in them whose minds are fixed upon Him and whose intellect dwells in Him. However, not everyone can think of God constantly. Therefore, if one cannot fix one's mind upon Him, one can practice meditation (*abhyasa yogam*). If that also cannot be done, one should perform actions for the sake of God and attain perfection. If one cannot do even that, one should take refuge in God, and renounce the fruit of one's actions to God with self-control.

The *gunas* also play an important role in shaping our devotion. Sattvic devotion is the purest. It is free from desires, egoism, vanity and selfishness. A sattvic devotee seeks nothing but the company of God. He worships Him without attachment and doership. He remains equal to pain and pleasure, and success and failure. A rajasic devotee worships God to satisfy his passions, and to fulfill his desires. He sees God and his manifestations as distinct and separate from himself. He is easily disappointed and distracted. He worships God with expectations and strives hard to please Him through his service. He also has poor understanding of good (*dharma*) and evil (*adharma*) and what should be done or not done (18.31). A tamasic person worships God conditionally with evil intentions, even to hurt and harm others. He is ignorant and delusional about his methods and practices. He worships out of vanity, egoism, pride and envy with ulterior motives. He resorts to extreme measures to please God and obtain His favors. He is unskilled, imperfect, crude, stubborn, deceitful, malicious, depressed and procrastinating. He holds perverted opinions and usually ends up hating God and opposing Him.

Atmayoga, Realizing the Self by the Self

Atmayoga or *atma-samyama-yoga* is the yoga of knowing the Self by controlling the Self, through concentration, meditation and self-absorption. In *atmayoga*, you align the mind and body, through intense self-purification, according to the demands of spiritual practice so that you are in perfect harmony with yourself. By restraining the egoistic self and its natural inclination to seek sense-objects, you transcend the limitations of your mind and body and their modifications to experience peace and stability that are essential for stabilizing the mind in the contemplation of the Self. The aim of *atmayoga* is to remove the impurities from the lower self and silence its craving and striving so that one may perceive the Self that is hidden deep beneath layers of accumulated memories and habitual thought patterns. This is accomplished through the various limbs of yoga by practicing rules and restraints, controlled breathing (*pranayama*), withdrawal of the senses (*pratyahara*), concentration (*dharana*), meditation (*dhyana*) and self-absorption (*samadhi*). When you achieve perfection in these discipline and practice the last three simultaneously, it becomes *atma-samyama-yoga*.

We do not experience peace if we are in conflict with ourselves. We cannot achieve perfection in yoga with halfhearted measures. We may seek the grace of God (*Isvara-prasadam*) but it comes with self-effort only. The Gita says that first we must renounce our desires and attachment to the fruit of our works. None becomes a yogi without renouncing the thoughts of the world. For a sage (*muni*) on the path of self-realization, selfless work is the means to unite with the Self. (Ch.6.3). Once he has accomplished perfection in work by means of renunciation, serenity is the means. One should uplift the Self by the self, by not degrading himself and by not doing things that are in conflict with the goal of self-realization. This advice is relevant to the practice of *atmayoga* because, as the Gita says, the self only is the friend of the Self and the self only is the enemy of the Self. For him who has conquered the lower self by the higher Self, the Self is the friend and for him who has not done it, it is his enemy.

Therefore, self-discipline is at the crux of *atmayoga*. A self-disciplined and serene person (*jitatma*) becomes established in the contemplation of God and remains equal to the pairs of opposites (6.7). Indeed, discipline is vital to any practice. It is hard to imagine whether progress is possible at all in any field without discipline. While indiscipline may not pose problems in some aspects of worldly life, there is no place for compromise or complacency in spiritual life. Discipline is important in spiritual practice because one can realize the Self only when the mind and body are completely pure and filled with *sattva*. For mental stability and inner peace, which are imperative for the practice of *samyama*, there must be no trace of *rajas* and *tamas* in one's mind and body and no thought of desire or attachment.

How one can practice *atma-samyama-yoga*, is also described by Lord *Krishna* (6:10-19). He states that a yogi should select a clean place and arrange his firm seat (*sthira asanam*) there, which should be neither too high nor too low and cover it with *kusa grass*, deerskin and a cloth one over the other. Sitting on that seat, keeping his mind and sense organs under control, he should practice yoga for self-purification (*atma visuddhi*). Holding the body, the neck and the head in one straight line, stable and still, concentrating on the tip of his nose, undistracted, with peaceful mind, without fear, practicing celibacy (*brahmacharya*), subdued in passions, mind engaged in *samyama*, with mind firmly in God alone, he attains peace and the Supreme Goal of liberation (6:10-15).

There is no place for extremities in this yoga (6.16-18). Moderation is the ideal in both actions and practice to achieve balance and equanimity. This yoga is neither for those who eat excessively nor for those who do not eat at all. It is neither for those who sleep for long nor for those who remain awake. Controlling his eating and enjoyment, controlling his sleeping and waking time, an adept in the yoga of self (*yukta*) destroys all sorrow. Resting his controlled mind (*vinaya cittam*) in the Self, without desires and craving for sense-objects he practices absorption in the Self. Like a lamp in a windless place, in that state of equanimity his mind remains stable, without flickering. With his mind withdrawn from the external world, with his ego-self absorbed in his higher Self, he remains satisfied within in himself (6:20). Resting in the Self, he arrives at the ultimate goal of yoga, which is disassociation from union with pain and suffering (6.23). He enjoys the extreme bliss of union with Brahman and develops the unified vision of the Universal Self, seeing the Self in all and all in the Self.

This yoga is indeed difficult for those who cannot control their minds. Self-absorption and the practice of *samyama* are possible when the mind and body are still. Self-discipline is therefore important. One has to keep one's mind firmly under control and free from modifications. For that, he has to restrain his senses and withdraw them into his mind. What happens if a yogi fails to control his wandering mind? Would he fall into darker worlds? When Arjuna asks this question, Lord Krishna replies that any effort in the yoga of self does not go waste. Neither downfall nor destruction is foreseen for those who are engaged in auspicious deeds, here or hereafter. (6.40). If he falls from the yoga, he may not attain liberation, but he would go to heaven or the world of righteous people and live there for long, enjoying the merit of his actions. Once his *karma* is exhausted, he would return to the earth and takes birth in the house of pious or prosperous people (6.41 & 42). There, he regains the knowledge and intelligence of his previous life and strives again with greater vigor and determination to achieve liberation (6.43).

In terms of principles and practice, as well as goals, *atma-samyama-yoga* as described in the *Bhagavadgita* bears close resemblance to the classical yoga of *Patanjali*. It has all the ingredients of *Patanjali* yoga, but unlike the other, it is theistic. The purpose of *atma-*

samyama-yoga is to attain Brahman or union with God, while that of *Patanjali* yoga is to attain union with *Isvara* or self-absorption. Lord Krishna declares the yoga to be higher than the yoga of knowledge and the yoga of action and advises Arjuna to become its practitioner. He further adds that among the yogis, those who practice this are considered the most skilful. They are superior to ascetics, men of knowledge, and men of actions (6.46). Even among them, those who are full of faith and whose thoughts are absorbed in Him are considered the best. The practice of this yoga also requires the cultivation of divine qualities, which would lead to the predominance of *sattva*. This is the same as the practice of *yamas* and *niyamas* in classical yoga for self-transformation. The divine qualities, which are vital for the practice of this yoga, are listed in the 16th and 17th Chapters.

Transforming the Physical Self

The *Bhagavadgita* is essentially a book of self-transformation. It suggests the ways and means to transform your mind and body, and achieve liberation, making your life a continuous offering to the Supreme Brahman, practicing the three principal yogas, namely the yoga of action (*karmayoga*) the yoga of knowledge (*jnanayoga*) and the yoga of devotion (*bhaktiyoga*). They are meant to purify and divinize the physical, mental and spiritual aspects of our personalities and make them fit for higher and purer states of consciousness. The scripture describes other yogas also, which are equally important. We may regard them as part of a comprehensive program of self-transformation.

In the context of the *Bhagavadgita* as well as *Patanjali* yoga, purification or self-transformation means suppressing the impurities of *rajas* and *tamas* and replacing them with *sattva*. *Sattva* is a divine quality. All the divinities and bright objects in the universe have *sattva* in predominance. If we increase *sattva*, we become divine like and reflect the qualities of God. *Rajas* and *tamas* make us more egoistic and gross, whereas *sattva* refines our subtle bodies and brings us closer to our divine potentials. Intuition and other paranormal powers (*siddhis*) arise from its predominance only. It is also responsible for rationality, wisdom and intelligence in us. *Sattva* elevates our thinking where as *rajas* and *tamas* degrade it. Rajasic nature makes people increasingly this worldly and selfish, while *tamas* brings out the worst in them and leads to demonic and destructive behavior.

The *Bhagavadgita* emphasizes the importance of self-transformation and inner purity to overcome ignorance and attain liberation. It prescribes the yoga of action (*karmayoga*) to overcome desire for sense-objects, the yoga of knowledge to overcome ignorance and delusion, and the yoga of devotion to subdue egoism and evil tendencies. The various yogas suggested in the scripture are meant to transform the gross physical body, the breath body, the mental body and the intelligence body, so that lower self controlled by Nature becomes a friend of the higher Self in the journey of liberation. In the human personality, the body is the animal component, the mind is the human component, and the heart is the spiritual component. The body is a playground of the elemental forces. The human mind with its reasoning power is unique while in the heart alone, we experience the bliss of the Self and subtle feelings and emotions that are peculiarly human. With the help of the three yogas, we can integrate these three basic components of our personalities into one harmonious whole and attain salvation. Integrating these three, we can experience peace and stability within ourselves and remain equal to all. However, the process is not easy, since to achieve freedom one has to escape from the hold of Nature, which does everything in its capacity to bind the beings to the earth and the cycle of births and deaths. It builds many walls around the Self and prevents it from attaining freedom.

The *Bhagavadgita* identifies the body as the playground of Nature and as the field (*kshetra*). It describes it as the city of nine gates, in which the Self, the Knower of the body, is held in bondage. For liberation and the practice of yoga, one needs to know the distinction between the two clearly. The body is made up of the five elements, ego, intelligence, the triple *gunas*, the senses and the mind. It is subject to desires, repulsion or hatred, happiness or pleasure, pain or suffering, liveliness or dynamism, consciousness and modifications. It is perishable and unstable. It needs to be transformed so that it will become a vehicle of humility (absence of pride), honesty, non-violence, tolerance or forgiveness, purity, sincerity, stability, self-control, detachment, dispassion, absence of ego, equanimity, even-mindedness, unwavering devotion to God and preference for loneliness. When these are firmly established through inner purification, one attains immortality. The body is a battlefield in which both the good and evil battle for supremacy whiles the Knower of the field remains in the background as the Witness and Enjoyer. The conflict between these opposing forces is essentially a conflict among the three *gunas*, which try to suppress each other. Our aim should be to cultivate *sattva* by practicing virtues and suppress *rajas* and *tamas* by regulating the food we eat, the actions we perform and the virtues we practice. One should also abandon the triple gates of hell, namely lust, anger and greed. Whoever is free from them acts for the welfare of his Self and reaches the highest goal (16.22).

The ultimate aim is to rise above the *gunas*, but until then one needs to cultivate purity (*sattva*). Purity is said to be the fruit of pious and selfless actions (14.16). Therefore, to cultivate purity a yogi should practice the yoga of action, performing sattvic actions and cultivating sattvic qualities. He should follow the sattvic ideals in matters of faith, worship, sacrifices, austerities, penances, charity, eating, speech and thinking, as described in the 17th Chapter. From *sattva* arise knowledge and the wisdom to practice the yoga of knowledge. With increasing *sattva* he attains good births and purifies himself further until he become adept in the yoga of devotion and transcends all the *gunas*. Knowing that the *gunas* alone act, he remains unconcerned and unmoved by their activities. Same in sorrow and happiness, self-reliant, equal to all, stead, balanced in censure and praise, equal in honor and dishonor, equal to friends and foes, renouncing doership, he serves God with unwavering mind.

The *Bhagavadgita* prescribes various methods to transform the mind and the body. The aim is to cultivate even-mindedness, detachment and divine qualities that facilitate samyama or the advances states of self-absorption. Based upon the various methods of transformation suggested in the *Bhagavadgita*, it can be accomplished by purifying the various component parts (*tattvas*) of Nature in the following manner.

The organs of action

They should be restrained and purified by performing actions without desires, offering their fruit to God. The organs of action cannot be silenced forever. No one can live by remaining inactive because of the *gunas*. It is also not good if the mind keeps dwelling upon sense-objects while the organs of action remain inactive or restrained. One should therefore excel in the practice of the yoga of action, restraining his organs of actions by his mind, unattached (3.7).

The organs of perception

The sense organs of perception (*jnanendriyas*) are difficult to control. They disturb the minds of even those wise people who practice self-control. They are responsible for the turbulence of the mind, attachment, desires, delusion, confusion of memory (*smrit-bhrama*) and loss of discrimination. Withdrawal of the senses (*pratyahara*) is the best way to restrain them and purify them. When one withdraws one's senses from the sense-objects as a tortoise withdraws its limb, one becomes a person of stable intelligence (*sthita-prajna*) (2.58). The sense-objects stop bothering those who do not enjoy them through their senses. The taste for them may last for a while in memory; but even that will fade when one sees the Supreme Self.

The mind

The mind (*manas*) is the eleventh sense organ. It is influenced by the senses. By nature it is fickle (*cancalam*), turbulent and difficult control. It is a major obstacle on the path of yoga. Without controlling the mind, it is difficult to obtain the state of equanimity in yoga. The ideal state of mind portrayed in the *Bhagavadgita* is that which is stable, balanced, even-minded, sameness and free from the modifications arising from impurities, delusion and ignorance. A yogi of subdued mind is likened to a lamp in a windless place. The methods suggested to subdue the mind and achieve lasting peace are withdrawal of the senses, concentration, meditation, self-absorption, living in solitude, self-control, celibacy, moderation in eating and sleeping and freedom from desires (6.1-10-16). A yogi should rest his disciplined mind in himself alone. Seeing himself abiding in his Self, he should remain satisfied within himself.

Intelligence

Discerning wisdom arises from intelligence (*buddhi*) that is stable, one-pointed and free from attachments and the impurities of *rajas* and *tamas*. Intelligence is the highest aspect of Nature present in us; but the Self is higher than the intelligence (3.42). When it is pure, it radiates the brilliance of the Self. Delusion and ignorance arise when the mind is restless and subject to craving and attachments. Deluded people do not worship God, or worship other divinities, pursue wrong aims and identify themselves with their minds and bodies. The *Bhagavadgita* states that there is no intelligence for those whose minds are unsteady (2.66). Their wisdom is carried away by their disturbed minds as a boat is carried away by turbulent waters (2.67). Therefore, one should aim to keep the mind steady and concentrated. When the mind is stabilized through withdrawal of the senses, selfless actions, detachment and sameness, intelligence becomes stable and one-pointed, whereby we distinguish right from wrong and knowledge from ignorance. With increased wisdom and knowledge, we become aware of the eternal nature of our existence and work for our liberation.

The ego

The ego (*aham*) is the false self. It is our individuality and our identification with our minds and bodies whereby we become deluded about our eternal nature. The ego is both the friend and enemy of the Self. It is friend when it pure and enemy when it is impure. For liberation, cooperation of the ego is very vital. Detachment, self-restraint, the yoga of action and knowledge, surrender to God and devotion are the best means to transform and purify our ego consciousness. Even mindedness is important. It can be practiced by restraining the senses, doing selfless service (12.4) and practicing devotion. Surrendering all actions to God, worshipping Him and meditating upon Him with single-minded devotion, one should practice devotion and work for his liberation. These methods increase *sattva* and suppress *rajas* and *tamas*. What makes a person divine or demonic is the purity of his physical self. An impure person comes under the influence of dark and demonic nature and its leads to his delusion and downfall. The practice of *karmayoga* and *jnanayoga* are therefore important to achieve perfection and stabilize the mind and the body in the practice of *bhaktiyoga*, which will ultimately lead to liberation.

Liberating the Self with the Self

We learn from our enlightened masters that liberation is not a learning process, but an unlearning process. You practice yoga to withdraw from the world with which you form an attachment, and let your mind and senses become still so that you will have an uninterrupted opportunity to look within yourself and know who you are truly. Logically, it is an inverse process of returning to the point from where you began the journey as an embodied Self. You may return to that state in a thousand ways, but eventually return you must. When you look at the colorful diversity of the world, in a state of duality, you are drawn into an alternate reality that binds you and does not let you discriminate truth from falsehood. However, when you withdraw from it and look within yourself, you will suddenly realize in a state of unity that you have been an eternal Self all along. Transformation and purification are for the mind and the body only. In this transformation process, you do not destroy anything. You bring the various aspects (*tattvas*) to their perfect best so that they can be closest to the divine in terms of their purity and divinity. Even God is associated with Nature in His manifested aspect. *Isvara* is a pure Being (*Isvara tattva*), having Nature as His playground of activity. Our objective in yoga should be to attain that level of purity so that we reflect His qualities in ourselves.

The individual Self is always pure, eternal and immutable. When you become a *jiva*, you do not know who you are or what you represent. When you remember it, you become Siva. As a *jiva*, you enter into a state of ignorance and forgetfulness as to who you are. When you overcome them, you revert to your original state and become free. The *Bhagavadgita* teaches you how to return to that pure and resplendent state, not by avoiding the battles of life, or escaping from their consequences, but by staying right in the middle of the battlefield of life and doing your duty with peace and equanimity. It suggests how you may lead a divine centered life, working for your salvation with knowledge and awareness in a state of surrender and devotion. The scripture is not a dogma. It is a practical philosophy, which can be practiced and tested by anyone. It has been a source of inspiration since ancient times. Countless devotees followed it to transcend their ignorance and achieve liberation. It continues to enjoy a special place in the hearts of millions of Hindus even today.

Stable Mind and Self-Realization

The human mind is the most amazing, powerful and complex creation of Nature. It enables us to know our individuality and the world in which we live, and use that knowledge intelligently and rationally to regulate our lives and actions according to our needs and desires. Our self-awareness, knowledge and intelligence arise from the various faculties of our minds, which are collectively mentioned in our scriptures as the internal organ (*antahkarana*). With our minds, we can fathom the depths of our own being and the universe and understand their structure, mechanism and relationships. We may not be always right in our knowledge and actions and we may not always have complete knowledge of everything, but we have the ability to discern the right way and right knowledge through effort and by trial and error.

From an evolutionary perspective, we may consider the human mind the most developed instrument of Nature; but our scriptures indicate that the human mind is still an incomplete and imperfect evolute of Nature, having both light and darkness or shades of gray and subject to instability, impermanence and disintegration. It is vulnerable to modifications (*vrittis*) and afflictions (*klesas*) and susceptible to both ignorance and delusion. Unless you train it vigorously, you cannot keep it stable or peaceful. You cannot concentrate your mind if you cannot control your senses. You cannot hold peace or light in it if you cannot free yourself from doubt, delusion and despair. Your existence upon earth is defined greatly by the state of your mind and your perceptions. With the help of your mind, you may soar to the heights of heaven or plunge into the depths of sorrow and depression.

One of the chief weaknesses of the human mind is its instability caused by desire, duality, and attraction and aversion to the pairs of opposites. In seeking what gives us pleasure and happiness and in avoiding what is unpleasant and painful, we become caught in the phenomena of life and experience diverse feelings and emotions. They keep our minds restless and carry away our wisdom and discernment. Caught between attraction and aversion to things, caused by our attachment, we allow our minds and bodies to experience pain and suffering. If we feel happiness and pleasure in between, they will be fleeting because although we have some ability to control our destinies through our actions (*karmas*), our lives are also shaped by acts of God (*adhidaivam*) and Nature (*adhibhutam*). When we do not get what we like, or when we get what we do not want, we become disturbed, anxious and emotionally upset. When we are disturbed, our intelligence fails to discern the truth and make right decisions.

The *Bhagavadgita* recognizes human intelligence (*buddhi*) as the higher mind different and distinct from the ordinary mind (*manas*), which is considered a mere receptacle of thought forms and accumulated memories. Intelligence (*buddhi*) is the highest evolute of Nature. In the universe, it manifests as the Great Intelligence or the Material Mind (*Mahat*), distinct from the Pure Mind or the Pure Consciousness (*satcit*) of the Self. *Mahat* in the universe is equal to *buddhi* in a being. As an aspect of Nature it is part of the field (*kshetra*) whereas Pure Mind or Pure Consciousness is the eternal and immutable state of the Knower of the field (*kshetrajna*) and stays above all.

According to the *Bhagavadgita*, our consciousness (*citta*) is prone to disturbances when our minds and intelligence (*buddhi*) are corrupted by the impurities of *rajas* and *tamas*. In a deluded state, driven by desires and subject to duality, we fail to discern truth. Caught between the polarities of life and acting under the influence of senses, we develop attachment to the sense objects. It leads to craving, and attraction and aversion to the pairs of opposites. If our cravings are not satisfied, we experience strong emotions such as anger, fear and frustration. Under their influence, we suffer from the delusion that we are mere mortal beings, forget that we are immortal selves and indulge in indiscriminate actions, which lead to *karma*, rebirth and bondage to the earthly life. Instability of the mind induced by modifications arising from desires and attachment is thus the real problem.

Mental disturbances are part of our daily experiences. We are never free from them. Our minds are in a constant state of flux. Unless we train them, we cannot bring them to rest. Most of the time we are not even aware that we are restless because we become accustomed to it and accept it as a natural condition. We cannot resolve this problem with our mental or intellectual knowledge. They may help us to some extent to experience peace and stability, but they do not provide everlasting solutions. Our knowledge of the world and ourselves (*vijnanam*) arises from our perceptions and memories stored in our minds. It is incapable of resolving our existential problems associated with our bondage and find solutions to the problems whose causes we cannot easily ascertain. In fact, instead of resolving our restlessness, often this knowledge aggravates our hopelessness and despair by exaggerating our fears and fueling our doubts. Besides, it cannot help us fathom the memories that remain deeply buried in our consciousness and contribute to our mental afflictions to understand their causes. Therefore, whatever solutions we may find with the help of our perceptual knowledge are inadequate. If this were not so, today people would not suffer so much from mental afflictions and resort to drugs and other chemicals to keep themselves calm and sane. We need more comprehensive and lasting solutions to resolve the problem of mental instability and restlessness. For that, we need to stop looking outwardly and look within ourselves to study our consciousness, observe it dispassionately and understand the causes of its modification and their remedy. We must look for that center in us which is impervious to the disturbances created by our senses and remains calm even amidst storms and tempests of life.

The *Bhagavadgita* portrays the restlessness of the human mind as a natural condition and an intentional design of Nature (*Prakriti*) to keep us deluded, distracted and subdued. In a deluded and disturbed state, we do not know who we are and we do not care to be other than what we are. Thus, both these attitudes perpetrated by Nature serve its objectives, while it works entirely against our spiritual wellbeing, peace and happiness. The scripture goes to the root of the problem and suggests that our suffering, bondage, delusion and ignorance, arise from the triple *gunas* that are pervasively present in our minds and bodies. You cannot see them or feel them. You can know them only by the results or the effects they produce. Lord Krishna states categorically that the *gunas* are responsible for our desires, attachments and desire-ridden actions. Since our actions lead to *karma*, they are also responsible for our bondage and our continuation in the mortal world as subjects of Nature and beings of delusion and ignorance. You may think that you are performing your actions, whereas the truth is your actions arise from the predominance of the *gunas* present in you. A wise person knows it and thereby remains undisturbed by his experiences, circumstances, actions and their results. He does not assume doership because he knows that he has acted only under the influence of his *gunas*.

The *gunas* tend to compete and suppress one another in their struggle for predominance. In the process, they induce in us desire for the sense objects in which they are present predominantly. Thus, *sattva* prompts you to seek objects that are predominantly sattvic, *rajas* that are predominantly rajasic and *tamas* that are predominantly tamasic. In this internal struggle, without knowing that we are acting under the influence of our predominant *gunas*, we indulge in actions, develop desires and habitual thought patterns, form attachments, and become bound to the cycle of births and deaths.

The three *gunas* bind us in their own ways. *Sattva* binds us through pleasures, *rajas* through passions and *tamas* through ignorance. Ideally we have to transcend all the three; however since it cannot be accomplished without years of strenuous effort, we must try to cultivate *sattva* to the extent possible so that we can stabilize our minds and intelligence and experience peace and stability. When *sattva* predominates, we become spiritual in our thinking and attitude. We turn to God and work for our liberation. As we advance on the path of self-transformation, we experience unity and absorption in the Self (*atma samyama*), which will gradually burn away all the latent impressions and seeds of *karma*.

It may not be an exaggeration to say that the primary goal of the *Bhagavadgita* is to teach us how to live spiritually and experience peace and stability, without renouncing the world or our basic human responsibilities as members of our families and society. The teaching itself is to calm the nerves and address the problem of ignorance, delusion and human suffering as exemplified by Arjuna. Indeed, the objective of the *Patanjali* yoga is also the same, how to achieve peace and stability through self-transformation. It is a major challenge in any age or society. Yoga is one of the simplest and direct means to address this problem. The *Yogasutras* begins with the assertion that the purpose of yoga is cessation of the modifications of the mind (*yoga cittavritti nirodhaha*). Thereby it brings the central purpose of human life to the forefront.

The *Bhagavadgita* equally and repeatedly emphasizes the importance of equanimity, stability and sameness in the pursuit of liberation. The purpose of *buddhiyoga* is also the same. If you do not have mental stability, you cannot be free from the modifications of your mind and body. A disturbed mind cannot focus on anything in particular for long. In a disturbed state, we cannot also withdraw from the world and remain focused upon ourselves. One may escape from the world, but without training, one cannot escape from the thoughts and memories of it. You may escape from the world to the *Himalayas*, but if you have not trained your mind, you will not be at peace with yourself, except perhaps when you are in deep sleep. If you have attachments and desires, the world will follow you even into the deepest caves or the recesses of your mind. There is no sanctuary for him in the entire world whose mind is disturbed and whose senses are not under his control. If you want to achieve perfection in yoga, and address the problem of fickle mindedness, you must deal with your desires and attachments before you can live alone and self-absorbed.

According to the *Bhagavadgita*, when we are disturbed, we cannot concentrate or think clearly. We make wrong decisions or discern things incorrectly. We take refuge in our egos view ourselves as physical beings subject to death and destruction. This is the state of delusion. This is what happened to Arjuna also. He used his knowledge of duty and religion to justify his cowardly decision to escape from the harsh realities life. He cleverly manipulated his own thoughts to create a justifiable philosophy of virtue and social responsibility to avoid his difficult and unpleasant duty as a warrior. Our scriptures say that the mind is conjurer. It creates its own magic of make believe reality or self-induced delusion, to avoid dealing with the complex problems of life and the pain and suffering that arise from it. This state of mind (*prvritti*), which is so natural to us, and which we may not even notice, is a major obstacle in our quest for peace and liberation. With it, we cannot really resolve any problem or find happiness on a lasting basis. For that, we need a stable mind that can focus uninterruptedly, think intelligently and free us from own ignorance and delusion by readjusting our thinking and behavior.

Our problems are self-created. We create them largely because of our ignorance and inability to think clearly and wisely. Our wisdom becomes evident in our decisions and actions. Disturbed people make disturbing decisions. We aggravate our problems and suffering when we are not peaceful and when we are not in harmony with ourselves. Wise men, skilful in yoga, choose to be part of the world, but they never get involved with it or lose their freedom through indiscriminate actions. They restrain their senses, practice detachment and remain undisturbed by external events. Things in themselves have no power over you. You put power into them with your own desires and involvement. You willingly seek them in the hope and illusion of securing them and making them your own. Caught between attraction and aversion to them, you barter away your freedom, peace and happiness.

You do not realize how deeply you have become involved with the world and how much freedom you have lost until you become introspective and observe your cravings and longings with the intelligence and awareness you acquire through yoga.

A silent mind is ideal for liberation. When we are calm, we allow our intelligence to shine. When we are free from disturbances, we think clearly and focus firmly. The *Bhagavadgita* shows us the way to attain this ideal. It states that mental stability (*sthithaprajna*) arises from one-pointed intelligence. If you want to control your mind, you should sharpen your intelligence with knowledge and wisdom and purify it with *sattva*, so that it can penetrate into the nature of things and discern the truth hidden in them. A person of stable intelligence is not fooled by the appearance of things. He knows what is happening around him and inside him. Established in yoga, performing actions such as seeing, hearing, touching, smelling, tasting, walking, dreaming and breathing, he thinks he is doing nothing (5.9). While engaged in actions and dealing with the world, he remains untainted like a lotus leaf in the water. (5.10). He looks upon things equally, and with his intelligence firmly fixed in his inner Self, he attains the state of non-return (*apunahvritti*).

The *Bhagavadgita* rightly identifies desire as the root cause of our suffering. Out of desire, we become bound to the world. We keep seeking objects or try to avoid them in the hope of finding peace and fulfillment through accumulation of things that we desire most. When our actions do not yield expected results, we suffer from frustration and negativity. On this perilous path, we may experience pain and pleasure intermittently, but we cannot secure peace permanently because we have little control over the world. Happiness arising from the external world is limited in its ability to stabilize the mind; but that which arises from within you, independent of the external world, is more lasting. It has firmer foundation and therefore more reliable as a solution to the problem of human suffering. You have greater control over the world that exists in you than the world in which live. By controlling it and stabilizing it, you can experience peace and stability even when the world is disturbingly chaotic.

Thus, mental stability is achieved by knowing what is important in your life and how best you may empower yourself by securing it. Extending our influence over the world is not as important as withdrawing from it and remaining detached from it with mental and spiritual discipline. You conquer the world not by rushing into it but withdrawing from it. You cannot control that which you seek out of desire. You cannot control that upon which you depend. Happy is the person who restrains his senses rather than gives them inexcusable freedom. Those who want to rule the world are its slaves, but those who have restrained themselves are its true masters. You do not exercise this control with egoism or tamasic cruelly, but with detachment, tolerance and gentle firmness. Peace comes to us not by having things or controlling them, but by relinquishing our desire and dependence upon them. True freedom arises from absence of desires. Whoever is free in the body is free from the world.

Liberation may be difficult, but not impossible if you have sattvic resolve or firmness (*dhriti*), which according to the *Bhagavadgita* (18.33), arises when through yoga a yogi stabilizes his mind, life breath, senses and actions. Practicing sattvic actions with detachment (*vairagyam*) and controlling your desires with sattvic resolve (18.26) you can cultivate pure intelligence (18.30), which enables you to know the difference between indulgence and abstinence, action and inaction, and bondage and liberation. These eventually lead you to stability and sameness. With mental stability comes undisturbed and unending calm. All sorrows cease for a yogi whose mind is stable and whose craving has ended. In the absence of desires and craving, he remains equal to all. He accepts every condition in his life as providence (*yaddruchcha-labha-samtushta*) and deals with it with sameness and indifference. By conquering his inner world, overcoming his limitations and becoming disinterested in the world, he overcomes duality (*dwandatitha*) and egoism and remains undisturbed and indifferent always. Free from ignorance and delusion he sees clearly the beauty and splendor of his very Self that is hidden in him. Having become united with it, he sees himself in all and all in himself

Living in a complex world, we know how important peace and equanimity are in our lives. In this regard, the *Bhagavadgita* is very clear. It says that you can look for solutions to the problem of your suffering within yourself. You have the knowledge and wisdom to achieve this goal. You cannot reach it in your present state because they are veiled by the delusion (*maya*) cast by Nature. If you purify your mind, you can tap into that eternal source and use that knowledge for your liberation and everlasting peace. To experience peace, you do not have to escape from the world, but you have to renounce your attachments. You do not have to give up your actions or responsibilities, but only your egoistic attitude in performing them and your desire for their fruit. If you do not live for yourself or for your selfish desires, you will not be touched by the impurities of your life. If you offer your actions to God, He will assume responsibility for their consequences. If you bring God into your life, He will become your Guide and lead you safely to the world of eternal freedom.

Purusha and Prakriti

In creation, all things come in pairs. Like the positive and negative charges of electricity, they act like twins and together complete the circle of life. We call them the pairs of opposites. They exist even at the highest level of manifested realities. Although Brahman is one, He manifests in the world as two. He creates His twin aspect, an opposite, which is responsible for the materiality, dynamism and diversity we find in our world. We recognize them as Nature and the Supreme Self respectively. They also go by different names as *Prakriti* and *Purusha*, Universal Male and Universal Female, Mother Goddess and Father God, or Energy and Pure Consciousness. They are the twin realities of the Manifested Brahman, who is also known as the Lord of the Universe (*Isvara*). Even in the physical dimension of the universe, we can see them as matter and space. Both are said to be eternal, but *Prakriti*, in contrast to *Purusha*, is dependent reality. In other words, it needs the support of God. However not all agree with this assertion. Some believe that both are eternal and independent. Whatever may be the truth, they participate together to initiate, implement and regulate the universal creative process. If *Purusha* is the source, *Prakriti* is the means. According to some schools, Purusha is both the efficient and the material causes of the creation; while some, like the school of *Samkhya*, believe that He is the efficient cause while *Prakriti* is the material cause. The *Bhagavadgita* upholds the former view that God is the source of all, including *Prakriti*, and considers it a dependent and eternal aspect of Brahman only.

Etymologically, *Prakriti* (pra + akriti) means, the power or the intensity (*pra*) hidden in the forms (*akriti*) or the power that creates forms (*akriti*). It also means that which gives life (*pra*) and form (akriti). Its popular meaning is natural condition, state, disposition, or form of anything. In philosophy, it is generally used to refer to Nature or material universe. Its opposite is *vikriti*, meaning artificial, ugly, changed or modified. *Purusha* (puru +

usha) means "the eastern dawn," signifying the rising Sun as the Manifested Brahman, who heralds the dawn of creation by appearing in the endless space (*akasa*) and sets in motion His dynamic energy and creative consciousness to bring forth all beings and worlds. *Purusha* and *Prakriti* constitute the two distinct realities of creation and our very existence. In each of us, *Purusha* is represented by the Self or pure consciousness, while *Prakriti* is represented by our minds and bodies.

Prakriti operates at two levels. Its lower nature consists of the eight fold divisions namely, earth, water, fire, air, ether, mind and reason and also the ego (7.4), while its higher nature consists of that (life force) by which all the living entities are upheld (5.5). All the beings in the universe originate from this twofold Nature (5.6). The *Adhibhuta*, which is responsible for all physical events, represents the elemental aspect of Nature (8.4). At the end of each cycle of creation, all manifested things and beings dissolve in Brahman. When the next cycle begins, He manifests them again (9.7). Seated in *Prakriti*, *Purusha* creates all the living communities (9.6), and the whole creation itself, both moving and non-moving (9.10). Their relationship is symbolized creatively in the *Sivalinga*, a representation of Siva as the Lord of the Universe, in which they are shown as organs of creation embraced in perfect union. All living beings are living examples of this great union. Nothing happens until the two come together and work together. A being (*jiva*) arises from Non-Being (*Siva*) when he becomes associated with beingness (Nature) and experiences duality and delusion.

In an individual being, the mind and the body complex represents *Prakriti*, while the Self represents *Purusha*. The former along with its realities or aspects (*tattvas*) is known as field (*kshetra*), where as the Self is known as the Knower of the field (*kshetrajna*). The field has parts and diversity. It is subject to modifications, where as *Purusha* is indivisible and free from modifications. *Prakriti* is subject to duality and change, while *Purusha* is indestructible, immutable and inexhaustible. *Purusha* exists in the being as the pure, egoless consciousness beyond the senses and the mind. Even though He is bound to the phenomenal world and enveloped in delusion, He is not subject to any modifications. *Purusha* is the *Adhidaiva*, the Great God (8.8), the Ancient, the Omniscient, the Universal Enforcer of Law, and the Supporter of All (8.9). In the body, as the indwelling Spirit and inner Witness, He becomes *Adhiyajna*, the Lord of the Sacrifice (8.4). He is the Witness, the Guide, the Bearer, the Enjoyer, the Great Lord and the Supreme Self (13.22).

Purusha is the universal Cosmic Male, the supreme Brahman, who emerges out of nothing to manifest the worlds and beings for unfathomable reasons. He is the subject as well as the object of sacrificial ceremonies. According to the *Vedas*, His self-sacrifice in remote antiquity resulted in the manifestation of the worlds and beings. Since He is the source of all, and considered the Sacrificed as well as the Sacrificer, by making sacrifices to Him, one gains entry into the world of gods or immortal beings. The concept of *Purusha* as the Creator and Nourisher is well documented in the Vedic hymns, especially in the *Purushasukta* of the *Rigveda*, which describes how *Purusha* manifested the worlds out of Himself and established social order.

The *Bhagavadgita* describes two types of *Purusha*s, the perishable and the imperishable. The body is the perishable *Purusha*, while the soul is the Imperishable One (15.16). In other words, it acknowledges *Prakriti*, which stands for the body in the beings, as an essential aspect of the eternal Brahman. In a living being, *Prakriti* is the physical self or the perishable *Purusha*, while the individual Self (*atman*) is the imperishable *Purusha*. The Supreme Purusha, God (*Isvara*) Himself, is however said to be neither of these, because He is beyond the perishable (*Prakriti*) and higher than the Imperishable inner Self, and sustains the three worlds by entering into them (15.17). Since He is beyond the perishable and higher than the Imperishable (Self), He is called the Supreme *Purusha* (*Purushottam*a) (15.18). It means, although the individual Self has the same essence as the Universal Self, just like *Prakriti* it is considered an aspect (*amsa*) of the Universal Self only. The

Universal Self pervades the whole creation. There is no end to His manifestations (*vibhutis*) (10.40), which He holds by a single fragment (*ekamsam*) of Himself (10.42), including the individual Selves.

Prakriti is responsible for the illusion and the duality we experience in our perceptions and interactions with the objects of the world. All modifications (*vikarams*) and modes (*gunas*) arise and exist because of *Prakriti* only (13.19). With the help of the *gunas*, it binds the indwelling Purusha to the sense objects and causes His birth in both good and evil wombs (13.21). The Bhagavadgita declares that in the performance of actions, *Prakriti* is the cause, while in case of pleasures and pain, *Purusha* is the cause (13.21). Our ignorance and attachment arise largely due to the impurities present in our minds and bodies. As long as they are present, we cannot discern truth clearly. Our senses are imperfect instruments. With their help, we may perceive things, but only superficially. We cannot penetrate into the nature of things and experience them not only perceptually but also as they are in their essential state. We cannot know things experientially because of duality and the distinction between the knower and the known or the subject and the object As long as the object remains in our perception, the experience of knowing remains incomplete. The same is the case with knowing the Self. To know it really, we have to overcome duality and become absorbed in it.

The soul in the body is known as the indwelling witness and lord of the sacrifice (*Adhiyajna*). We learn from the Bhagavadgita (8.4) that when *Purusha*, who is also known as the Controlling Deity (*Adhidaiva*), resides in the body as the inner witness, He becomes the Lord of the Sacrifice (*Adhiyajna*). He is the lord of the sacrifice because in the sacrifice of life, He (the Self) is the ultimate recipient of all offerings. Perceptions, life breath and food are enjoyed by Him only. It means that *Purusha* and *Prakriti* manifest in both the macrocosm of the universe and the microcosm of each being as inseparable twins. In their highest and lowest aspects, they represent the two faces of One Absolute Reality.

The indwelling Self is also known as the embodied Self (*jivatama*). In its essential nature, it is the same as the liberated soul (*muktatma*). However, it is bound to the body (*Prakriti*) and caught in the field of illusion from which it cannot easily escape without persistent spiritual effort. To perceive the Self in the body, you need knowledge and discernment. You have to detach yourself from your beingness and identify yourself completely with your spiritual nature. As the *Bhagavadgita* states, a striving yogi perceives Him, as the Lord seated in the body enjoying the sense objects, while the ignorant ones whose hearts are impure, cannot perceive Him even after much striving (15.11).

For the Self the body is like a garment. Until liberation is attained, He keeps returning to the earth to attain new bodies and continue His association with Nature. When a being dies with unfinished *karmas*, its elemental body (*bhutatma*) returns to Nature. The indwelling Self leaves the body and goes to the ancestral world. While departing He takes away with Him the mind and the senses like the wind carrying away the fragrances so that He may continue to enjoy the objects in his afterlife (15.8). The final moments are crucial. The *Gita* says that whatever a person thinks, at the time of his death, he attains it (8.6). Whoever departs from the body thinking of God only attains Him without doubt (8.5 & 8.13). One should therefore train the mind well so that one can think of God and remember Him always (8.8).

The time of death is also important since it has a bearing upon where one would go. A yogi who dies during the period of northern solstice goes to the immortal world of Brahman by the sunlit path and lives there forever. He never returns to the mortal world of suffers from bondage to Nature. Those who depart from here during the southern solstice go to the world of ancestors by the moonlit path and return to the earth again after exhausting their karmas. They take birth variously according to their past merit. However, those who are demonic by nature perish. They fall into the lowest hells (16.16) and suffer there.

According to the *Bhagavadgita*, the eternal Supreme *Purusha* is said to be neither Being (*sat*) nor Non-Being (*asat*). He is omnipresent with hands and feet, eyes, heads, faces and ears everywhere. He envelops everything without moving. He is the source of the sense organs, but does not have them, detached but sustainer of all, without qualities but their source. He is within and without all beings, moving and unmoving, very subtle and incomprehensible, far away but also very nearer. Though Undivided, He is also situated in the beings as divided. Bearer of beings, who is also known as the devourer and the illuminator. Among the illuminated, He is the very illumination and said to be beyond the darkness also. He is the knowledge that is known, that is yet to be known, and the goal of all knowledge also. He resides in the hearts of all. The scripture declares that that *Prakriti* is for performing actions, but *Purusha* is for enjoying the pleasures and pains of life. Indeed, He is said to be the Overseer, Regulator, Bearer, Enjoyer, the Great Lord, and the Supreme Soul. He is *Purusha*, the transcendental Soul (13. 12-22).

The knowledge of *Purusha* and *Prakriti* is helpful to know the perishable and imperishable aspects of our personalities and the world in which we live. By knowing the distinction between the two, we know where to focus our efforts and what we should do to achieve liberation. When we know that the body is a temporary dwelling place for the embodied Self, we develop dispassion and detachment towards it and turn our attention to the Self. The *Bhagavadgita* affirms that he who knows *Purusha* and *Prakriti* with its *gunas*, even if engaged in actions will not take birth again in this mortal world (13.22). They go to the Supreme (13.34).

Conquering the Ego, the False Self

In this world, it is very difficult to live without identity and individuality. These two define us and introduce us to the world. Without them, we cannot manage our lives or relate to others meaningfully. Imagine what happens, if you wake up one day and forget who you are. Your life will be chaos. It happens to some unfortunate individuals when they wake up from coma or suffer severe brain damage. Your identity grows with you; so does your individuality. They keep changing as you accumulate knowledge and experience and learn to manipulate your way through the world and relationships. Your individuality is what you build and live with. You may consider it an asset or a burden. For spiritual people it is a problem as well as a burden, but for the worldly, it is an asset and the means to draw their respective territories and establish their zones of influence. People spend their whole lives, defending it, upholding it, promoting it and protecting it. You do not know how your life would be if you silence you individuality, if you do not know who you are or if you become a different person by chance.

The ego is the sum total of the experiences, perceptions, memories, knowledge and relationships gathered by each being in the course of its existence upon earth. It is an illusion created by their aggregation. It does not actually exist except as a notion in the consciousness of each being. You will not find the ego in its parts, but only in the association of things and experiences. The ego thus survives by attachments and relationships. You remove them from the equation and the ego disappears instantly. Your individuality is a myth, which you create and perpetuate for a lifetime. You defend it, uphold it and promote it as if it is all that matters. In the end, you pay the price. When the diverse components of your individuality disperse or return to their sources, your ego vanishes. What is left after that is a mystery, which we have been trying to understand since the dawn of our civilization. Is there anything beyond it? "Yes," say the Hindus;

and "No," say the Buddhists. You do not have to agree with either of them. You have a choice. You can wait until Nature disintegrates and disperses your ego and all that you build in the vain hope of surviving death; or you can do it yourself through yoga and self-transformation and see what happens. The yogis do it. Painstakingly, they remove the threads that keep their egos intact. When they do it, they fall into silence. They become the silent ones (*munis*) because their egos die before their bodies. They have no interest to tell you what is happening to them. They have no being in them to tell you what is going on.

In worldly life, the ego is the facilitator; but in spiritual life, it is an obstacle. It is also often described as the false self or the lower self, which is even compared symbolically in some traditions to the enemy within or the demon. It is responsible for our individuality, duality and beingness. It creates and perpetuates in us the idea that individually we are distinct and different from the rest of the world and we need to work for our own survival and wellbeing. Because of egoism, we assume ownership and doership and perform actions to satisfy our desires and secure our attachments. The ego touches every aspect of our worldly existence. It is our spokesperson, our message and our front. The life that we lead here upon earth is essentially its creation. The *Bhagavadgita* is very much a conversation between human ego and the eternal Self. Arjuna stands symbolically for the ego-self, while Lord Krishna represents the individual Self or the Supreme Self. Arjuna's suffering is the suffering of an ego bred on ignorance, delusion, pride and passions. It arose from his limited knowledge, his sense of separateness, his identification with name and form, his attachment to his body, his belief that he was the doer of his actions and his anxiety about the outcome of his actions. He suffered from doubt and despair when he took upon himself the entire responsibility of waging a terrible war and thought of its consequences as directly influencing his life. In that state of anxiety and confusion, he did not remember the role of God in his life, even though Lord Krishna, God-incarnate, was right in front of Him, acting as his charioteer. Because of its limited knowledge, the ego suffers from anxiety and uncertainty. Conflict and confusion are rooted in its consciousness. These qualities are well reflected in Arjuna's suffering and the doubts and moral problems he expressed about fighting the war against his own relations and acquaintances. He had delusion about his own identity as he identified himself with his name and form and thought about the same with regard to others.

Identification with one's own name and form is considered egoism. However, identification with the inner Self or the Supreme Self is not considered so, although the Self is also an ego (*aham*) of the transcendental kind. When you identify yourself with it completely in a state of withdrawal and self-absorption, it leads to your transformation and the realization that you are none other than Brahman only (*aham Brahmasmi*).

According to the *Bhagavadgita*, the earth, water, fire, air, mind, intelligence and ego constitute the eightfold division of the material Nature of Brahman (7.4). Lord Krishna describes it as His inferior Nature. In the individual being, it is equivalent to the physical Self or the ego-self. At the highest level in creation, it is the Supreme Being, *Purusha*, *Brahma*, or the Manifested Materiality (*sambhuti*), which consists of His creative energy, numerous manifestations (*vibhutis*), worlds and all the living beings (*jiva-bhutam*). The dualistic schools refer to it as His universal body (*visvarupam*). Higher than the ego-self is the inner-Self in each being and the Supreme Self or Pure Consciousness at the universal level, which pervades and envelops everything. In mortal life, the ego-self and the eternal-Self represent two opposite and distinct realities, with no correlation whatsoever between the two. However, when it comes to liberation, their relationship assumes great significance. The physical self is either a friend or enemy of the eternal Self, depending upon how it conducts itself upon earth and whether its actions lead to liberation or bondage. In case of those who are deluded and ignorant, it is the enemy of the Self, where as whoever conquers his lower Self by his higher

Self, it becomes His friend. Therefore, says the *Bhagavadgita*, one should uplift one's Self by oneself (6.5), and become a conqueror of one's mind and body (*jitatmana*), remaining the same in cold and heat, pain and pleasure and honor and dishonor (6.7). One should take refuge in the inner Self and surrender to God, performing selfless actions, renouncing their fruit. When you do not feed your ego with pride and vanity arising out of your actions, and when you take refuge in the Supreme Self, your ego becomes a friend in your journey to the world of God.

In the *Bhagavadgita*, we find many references to the ego (*aham*) and the importance of transforming it for perfection in yoga. It identifies the ego as an aspect (*tattva*) of Nature and beingness as the field (*kshetra*) (13.6), which is subject to modifications such as aging, sickness, birth, death, rebirth, sorrow, anger, and the duality of attraction and aversion. The ego is subject to the influence of the *gunas*. It is responsible for the modifications (*vrittis*) of the mind and actions performed out of desire and attachment. A person who is without ego (*anahamvadi*) is dearer to God. Egolessness (*nirahamkaram*) is a divine quality (13.12), which arises from the predominance of *sattva* (18.26), and leads to peace (2.71) and equanimity. He alone is fit for self-realization, who is without ego (18.54). Actions do not taint him because whoever acts without egoism (*ahamkritva bhava*) does not act even if he acts (18.18). Therefore he is not bound. In contrast, performing actions for the sake of oneself (ego) is a demonic quality (17.6), which leads to ignorance and downfall. Men of demonic resolve perform severe penances and torture their minds and bodies without discrimination, out of vanity and egoism, (17.6). Such actions lead to bondage rather than liberation.

The ego makes us to believe that we are the doers of our actions and responsible for them and their outcome. Because of it, we crave for things and perform actions out of desires and attachments. In the process, we become bound to the mortal world. The *Bhagavadgita* says that it is a delusion to think that you are the source of your actions. You perform actions because of the desires induced by the *gunas* that are inherent in you. All actions are performed by the *gunas*, which have a tendency to compete and dominate one another. An egoistic and ignorant person wrongly believes that he is the doer (3.27), whereas he is actually acting under their influence. The first step to overcome the problem of *karma* is to recognize this fundamental truth and offer your actions and their fruit to God, not taking any credit or discredit for their outcome. A *karmayogi*, who is pure in his heart and restrained his mind and senses, overcomes his egoistic thinking and limited vision. He sees his Self in all living beings and remains free even though he is engaged in actions. (5.7)

Depending upon how we approach it, the ego-self, can be either a help or an impediment in our spiritual liberation. If we purify it and align it with our spiritual values, it facilitates our liberation. Conquest of the egoistic Self, therefore, is very important for perfection in yoga. He, who conquers his ego or the feeling of individuality and separation, earns the right to enter the Abode of the Supreme Self. He remains stable and serene in all circumstances. When he reaches this state, he becomes free from anger, pride, greed, envy, fear and delusion. Freed from all desires and attachments, he believes that he does nothing while seeing, hearing, touching, smelling, tasting, walking, sleeping and breathing (5.8). With his ego subdued, he attains union with the Universal Self and develops a unified vision through which he sees the Self in all and all in the Self (6.29). He finds God everywhere and worships Him as the Inhabitant of all beings (6.31). He reaches the profound conclusion that he is indeed none other than Brahman Himself.

Achieving egolessness

How can we achieve egolessness? The ego manifests in many ways and perpetuates itself in many guises. It fights to survive until the end. The problem we have in subduing our egos is we have to do it within ourselves using the very faculties that tend to support it or that are influenced by it. In other words, you have to subdue the self by the self. This is indeed very difficult. You can fight with external enemies. However, fighting against yourself within yourself and living as if you do not exist and you do not matter is a challenge. Many advanced yogis, who spend years transforming their personalities, betray their egoism when they feel disturbed, opposed or challenged. Egoism is not just having pride in your identity and individuality. It is the very notion of you as an individual and any thought or feeling to which you may be particularly drawn. In other words, if you have an opinion, know that you have ego. If you feel the urge to defend your opinions or views, know that you have ego. If you react to the world in any manner, even for righteous purposes, unless it is arising from your pure consciousness, know that you have ego. In short, if you defend yourself, promote yourself, speak for yourself, take credit, seek recognition, have expectations, claim ownership, or experience fear, anger, greed, envy or pride, know that you are not free from your ego. We know from observation that even after spending years in purifying you may still experience traces of egoism in your thinking and behavior. The *Bhagavadgita* touches upon some very important truths concerning our existence. By meditating upon them, we can develop deep insight into the nature of ego and its transformation.

1. Ignorant people identify themselves with their minds and bodies; but in truth, you are an eternal and indestructible Self.
2. The body is like a garment, worn by the Self in its embodied state. In the course of its existence upon earth, it assumes many bodies and goes through many experiences in a state of ignorance and delusion.
3. Actions arise from the *gunas*; but the real source of all actions is God because He is the source of the *gunas* also. Therefore, He is the real doer and all actions should be attributed to Him and offered to Him without desiring their fruit.
4. The ego is strengthened by the impurities of *rajas* and *tamas*. One should therefore cultivate sattva.

5. You can transcend your ego by renouncing desires and attachment to your actions and things, doing selfless work, surrendering to God and cultivating sameness.
6. If you absorb your mind in the thoughts of God, your mind will soon be filled with the rare brilliance of God and reflect His qualities. Therefore, restraining your senses, withdrawing from the world, concentrate your mind and intelligence upon God and worship Him with unwavering mind. When you saturate your mind with the thoughts of God, you become one with Him.
7. Knowledge and wisdom are essential to discern things clearly and overcome ignorance and delusion. When they are removed, you become centered in your inner Self and experience oneness with it.

The Divine Qualities of a Sattvic Person

The *Bhagavadgita* puts significant emphasis on inner purity and unwavering sincerity in the practice of yoga for liberation. The inner Self is the witnessing Self. It is ever awake and attentive to our actions and mental formations, but completely untouched by them and the phenomenal world. It is forever pure even when it exists in the body of the lowest organisms. It watches our actions, interactions and modifications, enjoying the perceptions brought in by our senses. In contrast, the mind and the body are very vulnerable to our actions and impurities. Even a simple thought in the form of a subconscious suggestion can hurt you and delay your progress. A spiritually active person must be therefore very careful about his thoughts and actions and remain on guard always, examining his motives and paying attention to his hidden desires and unresolved passions.

In the practice of yoga, sincerity and honesty are very important. You must be true and honest with yourself, acknowledging your faults and mistakes, without deluding yourself. You must make necessary effort to correct yourself, going the extra mile if necessary. Self-realization is a mirage for those who indulge in outward religiosity, without making necessary effort to purify themselves. To experience peace and equanimity you must fill your mind and body with *sattva* and suppress *rajas* and *tamas*. Without it, you may practice yoga for years, but you will remain a slave to your passions and desires. A yogi who is balanced (*yukta*) is always on guard. He would not allow his ego to take control or defend him. A spiritualized ego is a much a bigger problem in overcoming selfishness and attachments than an ordinary and simple ego that is largely ignorant of its spiritual purpose. Unless we are careful, we may become deluded by the very religion that intends to deliver us from sinful actions. When we bring our worldliness into our religious practice and develop attachment to a particular religion, god, scripture, *guru* we delay our liberation. Alternatively, we may also develop hatred towards other paths and religions and become involved in egocentric clashes and vengeful attitude. It equally detrimental to your spiritual progress. You should stay away from these negative and destructive emotions. As the *Bhagavadgita* declares clearly neither you should be the cause of disturbance to the world nor you should be disturbed by it. The purpose of yoga is to transcend both attraction (*raga*) and aversion (*dvesha*) not only in worldly matters but also in spiritual life. Our success on the path depends very much upon our transformation and development of certain qualities that enhance our purity and bring us closer to the essential nature of God.

Self-purification is very important in spiritual life. We may read scriptures or perform rituals and sacrifices out of genuine interest, but they are of no value unless we remove the impurities of *rajas* and *tamas* from our minds and bodies, and practice virtue unconditionally. Without purity, none can achieve self-realization. None can cross the ocean of phenomenal existence with sinful attitude. None can see the Self if the mind is filled with passions and emotions. On the path of yoga, inner cleanliness (*antar-suddhi*) is more important than even physical purity. A yogi may live in an unclean place or ignore his bodily care out of pure indifference, as followers of some ascetic traditions do, but they keep their minds clean. If the mind is enveloped in ignorance and delusion, it remains this worldly, bound to Nature and its modifications. The impure cannot join the pure in the pure world of Brahman. This is an undeniable spiritual truth. Unless one practices self-discipline and cultivates divine qualities that are enumerated in the *Bhagavadgita*, it is not possible to experience self-absorption (*atma samyama*) and oneness with the Self. Unless the higher mind (*buddhi*) is made pure like a clear diamond, with virtue (*yamas* and *niyamas*), restraint of the senses, concentration and meditation, it cannot reflect the radiance of the Self, and reveal the secrets hidden within the depths of one's consciousness.

Man is a mixture of both divine and demonic qualities. We are part animal, part human and part divine. Our consciousness is permeated with the qualities of all the three. Applying our will, we can either strengthen or dissipate them according to our aims and aspirations. We may either bring light into our lives or plunge ourselves into utter darkness, with our thinking and attitude. The Bhagavadgita therefore offers us a choice to achieve liberation and escape from this world through yoga or keep ourselves bound to it and continue our mortal existence. The paths to Brahman are many and we may reach Him by any path and from any direction, but reaching is what matters. Lord Krishna affirms clearly in the scripture that in whatever way He is worshipped, He strengthens the faith of His devotee in that direction. Our devotion is of three types, sattvic, rajasic and tamasic, just as our firmness and our actions are. Each has its own consequences. In the first, you worship God; in the second, you worship yourself; and in the third, you worship darkness and ignorance. Therefore, the first one leads to salvation, the second one to bondage and the third one to delusion and downfall.

To achieve liberation we need to purify our lower egoistic selves and align them to our higher Selves, so that we remain in harmony with our noblest and highest ideals and experience peace and equanimity. The lower self needs to be divinized so that it acts like a friend to the higher Self rather than its enemy and uplifts it from the mire of delusion by which it is surrounded. In simple and practical terms, you have to lead virtuous life and follow the best and the purest thinking you can ever imagine. Whenever there is a conflict within yourself, you have to listen to your higher thinking, align with divine forces and allow yourself to err on the right side rather than on the wrong. A true devotee does not compromise his ideals. He will not forsake virtue. He will remain loyal to God by practicing the divine qualities He represents in His own being. Thereby, he gradually removes all notions of separation and distinction from Him and emits His radiance. When your mind becomes pure and divine, it opens up to the higher intelligence and becomes stable in the contemplation of Brahman. True knowledge arises from sattva. Devotion becomes possible only when your mind and heart are filled with it. We will be able to perform desireless actions without seeking their fruit, only in a sattvic state.

Divine qualities

The *Bhagavadgita* provides ample information on the role of the triple *gunas* and their manifestations. It lists the divine qualities that lead the beings towards light and liberation as well as the demonic qualities that result in their downfall. By explaining clearly what leads to liberation and perdition, it encourages us to lead austere lives, cultivating divine qualities instead of the demonic ones, and work for our final liberation. The scripture exhorts us to cultivate qualities (*daiva sampada*) like the ones listed below.

- Fearlessness (*abhayam*)
- Predominance of sattva (*sattva sumsuddhi*)
- Knowledge (*jnanam*)
- Charity (*danam*)
- Self-restraint (*damah*)
- Study of scriptures (*svadhyaya*)
- Austerity (*tapah*)
- Simplicity (*arjavam*)
- Non-violence (*ahimsa*)
- Truthfulness (*satyam*)
- Free from anger (*akrodha*)
- Self-giving (*tyaga*)
- Peacefulness (*santih*)
- Non-slandering (*apaisunam*)
- Compassion (*daya*)
- Without greed (*aloluptam*)
- Gentleness (*mardavam*)
- Modesty (*hrih*)
- Unwavering (*acapalam*)

- Radiance (*tejah*)
- Forgiveness (*ksama*)
- Resoluteness (*dhritih*)
- Cleanliness (*saucam*)
- Without malice (*adroham*)
- Without self-importance

Apart from these, Lord Krishna also describes the qualities of people who are fit for liberation or who have perfected themselves in the practice of yoga. They are described below.

- They are non-deluded. They know Brahman as the unborn (*ajam*), without a beginning (*anadim*) and Lord of the world (*loka mahesvaram*) (10.03).
- They know Him, His manifestations (*vibhutis*) and divine powers (*yogas*) and worship Him with utmost devotion (10.07), as the source and origin of all (10.08).
- Contemplating upon Him, with their minds forever absorbed in Him, surrendering to Him, speaking of Him and enlightening one another about Him, they live their lives devoted to Him (10.09).
- Restraining their senses, with sameness, they take delight in the welfare of beings (*bhuta hitam*).
- They are the most balanced (*yuktatamah*), endowed with supreme faith (*sraddhah*) and ever worshipful (12.2).
- They have intelligence, knowledge, compassion, truthfulness, sameness and mastery over their minds and bodies (10.04).
- They meditate upon Him as the Omniscient, the Most Ancient, Lord of the Universe, smaller than the smallest, upholder of all, of inconceivable form, golden hued and beyond darkness (8.9).
- They are free from hatred, compassionate, egoless, free from ownership, detached, forgiving, even minded, skilful, pure and impartial. They are free from sorrow, joy, impatience, fear and distress (2.13, 14 & 16).
- Their mind is placid and absorbed in Brahman. They free from impurities, and their rajasic nature is subdued (6.27).

- They are impartial, detached and free from desires. They look upon everyone equally, a *brahmana*, a learned person, a person of virtue, a cow, an elephant, a dog and even a lowly and unclean person (5.18). They are disinterested in gain and loss and treat all conditions in their lives equally (5.20).
- They live without making their presence felt. They are not disturbed by the world and they do not disturb anyone. They are free from joy, impatience (*amarsa*), fear and distress (12.15). They do not rejoice, do not hate, do not lament and renounce both the auspicious and the inauspicious (12.17).
- They worship God with faith, holding Him as their Supreme Goal (12.20) and the inexhaustible source of all beings (9.13). Always speaking high of Him, striving with firm vows, offering their obeisance to Him and striving to attain Him, they offer Him obeisance with undivided minds, forever absorbed in Him (9.13 & 14).

Demonic Qualities of the Wicked

Demonic qualities (*asura sampada*) are evil tendencies (*pravrittis*) that manifest in God's creation as part of the illusion of duality He creates with his manifesting power (*yogamaya*). They are opposed to good qualities and try to suppress them. They are the negative qualities whose manifest purpose is creating chaos and disorder, and hidden purpose is providing contrast and balance. They interfere with our spiritual practice by creating mental afflictions (*klesas*) and disturbances (*vrttis*) and lead us in the wrong direction (*durgati*). The demons are the dark forces of the universe. They are forever in conflict with gods, the forces of light. God is the balancing power. He makes sure that the demons stay in their ordained spheres and do not upset the universal order or spread chaos and terror, which they love to do whenever they get an opportunity. The demons not only live in the dark worlds (*asurya lokas*), they also live in various aspects of creation, including our minds and bodies, as tendencies and impulses. When they invade the bodies or prevail in them, men lose their virtue, knowledge and intelligence and indulge in senseless acts of violence, anger, cruelty, delusion, greed, pride and lust.

According to our tradition, the earth has a great significance in the creation of God. Liberation and ascent into higher worlds is possible only through a mortal body; so also the possibility of degradation and descent into the darkest hells. Whoever from the higher worlds wants to attain liberation, that being has to come here and take birth as an earthly being to move forward. Therefore, for the gods and demons, the earth is a battleground. The gods need the human beings for their nourishment; and the demons need them for increasing their strength. Both sides are always looking for opportunities to increase their influence upon earth. They do it mostly by influencing our thoughts and actions and guiding our lives according to their grand designs. Our lives are shaped mostly by what we do in relation to gods and demons, and which of them we support and nourish in our thoughts and actions.

We need to know how demonic nature arises and manifests in us and how it may interfere with our lives and liberation. Such knowledge helps us remain on the right side of things. By avoiding demonic qualities and staying away from those who possess them, we can minimize our chances of falling into degradation. If you know how demonic people live and act, you can shun their company and save yourself from a great calamity, for calamity it is to fall into the company of demonic people or become like them. We need to know the distinction between the divine and demonic qualities, so that we develop discernment and make right choices in guiding our lives towards light and liberation and of those who depend upon us or look to us for inspiration and guidance. By knowing the distinction between the two, and cultivating proper discernment, we can lead righteous lives, performing our obligatory duties in obedience to the will of God. At the same time, we can also avoid becoming vehicles of demonic forces and falling into depravity and degradation.

Being deluded and ignorant by nature, human beings have the potential to be good or evil depending upon the choices they make and the attitude with which they seek things and perform their actions. Since we are modeled in the manner of the Cosmic Being (Purusha) we contain within ourselves all the essential aspects of creation in the form of organs, components (*tattvas*) and energies. Depending upon our purity and propensity, we may nurture either the gods or the demons that reside in us. If we feed the divinities with sattvic food, and good thoughts and actions, we allow the divinities in us to grow in strength and help us in our self-transformation and liberation. On the contrary, if we feed the demons in us, they grow in strength and transform our minds and bodies into virtual hells. What we do and what we sow within our consciousness, therefore, is of utmost importance in our lives and our wellbeing. So also the food we eat. If we eat sattvic food, we grow into gods. If we eat tamasic food, we grow darkness in us.

The *Bhagavadgita* describes the demonic beings as destructive, cruel and deluded entities, who do not acknowledge God or His role as the Creator, Preserver and Destroyer of the worlds. Because of their ignorance, they do not worship Him or offer their respects. Instead, they hate Him or envy Him. Even if they worship Him, they do so out of egoism and vanity, to satisfy their personal desires and show off their power and status. For them the physical Self is the real Self and the material world is the only reality. If it suits them, they worship God but if they deem it necessary, they do not mind to oppose Him and fight with Him.

Impurity is for the mind and the body. The Self is always pure and resplendent, even in its embodied state. It is impervious to evil. However if one engages in evil actions, it remain bound to the mortal world, enveloped in ignorance. The physical Self and the inner Self, these are the two fundamental aspects of a living being. By its actions and attachments, the physical self binds the immortal Self to the cycle of births and deaths. Therefore, for the deluded and ignorant, their demon, or the enemy, exists but within themselves as their own being. Unless they purify their minds and bodies and surrender themselves to God, they will remain deluded and distracted from the goal of liberation. We find a reference to these two selves in the Upanishads as the two birds perched on the tree of life; one eats and enjoys the sweet and bitter fruit of the tree, while the other bird, the Self, calmly watches. The tree is a reference to the body; the enjoying bird is the physical self and the witnessing bird is the immortal Self. If they are in harmony, peace prevails. If they are not, chaos and disorder reign.

Due to the presence of impurities in our consciousness, we tend to indulge in actions that lead to our suffering and bondage. We live with the belief and the illusion that somehow the laws of life do not apply to us and somehow we remain untouched by the consequences of our own actions and the transience of life. With that assumption, we live as if Nature is going to make an exception out of us and keep us alive for long, free from the process of aging and dying. Alternatively, we do not believe in any of these and live as if God does not exist and nothing remains after death. If it were not so, a majority of people upon earth would live their lives responsibly and work for their salvation. Since this is not happening, it means most of us lack faith (*sraddha*) and remain wedded to our egoistic thinking and selfish actions. Some would even go to the extreme and become demonic. They completely give themselves over to demonic nature and create for themselves great misery.

Practice of virtue is necessary for our liberation. The rules and restraints prescribed on the path of yoga are vital to bring about a transformation in our selves. Studying scriptures like the *Bhagavadgita* and assimilating their teachings helps us greatly to cultivate right conduct and lead god-centric lives on the path of righteousness. Knowledge comes in two ways and both are essential to overcome our ignorance and suppress the latent demonic tendencies inherent in our nature. One is the intellectual knowledge, which arises from study (*svadhyaya*), and the other is the experiential knowledge, which arises from transcendental experiences arising from regular and persistent practice (*abhyasa*). Both lead to the refinement of character and discerning wisdom whereby we know what leads to liberation and what contributes to bondage.

In the 16th chapter of the *Bhagavadgita*, we find a very detailed description of the demonic qualities of the wicked people and the consequences arising from them. Lord Krishna explains that there are two types of beings in the world, the divine and the demonic. Divine tendencies lead to liberation and the demonic ones to bondage and suffering. The scripture declares that those who fall deeply into evil ways belong to the lowest of the humanity. Because of their demonic nature, they are cast forever into unclean and demonic wombs. Born thus in evil wombs, birth after birth, they sink into the lowest hells (16.19 & 20). What leads to such vile nature? Lord Krishna says that lust (*kama*), anger (*krodha*) and greed (*lobha*) are the triple gates of hell. They lead to one's downfall. Those who are liberated from them work for their spiritual welfare; but those who disobey the scriptural injunctions and act under the influence of their lustful passions attain neither perfection, nor happiness nor the Highest Goal.

The *Bhagavadgita's* (16.06) assertion about the two types of beings is also attested by other scriptures. We also get a fair view of their qualities by studying them. According to the Upanishads, in the beginning of creation Brahma created demons, gods and humans in the same order. The human beings not only share the qualities of both but also support them both by nourishing them with food, thoughts and actions. The demonic beings prefer darkness because of their tamasic quality; the divine beings prefer light because of their sattvic nature. The demonic beings perform actions selfishly out of vanity and egoism; the divine beings perform them selflessly as an offering to God. By nature the demonic beings are cruel and prefer pain to pleasure; the divine beings are pleasure oriented and prefer happiness and personal comfort. The demonic beings are opposed to God; the divine beings obey Him and follow His percepts. The demonic people love to spread chaos, confusion and disorder; the light beings are dedicated to spread peace, happiness and orderliness. The demonic people regard the mind and the body as the real Self, while the divine beings consider it a mere temporary construct prone to death, disease and destruction. The demonic people live as if there is no life beyond death. The gods are immortals and last till the end of creation.

The following list of demonic qualities is based on the teachings of the *Bhagavadgita*. They suggest why it is important to stay on the side of gods rather than that of demons.

Lack of discrimination: Demonic people lack discrimination since their intelligence is deluded by ignorance and impurities. They do not know what actions should be performed and what should be avoided (16.7). They consider enjoyment of desires as the highest goal instead of liberation (16.11).

Lack of balance: Demonic people lack balance. The go to extremes in performing their actions or voicing their opinions, with little consideration for their strengths and weaknesses and in disproportion to their wealth or power.

Lack of virtue: Demonic people do not believe in virtuous conduct. They do not know about cleanliness; nor do they know about traditions and customs (*acharam*). They lack truthfulness. Filled with lust, vanity, pride and arrogance, pursuing illusory things because of delusion, they engage in unclean actions. They are self-centered, selfish, egoistic, and narrow-minded and indulge immediate gratification without worrying about the consequences (16.14).

Lack of knowledge: They hold perverted opinions about the nature of the world and creation, thinking that the world is unreal, without foundation, and exists solely because of sexual activity (16.08). Deluged by ignorance, not knowing the true nature of their essential nature, they take pride in their birth, family lineage, wealth and religiosity (16.15).

Lack of compassion: Since they cannot discern the truth of their existence, they engage in hostile and cruel actions seeking the destruction of the world (16.09).

Lack stability: Demonic people suffer from countless worries until their death, as they give themselves completely to enjoyment of worldly pleasures (16.11)

Lack of respect for truth and justice: Driven by expectations and given over to thoughts of lust and anger, they try to amass wealth by unjust and unlawful means for the fulfillment of desires.

Lack of respect for tradition: Conceited, arrogant, proud, and intoxicated by wealth, they perform sacrifices for namesake only out of vanity and against tradition (16.17).

Lack of devotion to God: Given over to egoism, vanity, strength, lust and anger, they hate God and envy Him, who abides in them as well as in others (16.18). Carried away by delusion, they do not recognize Him as the supreme and Imperishable (7.13) and therefore they do not worship Him (7.15).

Lack of respect for the inner Self: Lacking in knowledge and intelligence, and not knowing His Supreme State as the Supreme Lord, they disrespect the Self that lives in the human body (9.11). Instead of taking refuge in the Self, they take refuge in the demonic nature (9.12)

Demonic people of the Age of Kali

In this age of Kali, the world will increasingly become vulnerable to demonic nature, whereby people lose their sense of right and wrong and become materialistic and excessively evil. As one saintly person once remarked, in the beginning the demons used to live in far away worlds of total darkness. Later they began to live in remote places upon earth, where light could not enter. Then they began to live amidst us, as our minds became polluted with impurities. Nowadays they live very much inside us as we have given over ourselves completely to the dominance of rajas and tamas. They are now not only ruling us from inside but also from outside as our leaders and role models. The demons have conquered the world, at least temporarily, until another incarnation manifests. Even the religions are under their sway. Hence, we have so much hatred and ill will arising from our religious beliefs and practices. In the *Mahanirvana Tantra*, Goddess *Parvathi* speaks about the evil nature of the present age, which is summarized below[1].

- It will be a sinful age, full of evil customs and deceit, as *Dharma* will be destroyed, and people will pursue evil ways.

- The *Vedas* will lose their power and *Smritis* (sacred books of revelations) will be forgotten. Many of the *Puranas*, which contain stories of the past, and describe the ways of liberation, will be destroyed.
- Men will become averse to religious rites. They will lose morality and virtue, and give themselves over to evil actions. They will become without restraint, maddened with pride, lustful, gluttonous, cruel... addicted to mean habits... thievish, calumnious, malicious, and quarrelsome...devoid of all sense of shame and sin and of fear to seduce the wives of others.
- The priests will live like the working class. Neglecting their own daily sacrifices, they will officiate at the sacrifices of the low. They will become greedy, given over to wicked and sinful acts... Eating unclean food and following evil customs, they will...lust after low women, and will be wicked and ready to barter for money even their own wives to the low. In short, the only sign that they are Brahmanas will be the thread they wear. Observing no rules in eating or drinking or in other matters, scoffing at the Dharma Scriptures, no thought of pious speech ever so much as entering their minds, they will be but bent upon the injury of the good.
- Since people of this age are full of greed, lust, and gluttony, by that they will neglect their *sadhana* (spiritual practice) and will fall into sin. Having drunk much wine for the sake of the pleasure of the senses, they will become mad with intoxication, and bereft of all notion of right and wrong
- Some will violate the wives of others, others will become rogues, and some, in the indiscriminating rage of lust, will go (whoever she be) with any woman.
- Overeating and drinking will disease many and deprive them of strength and sense. Disordered by madness, they will meet death, falling into lakes, pits, or in impenetrable forests, or from hills or housetops.
- While some will be as mute as corpses, others will be forever on the chatter, and yet others will quarrel with their relatives

and elders. They will be evil-doers, cruel, and the destroyers of Dharma

References

1. The *Mahanirvana Tantra*, Tantra of the Great Liberation, Translated by Arthur Avalon (Sir John Woodroffe), 1913.

The Body as a Vehicle of Self-realization

According to our tradition, that which is perishable with a beginning and an end and which is subject to modifications and impermanence is not real. The real has to be self-existing always not occasionally or conditionally. In other words, only that which is eternally and permanently independent, indestructible and stable counts as real and standard truth. Everything else is unreal and temporary, a mere appearance that appears and disappears in the phenomenal ocean of life like a wave in an ocean. The ocean of absolute and pure consciousness is real, but the waves that rise and fall in it are not. Pure consciousness is real, the formations or the colorations in it are unreal. In the world of God, we are like temporary waves, mere formations that rise and fall while the essence (*water*) in each of us is the same eternal consciousness. Based on this interpretation, we may consider the physical self, of which the body is the most important aspect, not the real self. So are the mind, the senses, and all that exists within its domain. They constitute the visible or the perceptible self or the outer sheath, inside which dwells the true Self (*Atman*) or the divine being. Identifying oneself with the physical self and accepting it as the true self is considered delusion. We all suffer from this delusion so long as we are subject to duality and rely upon our senses alone to discern things. This false identification, which arises from ignorance and the impurities present in our consciousness, is responsible for our bondage and continuation upon earth. We accept the false self as true because we cannot comprehend the truth that exists beyond the domain of the physical self and its instruments.

Arjuna was inundated with sorrow because he was steeped in duality. When he entered the battlefield and saw both the armies arrayed on each side ready to fight, he saw them as separate and individual entities having distinct names and forms of their own.

Therefore, he thought of the fate that was awaiting them and the extent of destruction the war was going to cause them. On both sides were his friends and family, people whom he knew for long and whom he loved and respected. Fate brought them together. Fate put them in opposing camps. Fate had drawn the lines between good and evil. It had drawn diverse range of people to the battlefield. Some came out of anger and vengeance to settle past scores. Some came out of social and family obligations. Some came at the command of their rulers and generals. Some came as part of their obligatory duties (*dharma*) to protect the lineage of *Kurus* to whom they declared their allegiance. Some came out of pure love and friendship for the people whose victory mattered to them. Whatever might be the reason, they were conditioned to fight and stand for their principles and beliefs, which they believed even if they were wrong. The war was precipitated by a number of causes. It could have been avoided if good sense prevailed; but it was not meant to be, because a war of such magnitude was necessary in the divine scheme of things to wipe out evil from the face of the earth and restore *dharma* so that the world could once again move forward and fulfill the Divine Will.

Those people were not much different from us in their reason to go to war. They resorted to the same approaches we follow in our lives to perform actions and resolve our problems and difficulties. At times, we are propelled by greed, desires, selfishness, anger, lust or fear. At times, we are inspired by noble intentions and higher ideals to help others or work for their welfare. Sometimes we become overly preoccupied with our interests and ourselves while sometimes we go out of the way to think of others and help them even at the cost of our own comfort and happiness. In all these situations, we act and react according to our worldviews, knowledge, intelligence and judgment. We act both rationally and irrationally. In resolving our problems, we do suffer from certain limitations that we cannot easily overcome because of our ignorance, attachments and our dependence upon our minds and senses. We may excel in the perception of things, but may feel limited in comprehending the ultimate truths of our existence. We cannot see the reality through the prism of our minds because we cannot free them from attachments, the *gunas* and the dualities of life.

These problems exist as long as we remain attached to our limited thinking and awareness and build our dreams and aspirations with egoism and selfishness to protect and promote our names and identities. If we spend our entire lives for the purpose of things that are impermanent in themselves, at the end of the journey we feel exhausted and wasted. It is like devoting your life completely to digging a deep only to know in the end that it cannot hold water. Most of us live our lives this way, striving and struggling for the sake of personal gains, taking pride in our power and position or our family lineages. Our achievements do not last forever. They do not accompany us to the next world except as under currents or unfulfilled desires. When we leave this world, we take but the residue of our actions and aspirations.

Arjuna suffered from sorrow in the battlefield because he falsely identified himself with his physical self, unaware that he was an eternal, inexhaustible and indestructible soul. He was concerned that the war would cause the death of many people including great souls like *Bhishma* and *Drona* and lead to the decline of his family. He thought so because he considered others and himself as physical beings and betrayed his attachment to his family and family members by expressing his concern about the impact of war upon them and the possible decline of his family. Like most of us, he lacked the conviction and the belief that he was an eternal soul who was immutable and indestructible. Most importantly, he ignored the role of God in creation. Until Lord Krishna explained to him clearly the difference between the destructible physical self and the indestructible inner Self, he did not look upon himself as an eternal self and consider his life upon earth as a mere interlude in the eternity of the God and the soul's existence. Until his mind opened to the new vision of him as an embodied self living in the city of nine gates as a temporary guest under the control of Nature, he did not consider his relationships and his attachment to his family an obstacle rather than a virtue in performing his duty and working for his liberation. We all suffer from this problem, right now at this very moment. It is hard for us to center ourselves in the belief that we are eternal souls. The idea may linger for a while in our minds when we read the scriptures or listen to a discourse, but we return to our physical mentality as soon as we get down to our daily routines.

For liberation and principle centered spiritual life, the distinction between the body and the Self is important. This knowledge alone has the potential to transform you and take you nearer to God. You must live with the conviction that you are an eternal soul and the body and the mind are just outer coverings, which will be discarded by you at the time of your departure from the world. The *Bhagavadgita* draws the distinction clearly. The body is the field (*kshetra*) while the Self is the knower of the field. It is an instrument of Nature, which acts as the vehicle of the soul. An impure body is like a prison house for the Self while a pure body is like a temple, where the Self radiates its brilliance and sanctifies everything that comes into its vicinity. The physical body is perishable, destructible, subject to the process of aging, sickness and disease. It is like a dress we wear. Just as people discard their worn out clothes and wear new ones, the soul discards worn out bodies and takes on new ones (2.22). Just as it passes its life within the same body from childhood to youth and to old age, after death it moves on from one body to another (2.11) Therefore, declares the *Bhagavadgita*, wise men are not deluded (2.13) and do not grieve over the dead or the living (2.11).

The body is an obstacle because it is made up of the *gunas* and aspects (*tattvas*) of Nature. It is also a facilitator in our liberation because with discipline and self-control we can purify it and experience oneness with the Self. For the disciplined and self-restrained, the body is a friend and for the irresolute and ignorant, it is an enemy. Liberation is possible only when the soul resides in the body as an embodied Self (*jivatma*). If it leaves the body without settling its past dues, it has to take birth again in another body. The body is thus a prison, but in that prison alone, you have an opportunity to practice yoga and work for your liberation. For a man of discernment, the body is a vehicle of liberation and a temple of God. By entering into that temple and closing all the doors, one can experience peace and unending joy. Therefore, one should treat the body with respect and reverence, without forming attachment to it and without subjecting it to cruelty or extreme austerities.

The body is an instrument of Nature. It is the source and support for the mind and the senses. It is a playground of the *gunas* and therefore subject to modifications. It is made up five great elements (earth, fire, water, air and ether), the ego, intelligence, the senses (the ears, the eyes, the skin, the tongue, the nose, the hands, the feet, the mouth, the anus and the sexual organ), the mind and the sense objects the sound, the taste, the touch, the smell and the shape). Apart from these, the body is also the seat of desire, repulsion, sorrow, bodily parts (*sanghatah*), dynamism (*caitanyam*), determination (*dhriti*) or will power (13.07).

In the phenomenal world, the body is a formation or secretion of Nature around the Self. Just as an oyster builds a pearl around the particles of dust in its womb, Nature shapes beings around the shining particles of the Supreme Self that are caught in its womb. Enveloping them in layers of ignorance and delusion, it continues its play, subjecting their minds and bodies to innumerable modifications, while the Self within them remains the Witness and the Enjoyer. The source of these modifications are the *gunas* (modes) namely, *sattva*, *rajas* and *tamas*. Their interplay and inherent tendency to dominate one another induce in the beings desires and desire-ridden actions. Thus, the triple *gunas* are responsible for our delusion and existence upon earth as mortal beings. Under their influence, we suffer from attraction and aversion towards the pairs of opposites and indulge in desire-ridden actions. By assuming ownership and doership for our actions and seeking their fruit, we become bound to the gunas and the results arising from the actions they induce (3.29).

In our practice of yoga, we must cultivate right attitude towards our bodies. Moderation is the ideal. The *Bhagavadgita* affirms that a *karmayogi* who engages his organs in desireless actions, keeping his body and mind under control, remaining mentally detached, offering the fruit of his actions to God, living only to perform bodily functions, becomes liberated from the bondage of birth and death and never returns to the mortal world (3.21-23). The body can be a source of liberation at the time of death also, for a yogi who has mastered his senses and controlled his mind. This is possible because whatever a person thinks and remembers at the time of his death, he attains that only (8.5). Thus, if a person manages to remember God only at the time of his death with complete devotion, practicing yoga and holding his breath between his two eye brows, he will easily reach Him (8.10). Discipline and sincerity are important. Whoever tries to restrain his organs of action outwardly without inner control and detachment from the sense objects is a man of deluded intellect and a hypocrite (3.06). One should aim for inner control and balance. By closing all the openings of the body, establishing the mind in the heart, fixing the life energy in the head, and uttering the syllable "AUM," a yogi can easily attain the Supreme Self (8.12 & 13). Therefore, a seeker of liberation should restrain his senses and train his mind, practicing buddhi yoga and continuously and thinking of God only.

The body has certain natural limitations. One should respect them. Those who ignore this instruction are considered men of demonical resolve, who practice austere penances not enjoined by the scriptures, under the influence of lust, power and attachment, and there by torture the body and God who dwells it (17.05 & 06). Moderation is equally important. The yoga of self-realization is not for one who is a voracious eater or a non-eater. It is also not for him who sleeps too much or who does not sleep at all (6.16). Moderation, regulated diet and relaxation, restrained actions, discipline in sleeping and waking, these practices lead to freedom from sorrow (6.17).

Thus according to the Gita, the body is where a yogi should focus his attention primarily and work for his transformation. Although it is perishable and changeable, since it keeps the soul in bondage, it needs to be purified and divinized to let the soul free. It is a means rather than an end in itself. It is not the sum total of our existence but only a part of it. While it may not last forever, it plays an important role in our liberation. The *Bhagavadgita* suggests that by detaching oneself from the body, by controlling one's mind, by becoming aware of the influence of the *gunas* and the senses, by constantly fixing the mind on the Higher Self, by performing daily duties with detachment, one should aim to overcome limitations and achieve liberation.

During spiritual practice, one has to learn to live with the pain and the hardship experienced in the body as it goes through various stages of transformation and purification set in motion by austerities and spiritual practices. Sometimes, it may even fall sick. A yogi should therefore pay close attention to his body. He should take care of it to the extent possible, keeping it clean and healthy, respecting its limitations and vulnerabilities, and protecting it from harm, injury and the disturbances caused by the impurities and evil forces. He should live, treating his body as a sacrificial altar, performing internal sacrifices with detachment, offering all his actions to God with surrender and devotion. He should give up bodily pleasures, renouncing his attachment to his body, cultivating *sattva*, practicing virtue and performing his bodily actions purely as an offering to God. Concentrating his mind upon Him with devotion, he should transform his body into a vehicle of truth, light and delight.

From the *Bhagavadgita* we also understand that apart from gods and beings, even God has a body of universal proportions, with numerous hands, eyes and ears and the effulgence of innumerable suns. His body is so vast that all His manifestations constitute but a small aspect of it. He is both the support and the womb for His creation. All the individuals souls are part of it. He awakens His body during the day of creation and puts it to rest during His night. Ignorant people cannot comprehend His universal nature or recognize Him in His aspects. At times, He may assume mortal body and incarnate upon earth to restore balance and destroy evil. On all such occasions, He remains firmly in control of His nature, free from delusion.

Making Sense of the Senses

The senses are our windows to the world. It is difficult to imagine life without them. We accumulate knowledge of the world through them and use them for our survival and continuity. In the spiritual realm the senses are viewed differently as obstacles to experience transcendental truths and overcome ignorance. The senses are called *Indriyas*, which denotes their association with Indra, the lord of the heavens. Symbolically, they are considered the agents of *Indra*. In the Cosmic Person (*Purusha*), they represent the divine forces. In a human being, who is considered a replica of God (*Purusha*), the senses belong to the realm of the mind, which is comparable to the world of gods (*bhuva*), while the body represents the earth (*bhuh*) and the Self the immortal heaven (*suvah*). At the individual level, the ego-sense represents Indra and acts as the lord of the mind (*bhuva*) while the senses represent the gods who are under his control and work for him. The senses represent the pleasure principle, just like the gods, and take delight in seeking things that produce pleasure and enjoying them. They are averse to painful and unpleasant aspects of life, just as the divinities are.

The sense organs are our only link to the external world. Without them, it is impossible to make sense of the world or relate to it. They are the means by which we overcome the limitations of space and extend ourselves well beyond our bodies into the world. They are responsible for our perceptions, dualities, relationships, desires and attachments. Our delusion, duality, ignorance of the transcendental truths, bondage and suffering arise from them only. In the physical plane, they are the main sources of our knowledge, but in the spiritual context, they are considered sources of duality, ignorance and delusion and obstacles to cultivate discernment, sameness and equanimity. The senses are the main sources of mental modifications (*cittavrittis*). Hence, withdrawing the senses and restraining them are considered important in the practice of yoga.

Our scriptures recognize eleven senses, five organs of action (*karmendriyas*), five organs of perception (*jnanendriyas*) and the mind, which is considered the eleventh. The eyes, ears, nose, skin, tongue and mouth constitute the organs of perception. They are responsible for our knowledge of the world and the material things. The mouth (as organ of speech), hands, feet, anus and genitals constitute the five organs of action. They are responsible for the actions a being performs for its survival and continuity. They are mostly body related actions. There is a fundamental difference between these two. The organs of perception are outgoing. They extend far beyond the body, while the organs of action remain attached to it and act according to the perceptions they bring in and the desires they create. Both are essential for the survival of the being. Together they constitute the ten physical senses (13.05). Then there is the mind (*manas*), which is likened to a sense organ in the *Bhagavadgita* (15.7). It is the Lord or the controller of the senses. They act under its influence and serve its interests. In addition to them, our scriptures recognize five subtle senses (*tanmatras*), which are also known as sense-objects. They represent the sensations, functions or actions pertaining to the organs of perception, namely the acts of smelling, tasting, seeing, touching and hearing. The five organs of perception have a fundamental affinity with the five great elements (*mahabhutas*), namely the earth, water, fire, air and space. In fact, the five subtle senses are considered their source because we know their existence through these subtle sensations only. Thus, the earth element is associated with the nose and experienced through the sensation of smelling. The water element is associated with the tongue and experienced through the sensation of tasting. The fire (light) element is associated with the eyes and experienced through the sensation of seeing. The air element is associated with the skin and experienced through the sensation of touching. Finally, the space or ether element is associated with the mouth and is experienced through the subtle sense of speech or sound.

The senses are responsible for our awareness and knowledge of the objective world with which we interact. However, they are not perfect. As instruments of truth and knowledge, they are not reliable in discerning truth from falsehood or realty from unreality. They are also not also very useful in knowing truths beyond the physical domain. In fact, while they are considered vital for our survival upon earth, as instruments of ignorance, duality and delusion, they are a major obstacle on the path of liberation. The senses limit our knowledge, vision and wisdom. They are responsible for our limited self-awareness and our attachment to our names and forms. By repeated contact with sense-objects they create in us desires, form which arise attraction and aversion to the pairs of objects. From them, we develop attachment. From attachment, we experience conflicting emotions such as anger, fear, anxiety, greed, envy and pride. They in turn lead to restlessness, instability and afflictions.

From experience, we know that we cannot always depend upon our senses to manage our lives or resolve our problems. We know from history how people believed erroneously for long that the earth was flat or the sun and moon revolved around it. They believed in what they saw and their senses mislead them. Now we know that we cannot totally rely upon our senses to know truths about our existence or our world. Even in case of ordinary perceptions, we have to be careful because our perceptions are colored by our thoughts, attitudes, emotions, beliefs, desires and prejudices. We create our own illusions. We see what we want to see or in what we are most interested. Our opinions and conclusions may not always be right since they are influenced by our egos and interests. Therefore, we need some additional means to validate what we perceive and arrive at truth.

The *Bhagavadgita* highlights the negative role the senses play and how they delude us into bondage and ignorance. It warns people not to rely upon them blindly, but cultivate discerning wisdom so that we know the truth and act accordingly. It explains how duality, desires and attachments arise because of them and how we may escape from their influence and transcend them to realize the transcendental truths. Cravings and the transitory feelings of heat and cold, pain and pleasure arise from the activity of our senses. We cultivate sameness when we learn to tolerate them (2.14), and suffer from duality when we indulging in them (5.22). When we keep extending ourselves into the material world through our senses and constantly deal with worldly things, we suffer from the feelings of attractions and aversion. A yogi and a seeker of liberation should not come under their influence at all (3.34).

In the second chapter of the *Bhagavadgita*, Lord Krishna explains how suffering arises from the activity of the senses. Repeated interaction between the senses and their objects lead to attachment, from which ensues anger. Anger leads to delusion and from delusion arises confusion of memory. From confusion of memory arises loss of intelligence and when intelligence is lost the breath of life is lost (2.60-63). The senses are responsible for our involvement with the world. They are responsible for our egoism (*ahamkara*) and our preoccupation with the transient things of the phenomenal world.

The scripture suggests withdrawal of the senses with detachment as a solution to stabilize the mind and cultivate equanimity and sameness towards the pairs of opposites. Since the senses are responsible for the instability of the mind and their delusion, they need to be silenced. They can be silenced only by withdrawing them form the external world into the mind and keeping restrained. Logically it makes sense, because the mind becomes restless in the first place because of the outgoing nature of the senses. When they are withdrawn, the mind gets temporary relief from the usual noise of the world and experiences peace and stability. The Gita says, by withdrawing his senses completely from the sense objects the way a tortoise withdraws its limbs, a yogi gains mastery over his senses (2.58). Freeing himself from passion and dispassion, keeping the senses that are acting on the sense objects under firm control, and by following the dictates of the inner soul, he can gain the grace of God. (2.64). Just as the winds blow away a boat floating on the waters, the senses also drive away the intelligence of a person whose mind is constantly engaged in the sense objects (2.67). Therefore, a yogi should firmly establish his intelligence by controlling his senses from all directions (2.68). Withdrawal of the senses (*pratyahara*) is one of the eight limbs of classical yoga. It is the foundation for concentration, meditation and self-absorption.

Withdrawing the sense from the sense-objects with a correct understanding of the role of the senses in our lives is the first step towards inner transformation and Self-realization. Withdrawing the senses is the first important step in stabilizing the mind. However, it alone does not guarantee perfection. We have to withdraw our minds also from the external world and concentrate them upon the contemplation of God or the Self. He whose mind is constantly engaged in the contemplation of God becomes stable and attains liberation. The senses create the bonds (*pasas*) and strengthen our egoism by extending its empire or sphere of influence as far as they can travel. The senses take refuge in the ego and follow its commands. Those who take refuge in the ego and perform actions indiscriminately incur sin and remain bound to the mortal world; but those who take refuge in the Self, practicing detachment and renouncing the fruit of their actions, attain the Highest Abode and never return. By controlling his senses dutifully, he becomes detached from the sense objects, and regains his freedom from the compulsion to act according to his desires. With the elimination of desires, he achieves equanimity of the mind, inner peace, and freedom from fear, lust, egoism, anger and such other ungodly qualities. Firmly established on the path of self-realization (6.24-29), he becomes stable like an ocean that remains undisturbed although water from numerous rivers enters into it from all directions (2.70).

If our senses act as barriers to self-realization, they also help us to overcome our ignorance and our limited self-sense. We can use our senses and our sensory knowledge to study the scriptures, perform selfless and virtuous actions, worship God, practice yoga, participate in devotional services or cultivate divine qualities. We can use them to practice concentration, meditation and self-absorption. Practicing dispassion and detachment from the body and subduing our egos, we can cultivate witness consciousness. By observing the world dispassionately without judgment and attachment, we can increase our knowledge and discernment. By paying attention to our own thoughts and actions, we can learn a great deal about ourselves and improve our thinking and behavior. By practicing mindfulness, we can develop self-awareness and establish peace within ourselves. Thus controlling our senses where necessary and using them for insightful awareness, we can lay firm foundation for our liberation.

Descriptions of the Self

One of the notable differences between Hinduism and Buddhism is with regard to the Self or the soul. Hinduism believes in the existence of eternal and indestructible Self or Atman where as Buddhism does not believe so. Instead, it believes in the non-existence of immortal soul or in no soul (*anatma*). It does believe in continuation of the physical or egoistic-self in the phenomenal world from birth to birth until it enters into a state of *nirvana*. The soul cannot be grasped through senses. Hence, we have many speculations about its essential nature. In western traditions, a soul is regarded as an entity having some kind of materiality or corporeality. In other words, it has spiritual or ethereal body that survives death and continues to exist in the astral realms. Hinduism regards the individual soul as pure intelligence or consciousness, devoid of any materiality. In fact, a soul is usually referred to as Self (atman) in Hindu scriptures to denote its transcendental and incorporeal nature.

The Self is a mystery hidden in the deeper layers of our consciousness. We cannot discern it with our minds or senses. We cannot experience it in a state of duality. We cannot relate to it except in transcendental states. Since it is indescribable and beyond the mind and the senses, we cannot comprehend its essential nature in human terms. We do not have definitive answers to many questions concerning the Self. How does it exist in the body? How can it be absolute and at the same time have individuality? Where does it exist after its liberation? What happens to it when a being dies? How does it escape from the body and where does it go after death? In a state of self-realization, do we become the Self or just become aware of its presence in the body? What is the state of a self-realized yogi and how is it different from ordinary consciousness. These and many other questions are difficult to answer to everyone's satisfaction. Speculative philosophies and ascetic traditions arose in ancient India to address such questions even before the birth of *Mahavira*, the last of the Jain *Thirthankaras* and the *Buddha*, the founder of Buddhism. They tried to probe into depths of human mind and understand the different state of consciousness, starting from the wakeful to the deep sleep state. The practice of yoga helped them induce different states of consciousness and experience duality and transcendence in varying degrees. The Vedas, especially the Upanishads, attempt to answer these questions by explaining what the Self is not, rather than what it is. They say that the Self is not the body, not the mind, not the senses, not the intelligence, not the ego, not the state of duality, not male, not female, not impermanence, not perceptible, not definable, not destructible and so on. Even with all these exclusions, it is difficult to comprehend what the Self is.

The individual Self and the Supreme Self

Today we have six schools (*darshanas*) of Hinduism, which deal with the cryptic nature of the Self and its relationship with the world and God. While these schools offer many alternative solutions, there is no unanimous opinion among them as to how the soul exists in relationship to God and His creation. According to some schools, the individual souls are different from God, but according to others, there they are the same or different aspects of the self-same reality. Some schools even go to the extent of denying the existence of God, stating that only the individual souls exist eternally in association with Nature or separate from it, with their number remaining constant forever.

Among those who believe in the existence of God, some believe that God creates the individual souls in the beginning of creation, while others believe that they exist eternally just like God, without a beginning and an end. Some traditions believe that while both souls and God are eternal and similar in their essential nature, they have some subtle differences, which make them distinct but not so distinct (*bheda-abheda*). It is difficult to prove which of these philosophies are correct in their assumptions and conclusions, because the human mind cannot discern transcendental truths definitively. Besides, when you deal with absolute truths with perceptual knowledge, there are bound to be differences and misunderstandings.

The problem is aggravated by the fact that the individual soul is beyond objective human experience and cannot be directly comprehended other than through subjective experiences of transcendental nature. Unfortunately, so far our studies concerning the Self have remained inconsistent and inconclusive, making it almost impossible to conduct any scientific enquiry into its essential nature and draw valid conclusions about it, which can be verified or validated universally. The Self cannot be discerned in a state of duality and when we transcend duality, we do not remember our experience, just as we do not remember any experience in deep sleep state. Thus, although the Self is theoretically within the reach of each individual, practically it is not within reach.

There is also no unanimous opinion among various traditions as to whether the soul is present in all living beings or only in human beings. Hinduism holds the premise that all living beings including plants and animals possess souls. Jainism goes a step forward and holds that not only all plants, animals, tiny insects and bacteria, but also even inanimate objects such as water, stones, pieces of dead wood and tubers grown underground possess souls. It also believes that souls may exist either individually or in clusters. The aggregate of souls makes the practice of non-violence even more difficult to practice.

The school of qualified monism (*vishistadvaita*) classifies souls into three categories based on their purity and degree of freedom, namely the bound souls (*baddhas*), freed souls (*muktas*) and forever-free souls (*nitya-muktas*). The bound souls are those who are caught in the phenomenal world. The freed souls are those who were once bound souls, but now exist in liberated condition. The forever-free souls are those who were never bound and who would never be bound. These last ones are again divided into *bhaktas* (devotees) and *bhagavatas* (servants of God). The *bhaktas* are devotees of God. They serve Him directly. The *bhagavatas* are also devotees, who as agents of God serve Him indirectly by serving His devotees. In fact, the teachings of Lord Krishna are especially meant for the guidance of this class of devotees.

Descriptions of the Self in the Bhagavadgita

The *Bhagavadgita* acknowledges the existence of both God and the individual souls. It believes in the rebirth of the individual beings, their delusion and bondage to the cycle of births and deaths because of the triple *gunas* and desire-ridden actions. It also suggests various solutions for the salvation of beings upon earth. It dwells upon various subjects like birth, death, delusion, desires, attachment, departure of the soul from the body, its upward journey to the higher worlds, it rebirth or return journey to the earth to continue its cycle of births and deaths, its relationship with God and how it can overcome ignorance and attain liberation. It declares that the Self is eternal and indestructible (2.18, which neither slays not can be slain (2.19). It is never born; it never dies; and after coming into existence, it never ceases to be. It is eternal (*nitya*), permanent (*sasvatah*), and very ancient (*purana*) (2.20). It does not suffer from afflictions; and it cannot be tainted by modifications. At the time of death it does not die, but leaves the body and enters into a new one (2.22). Weapons cannot pierce it, fire cannot burn it, water cannot moisten it and wind cannot dry it (2.23). It is impenetrable, incombustible, all pervading, stable and immobile (2.24). It is invisible, imperceptible and immutable (2.25). We find many such descriptions about the Self in the *Bhagavadgita*. They all convey the message that the Self is distinct from the body and is above all the constituents of Nature. It is a small part (*amsa*) of God, having all His attributes.

The *Bhagavadgita* is aware of the limitations of human mind in discerning the true nature of the Self. Therefore, it concurs with the Upanishadic notion that the Self is incomprehensible and indefinable. Speaking of the wondrous nature of Self, it makes these profound declarations. One looks at it with great surprise, another speaks about it with great surprise, another hears about it with incredulity and yet another after hearing about it knows it not (2.29). In a living being, the Self is superior to everything else. It is the highest. The senses are great, greater than the senses is the mind, greater than the mind is intelligence (*buddhi*) and greater than the intelligence is the Self (3.42). In these descriptions the scriptures sounds very much like an *Upanishad*.

The Self residing in the body is referred to as the Lord of the Sacrifices (*Adhiyajna*). We are told that when *Purusha*, the Supreme Lord (*Adhidaiva*), resides in the body as the inner Self, He becomes the Lord of Sacrifice (8.4). These descriptions refer to the internalization of the sacrificial rituals, which happened during the later Vedic period and their symbolic representation in the human body as various physiological and biological functions. The embodied Self is caught in the modifications of Nature (*Prakriti*). It cannot escape from it without making adequate spiritual effort and divine help, which comes to us in the form of grace (*Isvara prasadam*). At the time of death, it leaves the body and goes to either the immortal world of Brahman or the world of ancestors, depending upon its past actions and time of its departure.

According to the *Bhagavadgita*, the mental condition in which an embodied soul leaves the body at the time of death is very important, because it has a bearing upon its afterlife. Whatever a person thinks of at that time, that alone he or she achieves thereafter (8.6). Thus he who departs from the body thinking of God alone, he would undoubtedly attain Him (8.5, 12 &13). If he thinks of worldly things, he would return to them and live again as a mortal being. Therefore, it is important to contemplate upon God constantly and remember Him even when engaged in actions and worldly matters. Whoever remembers God only at the time of death is bound to reach the Abode of Brahman.

Liberated Self and the embodied Self

In its essential nature, a liberated soul is not different from the embodied Self. Although it is bound to the body, the embodied self remains immutable and impervious to the modifications of Nature. Thus, the difference between the two is situational. While the being undergoes change, the soul does not. Whatever changes take place happen to the being or the field, not to the Knower of the field. Just as the soot that accumulates upon the glass of a lamp may hinder the light shining within, while the light itself is untouched, the changes that happen to the body may veil the Self but do not taint it. However, the modifications and impurities bind the soul and keep it in bondage.

The embodied Self is also bound to Nature because of the activities of the egoistic Self, which is subject to modifications, desires and attachments. This worldly, it is entirely made up of the components (*tattvas*) of Nature, and subject to the triple play of the *gunas*. Caught in the snare of the causative world (*samsara*) through desires and attachment, it drags the Self also into its schemes and becomes responsible for its bondage. The egoistic Self suffers from the consequences of its actions for this very reason. Through its selfish and desire-ridden actions, it becomes responsible for the sin of keeping the inner-Self chained to Nature and delaying its liberation.

The individual Self, liberated from the snares of the world, remains free forever in the world of Brahman. It is never subjected to Nature again. What it does and in what state it exists as liberated Self, only the adepts know. According to some, it merges into the Supreme Self and loses its distinction. According to others, it remains as an individual Self in the world of Brahman in the company of other liberated souls and divine beings, enjoying close proximity to Him. At the time of the dissolution of the worlds, it may be temporarily withdrawn by Brahman, but it remains immutable. In future creations, it may move still closer to Brahman and play an important role as a divinity or emanation.

Realizing the Self

The Self is a mystery. It is the invisible and intangible aspect of our consciousness and beingness. Even though it exists in all of us, we do not feel its presence because we cannot reach it with our senses. We cannot feel its presence either because do not look within ourselves deeply or try enough. Distracted by the world, we do not allow our minds and bodies to stabilize and let the Self reveal itself. To feel the Self within, we need to withdraw our senses, silence our minds and purify our consciousness so that we can see the reflection of the Self in it. Just as you cannot see anything in murky waters, you cannot see the Self if your consciousness is filled with impurities. To see it clearly you have to purify it and make it transparent like pure glass. The *Bhagavadgita* declares that deluded people do not see their souls when they are present in their bodies or when they leave them in the end. Those with the eyes of wisdom see them. With intense effort, they see their souls seated in their bodies, while the imperfect and indiscriminate people cannot see them even with striving (15.10 & 11). The Self is luminous. It is the light of the lights. The same brilliance, which illuminates the Sun and the moon, also illuminates our being as our inmost Self. God is its source (15.12). It is also the source of our memory, knowledge and even their loss (15.15). We are able to know, think and remember because of the Self that is present in us. Our aims should be to know this and return to our essential nature.

Self-realization is the ultimate goal. It can be reached by restraining the senses and stabilizing the mind. For that, the body needs to be conditioned through intense self-purification. As the *Bhagavadgita* declares (6.19), the mind should be like a lamp in a windless place that does not flicker. When that state is reached, one sees the self abiding in the Self and one remains satisfied within the Self only. In that state, he does not deviate from truth or reality. He does not think of gain or loss and no sorrow is vexing or troublesome. This disassociation (*viyogam*) from sorrow (*dukham*) is yoga or the state of self-realization. It should be practiced with resolve and without despair and disheartedness (6.23), withdrawing the senses gradually, step by step, with firm resolve, fixing the mind in the Self, thinking of nothing else (6.25).

Apart from the senses, the triple *gunas*, namely *sattva*, *rajas* and *tamas*, play an important role in binding the Self to the body (14.05). *Sattva* binds through pleasure; *rajas* through attachment; and *tamas* through ignorance. The *gunas* are responsible for all actions and modifications. They propel the beings to seek objects and enjoy them so that they may grow in strength. One of the aims of yoga is to subdue the impure *gunas* so that the mind and body become free from their influence. When a seer sees that all actions arise from the *gunas* and realizes the Self, which is higher than they are, he attains liberation (14.19). Going beyond them, he becomes free from birth, death, aging and sorrow (14.20). He also becomes equal to all the pairs of opposites (14.24). With devotion to God and serving Him selflessly, he transcends them and qualifies for the state of Brahman (14.26).

The Wisdom of the Bhagavadgita

Every scripture contains some wisdom and a clear message to deliver. It may have a hidden purpose beneath a revealed one. Its authority may come from different sources, some obvious and some unknown. Its interpretation may change from time to time while its message may remain constant, bound by tradition and faith. It may represent the collective wisdom of multiple individuals who have seen light on the other side of the phenomenal world or just one individual who might have transcended human limitations and experienced oneness with the universal consciousness. The wisdom contained in any scripture is sacred, reverential and reliable as a spiritual guide for the humanity. However, that wisdom is supreme, which arises directly from God Himself, and comes to us in its purest form without any human fabrication. The *Bhagavadgita* contains the wisdom of God as spoken by Him. It contains wisdom that He claims to have revealed to the humanity from time to time whenever order and justice (*dharma*) declined in the world. It was spoken by Him in first person, without any agency in between. Hence, it is ideal for those who seek liberation.

Sacred dialogue

The scripture is a sacred dialogue, not a monologue or a speculative disputation. It is a conversation between a man and God in which there is a mutual appreciation of each other's view points. It is a revealing dialogue between God and His devotee. It is a two-way communication, not one sided, conducted by them in their wakeful states, in which mutual love, admiration and respect are maintained until the end.

As a scripture, it addresses directly the problem of human suffering as exemplified by the sorrow of Arjuna. The teaching is a direct response to it. It explores its causes and suggests possible solutions to deliver the bound souls (*baddhas*) permanently from the control of Nature. It encourages us to perform our obligatory duties as a sacrificial offering to God and not to abandon them even if they are unpleasant or difficult. It explains how we become bound to the world and offers various alternatives to escape from it without torturing ourselves with extreme ascetic methods. Delivered in the middle of a battlefield under extraordinary circumstances and divided into 18 sections, each under the name of a distinct yoga, the scripture contains revelations of God about Himself, His creation and our roles and responsibilities in it as His numerous manifestations (*amsas*). It is a book of practical wisdom, which shows us the way to overcome suffering without abandoning our duties and responsibilities. We can divide the teachings of the scripture into four main headings: the individual Self (atman), the Universal Self (Brahman), the relationship between the two and liberation of the individual Self.

The purpose of different yogas

Although on a superficial note the *Bhagavadgita* seems to favor devotion as the most effective path for liberation, a careful student of the scripture cannot miss the obvious connection among the various paths described in it. The path of knowledge (*jnanayoga*), action (*karmayoga*), renunciation of action (*karma-sanyasa-yoga*), wisdom (*buddhi yoga*) and self-absorption (*atmasamyama-yoga*) are all interrelated. The practice of one contributes to progress in others. We cannot say one is superior to the others because each has its own value in the transformation our minds and bodies. However, the path of action is considered the most basic because beings cannot exist upon earth without indulging in actions. Besides our bondage arises primarily from the actions we perform. Karmayoga addresses this problem at the most basic level by suggesting a way to escape from the cycle of *karma*.

The way of the world is to perform actions selfishly for one's own benefit; the way of liberation is perform them selflessly as offerings to God. The seeds of liberation are sown when we perform actions without desiring their fruit and consecrating them to God. The *Gita* gives us the assurance that when actions are performed selflessly, with detachment and discernment, renouncing their fruit, one does not suffer from their consequences. However, you cannot practice *karmayoga* effectively without practicing renunciation. In the context of the *Bhagavadgita*, true renunciation is not abandoning actions or your duties, but giving up the desire hidden in them and their fruit. This knowledge does not arise on its own. It arises from the study of scriptures, from knowledge concerning the Self and discernment, for which one needs to practice both the yoga of knowledge and the yoga of intelligence (*buddhiyoga*). Practice of concentration, meditation and self-absorption (*atmasamyama-yoga*) also helps one achieve perfection in desireless actions and contemplation of God. Thus in an integrated approach, actions, knowledge, detachment, intelligence, self-awareness, devotion and virtue together enable an embodied soul to escape from the cycle of births of deaths. When a seeker practices these different approaches or yogas for a long time, which may span over several lifetimes, he develops *sattva* or purity, knowledge, intelligence and divine qualities that are listed in the *Bhagavadgita*. With these refinements in his lower self or the ego consciousness, he eventually attains the fourth and the final stage of his spiritual development, which is the practice of devotion (*bhakti*) and selfless service to God and His manifestations. In this state, he experiences intense devotion and unconditional love for God. He surrenders to Him and spends his time in His service and contemplation. With his mind and senses fixed in Him, he loses himself in His contemplation, seeing Him everywhere and experiencing oneness with Him. Withdrawing mentally from the external world, he becomes absorbed in His thoughts, aspiring to be in His presence and in close proximity to Him always. When his devotion overflows, God reciprocates with His love and liberates Him from the bonds of mortal life forever.

Thus, we can see that the *Bhagavadgita* does not emphasize a single yoga but a holistic spiritual effort, which encompasses a whole gamut of approaches that are aimed to transform a devotee both physically and mentally and grow him in the image of God to the extent that the difference between the two become negligible. It places heavy emphasis upon physical and mental purity, pursuit of knowledge, discernment, wisdom, self-control, performance of duty, renunciation and devotion to God. While it does indicate that devotion is the most effective solution to achieving liberation, it also suggest that true devotion arises from perfection in other yogas, especially the yoga of action and knowledge. One is meant to purify the body and restrain the organs of action, while the other to purify the mind and restrain the organs of perception. With senses restrained and mind purified, one can practice concentration, contemplation and self-absorption and experience oneness with the Self. True devotion in which all sense of egoism becomes dissolved and only the thought of God remains arises after years of practice and self-discipline. It is possible only for those who restrain their senses, stabilize their minds, cultivate purity and perform their obligatory duties without desires, expectations and attachments.

Only those whose hearts and minds are pure and infused with the love of God can practice true devotion. If you are filled with desires and egoism, you cannot experience true love for God. When desires rule our minds and actions, our devotion to God would be a mere excuse to further our own interests. In fact, it is how a vast majority of people delude themselves into believing that they are devoted to God or their religion, whereas in truth they are serving none but themselves. Those who claim themselves as devotees of God should search their hearts to see how sincere they are in their devotion and aspiration. If you are in love with yourself, it will be difficult for you to love God unconditionally and surrender to Him. Until you reach that pristine state of devotion, you have to keep purifying yourself and perfect your actions with supreme intelligence. This is the goal for every seeker of truth in the initial stages. This becomes obvious when we try to build a coherent strategy using the divergent paths and practices suggested by the *Bhagavadgita* to achieve liberation and freedom from sorrow.

Different interpretations of the Bhagavadgita

In the past, the *Bhagavadgita* has been interpreted differently by different scholars belonging to various religious traditions (*sampradayas*). In the scripture itself, Lord Krishna mentions a lineage of scholars who received the knowledge of the *Gita* at different times in the long history of the earth spanning over several cycles of creation. The ancient scholars and commentators used their knowledge of the scripture to support their respective views or refute those with which they disagreed strongly. *Sri Shankaracharya* (8th-9th century A.D) wrote a commentary upon it in support of the advaita philosophy (monism), declaring Brahman to be the only reality and delusion as the main cause of our experience of duality and bondage. *Sri Ramanujacharya* (11th century A.D) interpreted in support of the *vishistadvaita* philosophy (qualified monism). He used the scripture to suggest that while God was the one and the only Reality, He was not without attributes. The individual souls were similar to Him in their essence, yet they were not identical, because there was a subtle distinction between the two, which was difficult to discern but equally difficult to ignore. According to him God and souls were the same, yet different, like an object and its reflection in a mirror. *Sri Machavacharya* (11th-12th century AD), a great proponent of the *dvaita* philosophy (dualism), wrote a commentary (*Gitabhasya*) and an interpretation (*Gitatatparya*) upon it. He argued that God and individual souls were distinct and different. While their essence was the same, they could not be treated as one because they represented two distinct and eternal realities. God was Supreme and none could equal Him. The individual souls were also eternal, but they depended upon Him. Those, which were caught in the phenomenal world, had an opportunity to achieve liberation through surrender and devotion to God. Once liberated they would live in the world of Brahman eternally. In other words, the distinction between God and the souls is permanent and eternal. Unlike the school of monism, the dualistic schools believe that the phenomenal world is also real and the duality exists not only between God and souls but also in every aspect of creation, all the way down to the pairs of opposites. Other scholars who contributed to our knowledge of the *Bhagavadgita* include *Nimbarka* (12th century A.D), his disciple *Kesavakasmirin*, *Vallbhacharya* (15th century A.D), the proponent of *suddhadvaita* (pure non-dualism), *B.G. Tilak, Sri Aurobindo, M.K.Gandhi* and in recent times *Sri Swami Prabhupada*. These scholars and great masters interpreted the *Bhagavadgita* according to their respective beliefs.

The seven fundamental instructions

As we have discussed before the scripture accommodates different and even divergent interpretations. At the same time, it adheres to some fundamental principles consistently that are deeply rooted in the Vedic tradition. Its main theme is liberation for which it provides different alternatives that are in many ways complimentary. For the spiritually inclined people, it offers the following seven fundamental perspectives or thinking points. They sum up the philosophy of the *Bhagavadgita* and its core teachings. The following account is written from a modern perspective, but it is based on the same teachings found in the scripture.

1. The world in which you live is impermanent. It is unreal. It is created and maintained by Nature to be the source of your bondage, ignorance, suffering and delusion. You should be careful when you deal with it because in many ways it is a prison house for the souls. It draws you in and binds you to things, keeping you engaged, distracted, and disturbed. Whatever escape it offers leads you in the end into a deeper trap and makes your life even more difficult. With each step forward into it, you distance yourself from yourself. With each thread of attachment you build with it, you increase your enmity with yourself. As you become attached to it deeply, you become your own enemy and delay your liberation. In the end, you are bound to suffer anyway because you cannot hold

on to anything here for long and when you are separated from things, you will experience sorrow, fear and anxiety.

2. Your identity and individuality are temporary constructions built around your name and form. They hide you from yourself and keep you disengaged from your true nature. Your name and form are illusions. In their defense, you spend several lifetimes only to realize in the end that you have been chasing false dreams. You are neither of them. You are an eternal and indestructible Self that can be neither slain nor injured. You are an aspect (*amsa*) of God and you will always be so. The body is like a garment. You wear it and discard it overtime. When the body dies, you wear another one to continue your existence in another body. Therefore, you should not lose your peace over the impermanence and the modifications to which we are subject. Think of yourself as an infinite being, with no limits whatsoever and look at this world and yourself from that perspective. You are here, but you do not really belong to the world. Living here, you have lost your way. You have to find it again to rediscover your true nature and stabilize in it. By practicing the yoga of self-absorption (*atma samyama yoga*) stretch your mind far into infinity. Enter into that limitless awareness of the Universal Self so that from that eternal perspective, your problems begin to fade away and you look at yourself and this world with wisdom, knowledge and discernment.

3. You are bound to the world. Your involvement with it arises from the activity of your senses. They draw you out and involve you with the world. As a result, you become attached to things and experience restlessness, anger, pride, fear, attachment and the like. Your involvement with the material world is the source of your suffering. It deludes you into accepting as true the duality and diversity of the world and believing that your happiness arises from having things rather than being yourself. This thirst for things and ownership is the cause of our suffering. What begins as a simple expedition into a magical world ends up as a servitude of many lifetimes. You

become a prisoner inside your own body, while every action you perform prolongs your sentence and delays your release. If you want to be free from the world, you should restrain your senses and retrain your mind to look within yourself to know who you are and what happened to you over time.

4. The world is not what it appears to be. It is a trap. If you live here ignorantly and negligently, you will be held in shackles. The world binds you to things and deludes you into believing that you can be secure and happy by having them. The spiritually blind are led into darkness. Those who live here with their eyes half closed suffer enormously. You cannot sleepwalk through this world. You must live here with your eyes wide open, and mind wide-awake, watching your steps carefully, as if you are lost in a forest that is full of traps and unknown dangers. You must cultivate discriminating wisdom (buddhi) to know the truth from falsehood and avoid making mistakes. You must live here wisely, making your way safely out of death and impermanence, avoiding sin and binding actions. True wisdom comes from knowledge and true knowledge is the knowledge of the Self. It arises not from perceptual experience but from transcendental experience, which is possible only when one achieves perfection in yoga.

5. You are responsible for your life, your actions and inactions. You are not bound to this world by them, but by your desires and attachments. Whatever you do or avoid doing in your life out of desires shape your destiny. Both action and inaction arise from the *gunas*. They are equally harmful when you indulge in them with desires. You cannot avoid *karma* by avoiding actions or your duties. True renunciation is not giving up actions or the world but giving up desires with firm resolve. It may be painful in the beginning, but in the end, it leads to liberation and freedom from death. You must live, but not for yourself and perform actions as if you are not performing them. It is possible when you perform them selflessly, without desires, not for yourself but for God or some divine cause. You should live here as if you do not exist

and do your duty as a sacrificial offering to God. Giving up your personal needs and comforts, you should live here for the sake of God and in His service, like a true a servant (*bhagavata*). Then you will be free from the consequences of your actions. Your living becomes an offering, a form of continuous worship. Instead of binding you, your actions will free you from their consequences. Therefore, perform your actions, without desires and expectations. Live as if you do not exist, you do not matter and you are no one.

6. The underlying causes of our bondage and ignorance are much deeper than we think. They are an integral aspect of our essential nature and so deeply hidden within our beingness that to know them we have to go all the way to the source of our creation. Our bodies are our prison houses. They are made up of Nature. We cannot escape from their influence easily because they are filled with the *gunas*, the primary qualities that determine our thinking and actions and thereby our destinies. We are good or bad, wise or foolish, knowledgeable or ignorant according to the *gunas* present in us. We act, react, and seek things because of them. We must therefore know what the *gunas* are and how they bind us through desires and actions. Wise people know it and thereby remain untouched by their actions or the changes that happen within them. We should also do the same. Knowing that the *gunas* are responsible for our desires, like wise yogis who have stable wisdom (*sthitaprajnas*), we should remain equal to the dualities of life with unwavering mind and let events of our lives unfold on their own.

7. When you live here, you serve many gods in the hope of finding peace and happiness. Propelled by your *gunas* and desires, you serve your own ego, worship your own interests and surrender to your whims. The result of this self-love is bondage. When you worship false gods of your own creation, you delude yourself and fall into greater ignorance. Instead of worshipping material things and taking refuge in your shadow self, you should take refuge in your real Self and the

Supreme Self, who is all pervading, eternal, indestructible and true liberator of all. He is the cause of everything and the real Doer of all actions. Those who are filled with *rajas* and *tamas* worship themselves or ignorance, but those who are filled with *sattva* worship the highest God. They offer themselves to God. They place themselves at His feet. Symbolically, they become His sacrificial food (*bhatka*) in the sacrifice of their lives. Therefore, cultivate purity (*sattva*) so that you can stabilize your mind in the contemplation of God, transcending your self-love, and experience oneness with Him. Restraining your mind and senses, focusing your mind upon Him, offer your thoughts and actions to Him. With surrender and gratitude, prostrate before Him and offer yourself to Him. If you persist in your practice, you will attain knowledge, wisdom and liberation quickly. When you seek refuge in Him, He assumes full responsibility for your life and guides you safely across the ocean of phenomenal life towards the world of light and delight.

The Triple Gunas

The *gunas* are the inherent modes or the primary qualities of Nature. They determine the state and behavior of things and beings. The *Bhagavadgita* is not the first or the only scripture to speak about them. They are mentioned in other scriptures and acknowledged by many religious traditions of ancient India, including Buddhism and Jainism. The *gunas* are the fundamental modifications of Nature. They are the first ones to become active in Nature at the beginning of creation. They are responsible for the dynamism, movements and properties of things and beings. They are three in number, namely *sattva*, *rajas* and *tamas* and distinguished primarily by the results or the effects they produce. They exist in all aspects of creation, both living and non-living, in various degrees of concentration, combination and dominance. Depending upon their relative strengths, beings exist in different states of purity and awareness, ranging from the highest state of light and knowledge to the lowest state of darkness and ignorance. The primary purpose of the *gunas* is to create modifications in beings and subject them to diversity, duality, attachment, delusion, ignorance, and bondage. According to the *Bhagavadgita*, the *gunas* arise from God only since He is both the efficient and material cause of creation. Deluded by the desires arising from the *gunas* (7.12), the world does not know God who is beyond all (7.13).

Although God is their ultimate source, He does not reside in them; but they reside in Him only (7.12). In Primordial Nature (*mula prarkriti*), they remain in a state of perfect equilibrium. When it is disturbed, they become active and produce modifications in the form of numerous states and conditions of existence. They propel beings into action and contribute to their bondage. Induced by the *gunas* the beings indulge in desire-ridden actions and suffer from their consequences. Deluded by their activity, they become bound to the cycle of births and deaths. All actions arise from the triple *gunas*, but due to ignorance and egoism, the deluded ones think that they are the doers. The *gunas* become active for the sake of Self only because seated in Nature He alone is the Witness and the Enjoyer.

The gunas and their modifications

In the 14th chapter of the *Bhagavadgita*, we find a very detailed description of the nature of the triple *gunas*. Knowledge of the *gunas* is supreme. By knowing it sages attained perfection in the past when they departed from here. Those who use this knowledge and attain the Supreme Self are not reborn again even at the time of creation, nor do they suffer during the destruction of the world. The *gunas* become active when God enters into the womb of Nature and places there the seed of creation. Having become active, they bind the embodied souls to their bodies. Of them *sattva* is illuminating and healthy. It binds the beings through attachment pleasure and knowledge. *Rajas* has the nature of passion (*ragatmakam*). Born out of thirst for things (*thrishna*) and attachment (*sanga*), it binds beings through attachment to actions. *Tamas* arises from ignorance (*ajnanam*). It deludes beings and binds them through negligence, sloth and sleep. The *gunas* have a tendency to suppress one another. *Sattva* prevails by subduing *rajas* and *tamas*, *rajas* by subduing *sattva* and *tamas* and tamas by subduing *sattva* and *rajas*. When *sattva* predominates, knowledge radiates through all the openings in the body. When *rajas* predominates, avarice in actions, restlessness and craving manifest. With the predominance of *tamas* arise darkness, sloth, carelessness and delusion.

The *gunas* also determine the fate of an embodied soul after its departure from here. When sattvic people die, they attain the pure worlds of those who know the highest Self. When rajasic people die, they go to the ancestral world. When they return from there, they are born among those who are attached to actions. When tamasic people die, they take birth in the wombs of the deluded (*mudha yonis*). Actions arising from them also lead to different ends. Sattvic actions lead to purity, rajasic actions to sorrow and tamasic actions to ignorance. *Sattva* leads to knowledge, *rajas* to greed and *tamas* to negligence, delusion and ignorance. Knowledge of the *gunas* and their influence is important in liberation. When you know that actions arise from the *gunas* and when seek the Self, which is higher than the *gunas* you attain liberation. Going beyond them, they become free from birth, death, old age and sorrow (14.20). Those who transcend the *gunas* become free from both attraction and aversion (14.22) to things and thereby experience equanimity and sameness towards all. Knowing that the *gunas* are responsible for all disturbances, they become indifferent and firm in their resolve (14.23). The scripture further states that the *gunas* can be transcended by serving God without distractions and practicing devotion.

The gunas in creation

The *gunas* permeate everything. Nothing in the manifested worlds is free from them. When you transcend them, you become liberated. Based on their predominance, everything in creation boils down sattvic, rajasic, or tamasic types (Ch. 18). Thus, you can divide actions into three. Actions performed as obligatory duties, without desire, are sattvic. Actions performed because of attachment and desires are rajasic; and not performing actions because of negligence or sloth is tamasic (18.7). Renunciation is also of three types. In sattvic renunciation, one renounces the fruit of one's actions; in rajasic renunciation, one gives up action because they are painful or difficult to perform; in tamasic renunciation, one gives up actions because of delusion. Sattvic renunciation leads to liberation; rajasic renunciation leads to bondage; and tamasic one leads to delusion. Those who do not practice true renunciation suffer from the consequences of their actions. Unpleasant, pleasant and mixed is the result of rajasic and tamasic renunciation (18.12).

Knowledge (*jnanam*), action (*karma*), and doer (*karta*) are declared in the *Gita* as the sum total of action (*karmasangraha*). They also arise from the *gunas* only (18.19); and they too are divided into sattvic, rajasic and tamasic types. Sattvic knowledge makes one see the Supreme Self universally in everything. Rajasic knowledge subjects one to duality and diversity. Tamasic knowledge leads to tunnel vision whereby one becomes excessively fixated with one thing only as if it were all. Sattvic actions are performed without desires as obligatory duties to uphold *dharma*. Rajasic actions are performed egoistically out of desire and with striving. Tamasic actions are performed out of delusion without due consideration for the relationship, ability and the destruction they may cause (18.25). In the same manner, the *Bhagavadgita* distinguishes intelligence (*buddhi*), firmness (*dhriti*), happiness (*sukham*), and castes according to the predominance of *gunas*.

Gunas and caste system

Justification for the caste system also arises from the *gunas*. It was probably the reason for its origin in the formative period of the Vedic religion. The system eventually gave way to a more corrupt and rigid system based on birth. However, it is not wrong to think of people in terms of their predominant *gunas* and group them accordingly. Based on the gunas people fall into three primary categories. However, since they are always found intermixed in beings their permutations and combinations may lead to even more. The Vedic system recognized four castes according to their predominant qualities: priests (*brahmanas*), warriors (*kshatriyas*), merchants (*vaisyas*) and workers (*sudras*). Purely sattvic people or those with the predominance of *sattva* are fit for religious duties and spiritual knowledge. People with the predominance of *rajas*, followed by *sattva* are well qualified for leadership positions, religious knowledge and spiritual life. People with the predominance of *tamas*, followed by *sattva* excel in materialistic pursuits such as business, trade and commerce. Finally, people with the predominance of *tamas* followed by *rajas* are better suited for professions involving manual work, sports and related activities.

Whether the *Bhagavadgita* supports caste system based on birth or the *gunas* is not clear. One may find in the scripture support for both arguments. Logically thinking, according to the *karma* theory the chances of a sattvic person taking birth in a sattvic family are high. It is also true in case of people having the predominance of the other two *gunas*. At the same time, we cannot ignore the importance of self-effort in one's *karma* and destiny. Family background and birth do not guarantee liberation. They may help, but persistent effort (*abhyasam*) has a greater role in one's liberation. Through practice and discipline, people may acquire *sattva* and qualify for liberation or acquire higher knowledge even if they are born in adverse conditions. It may not be appropriate to deny them opportunities for spiritual growth. Lord Krishna affirms very clearly that one should always pursue one's duties according to one's essential nature (as determined by one's *gunas*) rather than taking the duties of another, even if they are superior (18.47).

Transcending the gunas

The *gunas* are part of Nature. They bind people one way or another. They keep you engaged with the world and bind you to the body. Even *sattva* binds people in its own way and contributes to their ignorance. Therefore, ideally one should become indifferent to all the three. Liberation is possible only when you become free from their influence or inducement completely. However, for the purpose of liberation *sattva* is the most ideal because it is pure and conducive to the development of divine qualities such as dispassion, detachment and equanimity, which are essential for liberation,. Ultimately, we have to go beyond the *gunas*, by becoming indifferent to them, to transcend our lower nature and see the Self within ourselves (14.20).

What are the qualities of a person who has transcended the triple *gunas*? How does he behave and how does he actually achieve it? When a yogi overcomes the three *gunas*, he does not experience attraction or aversion to brightness, passion and delusion when they are present or absent (14.22). He remains indifferent and undisturbed, knowing that the *gunas* are doing their duty (14.23). He remains alike in pleasure and pain, censure and praise, and honor and dishonor. Alike in pleasure and pain, independent, he treats equally a piece of gold or a lump of clay. With equanimity and self-control, he remains equal to the desirable and the undesirable, defamation and self-adulation (14.24), honor and dishonor, and friends and foes. Without egoism in performing actions, he transcends them (14.25).

Knowledge of the triple *gunas* is important and very much relevant to the practice of yoga. It helps us understand the nature of our actions and the causes of our bondage. When we realize that the *gunas* are chiefly responsible for our thinking, attitudes and actions, we find solutions to the problem of *karma*. When we realize that it will lead to sameness (*samatvam*), equanimity, contentment (*santosham* and liberation (*mukti*), we will try to transcend them. Yogis practice self-purification to realize this state. With their latent impressions burnt away in the fire of detachment, their minds resting in their selves, they experience bliss and happiness even in their embodied state. Upon departing from their bodies, they attain the Supreme Self.

The Yoga of Sorrow

When Arjuna stood in the middle of the battlefield and saw the two great armies arrayed on both sides ready to wage a destructive war, he was suddenly overwhelmed with negative emotions. When we are confronted with a difficult situation, emotions invade our minds and fill us with conflicting thoughts. It happened to Arjuna. He was filled with remorse. He was filled with fear, doubt and confusion. Thoughts of violence and bloodshed arising from his actions overwhelmed him. He also thought of the consequences arising from the war upon him and his own family. It is very difficult for anyone to view things calmly and weigh the consequences arising from one's actions with a clear mind when confronted with a crisis. We tend to weigh actions in the light of the results they are going to produce and the likely scenarios that emerge out of them. Arjuna did the same. He weighed the consequences of the war and their impact upon others and himself. As he thought about it, he was filled with sorrow, fear and guilt. His knowledge and experience of warfare did not help him in that moment of crisis. They did not sooth his fears or his conscience.

At that moment in his life, he felt that the gains of warfare were far less significant, both morally and socially, than the losses and the destruction it was going to unleash. He was convinced that he was about to commit a great sin by participating in the war and causing the death of many some of whom were great souls and his close relations. He also felt that the war would leave its mark upon his own family and lead to its decline. With the death of male members, he reasoned, women in his family would lose their virtue and cause intermixture of castes. It disturbed him further and strengthened his resolve to leave the battlefield. In that fit of confusion he decided to renounce actions and live an ascetic life seeking alms from others. He reasoned that there was greater honor in seeking alms from other than waging war and killing one's own friends and relations for the sake of fame and kingdom.

The state of sorrow

Arjuna was educated, knowledgeable and scholarly. He was well versed in his profession. His ignorance was not of scholarly type. He studied the scriptures and trained under the best of the masters. He was well versed in the art of warfare and matters of governance. He had knowledge of virtue, mortality and religious duties. He was also mentally tough and courageous. He fought many wars and won them. He resolved many problems in the past and assisted his brothers greatly in securing victories and overcoming obstacles. However, his intellectual knowledge failed him at the most crucial time in his life. It did not adequately answer his doubts or address his fears and indecision. It did not give him the strength to bear the suffering silently and remain equal to the results of war. It exposed his weaknesses as a human being. The crisis demolished his long held beliefs about himself and brought out his vulnerabilities into open, exposing the most unstable part of his personality hidden behind layers of defenses built by him all along. It showed him that to address the complex issues of human life, one need to go beyond the mind and the intellect and look for solutions in the realm of the Self. What he lacked was spiritual awareness and his duties and obligations from a spiritual perspective. He needed a different approach, a major shift in his thinking and attitude, which would come later with the discourse of Lord Krishna.

One cannot blame Arjuna for his lack of conviction at a crucial moment in his life. It happens in many cases. People lose their courage when they require it the most. They become distracted when they are supposed to focus on their goals. They give up when they are expected to persevere. Although Arjuna was a great warrior and highly educated, he was not free from the dualities of life, more specifically from attraction and aversion to things. He also lacked proper knowledge, whereby he assumed that he could avoid sin by avoiding action. His mind was turbulent because of desires and expectations. He personified ordinary human consciousness, with which we are familiar.

Although he was well trained in concentration and mental discipline, like most of us, he could not suppress his emotions in front of his close friend and mentor, Lord Krishna, Whom he thought was an ordinary person. The same motives, desires and limitations, which assail our minds, as we deal with our routine tasks also weighed in his mind and troubled him, as he stood in the battlefield, confused, with his beliefs shaken, his fears aggravated, and his intelligence and judgment faltering. In the face of a grave emotional crisis, he spoke the same language, which we use when we feel like escaping from the harsh realities of life.

A great warrior, bred on the beliefs and values of his times, Arjuna was intensely religious, morally righteous, socially responsible, ambitious, earthly and humane. As he laid aside his bow and arrows and sank down in the back seat of his chariot shaken and dejected, there was no pretence in his thoughts or actions. He was neither cynical nor insincere nor vain in his approach. He did not try to evade the problem under some false pretext, hiding his real feelings. His feelings and doubts were genuine, which he expressed truthfully. Truthfully, he expressed his fear of sin and the bloodshed that might arise from his actions in the battlefield. As a person of great integrity and good human values, his sorrow was genuine and so was his concern.

Arjuna's sorrow makes sense from a human perspective. We love even those we hate if we see in them a reflection of our own ideals and values. Conditioned by society, we place greater emphasis upon certain social values, even if they are detrimental to the happiness and wellbeing of the individuals. We respect authority, even if it limits our freedom and opportunities. Arjuna's character and thinking were shaped by the conditions of his time. It would be inappropriate to judge him with today's standards. One cannot criticize him for his arguments about the admixture of castes or his lack of faith in the women of his family. He was but expressing the values and norms of his times and the conditioning to which he was subject.

Knowledge vs. Suffering

Worldly knowledge does not illuminate the suffering mind. It does not reflect truth adequately. It does not always provide correct solutions to the problems we face in our lives, because it arises from a limited field of experience and does not have the illumination of the all-knowing awareness. The knowledge, which arises from our interaction with the world, which we hold dearly and in which we take pride, is an ignorant force. It lacks purity of vision, strength and purpose, which can sustain us through crises. Since it is imperfect and incomplete, it does not suggest permanent solutions but only temporary fixes. Holding us within the walls of perceptual experience and accumulated knowledge of distorted perceptions, it binds us strongly to our habitual thought patterns, mental modifications, desires and attachments.

Perceptual knowledge is of the Nature, by the Nature and for the Nature. It is not a liberating force, but a deluding one. Its purpose is not to set us free but ensnare us deeply in the phenomena of the world. Its solutions are meant to perpetuate the status quo rather than changing it. It does not lead us towards light and salvation but into the world of egoism, ignorance and illusion. Its source, therefore, is not light but illusion. Its purpose is not to set us free, but hold us in bondage, and not to reveal truth but veil it and show us an alternate reality to keep us deluded and ignorant. Created, nourished and enriched by the senses, it holds in its view a very limited vision of life, upholding the values that are rooted in our desires and attachment. It does not show us the way but leads us astray, and does not establish divine centered living but self-centered activity.

Suffering, the ground reality

Sorrow manifests in our lives in many ways. Our lives are so infused with it that most of the time we do not even know that we are suffering. For an enlightened person, living itself is suffering. As the Buddha declared, every aspect of living is infused with a shade of sorrow. We may accept suffering but we cannot deny its existence or its relevance. An embodied self is an imprisoned self. Therefore, it is neither a happy nor an auspicious state. No doubt, for a materialistic person this may sound very depressing; but it is true that we are rarely free from suffering or its possibility. Suffering is the underlying theme of our existence and we spend our whole lives either addressing it or escaping from it. Sorrow does not mean mere crying and shedding tears, while it is outward and more visible form. It has many shapes, tones, hues, grades and colors. It arises in many forms such as agony, despair, anguish, physical pain, sense of separation, sense of loss, helplessness, depression, and the like. Some other manifestations include crisis of confidence, pangs of failure, self-pity, dejection, depression, mental breakdown, hysteria, self-deception, apathy, indifference, anger and frustration. These are numerous manifestations of sorrow, with which it overwhelms our minds and consumes our lives.

True freedom arises when we set our minds free from desires, attachment, accumulated knowledge and conditioning. We are free when we are free from attraction and aversion to things. We experience peace when we break out of the confines of our conditioned minds and its knowledge of limited light. Suffering helps us in this process. As long as we are not willing to go beyond sense gratification and sensory perceptions and as long as we are not willing to detach our minds from routine thought processes and habitual vibrations, we remain slaves to our minds and memory. Without the intervention of suffering and without knowing the causes of our suffering, we cannot establish a divine centered life that provides reasonable solutions to the problems of our existence. Without suffering and learning from it, we cannot change our responses and our unhealthy lifestyles.

Conclusion

Sorrow is a state or a condition. Hence, it is a yoga. It is the most natural state found in the living beings. Therefore, it is described rightly in the first chapter of the *Bhagavadgita* in the form of

Arjuna's sorrow. It arises from the afflictions and modifications of the mind and body, caused by desires, attachment, duality and the very nature of mind, which is fickle and restless. The purpose of spiritual endeavor is to overcome this state and enter into a higher yoga of equanimity, stability, peace and sameness, which lead to transcendence and immortality. There are many pathways to reach this august and supreme state. The *Bhagavadgita* explains them in the remaining seventeen chapters as different yogas.

The Causes of Suffering

Suffering is the first part. Understanding it is the second part. Resolving it is the third. In understanding our suffering, we not only have to discern the apparent causes, but also find their root cause. For that, we have to go deeper into our own consciousness and through study, observation and discernment realize how our suffering arises and subsides. We have to become familiar with both the thought process as well as the physical process involved in our suffering. We can do it by cultivating self-restraint, detachment and witness consciousness.. When we witness our own suffering in a state of detachment, we understand it and resolve it better than when we are involved with it and suffer from it like a victim. When we observe it dispassionately, we can understand it truly, without being influenced by our own desires, likes and dislikes.

Sorrow arises from various causes; but the most fundamental cause suggested in the *Bhagavadgita* is desire, which manifests as craving, attachment, and attraction and aversion to material things. Our suffering arises from gain and loss; and from association and disassociation with things to which we are attracted or averse. The *Bhagavadgita* defines yoga as a state in which we are permanently disassociated from pain and suffering. Gaining what you dislike or losing what you like leads to suffering. Coming into contact with the unpleasant or losing contact with the pleasant also leads to the same. Thus, our suffering arises from the delusion of ownership, union and separation, and our attraction and aversion to things caused by our desires and attachment. Desire is the manifest cause, but the real culprits are the *gunas*. They are responsible for our desires. They induce in us desire for sense objects, which leads to attachment, and attraction and aversion to the pairs of opposites. The *Bhagavadgita* reveals that human suffering arises from the following modifications, which arise primarily from the *gunas* only.

Ignorance: Knowledge leads to liberation; ignorance leads to bondage and suffering. Ignorance is of several kinds. The Ignorance, which we are specifically mentioning here, is spiritual ignorance, which leads to delusion and duality. According to the *Bhagavadgita*, it includes ignorance of the individual Self, the Supreme Self, the means to liberation, and ignorance about our phenomenal existence, the binding nature of actions and the *gunas*. Our ignorance arises from the impurities present in our minds and bodies. They veil our consciousness and prevent us from knowing the truth about ourselves.

Duality: Duality is seeing things differently and variously. We tend to understand things relatively in terms of relationships, groups, divisions and distinctions. That one is different from others is duality. When you see yourself distinct, you engage in duality and individuality. It leads to desire-ridden actions and self-seeking behavior. Distinction between the knower and the known, between oneself and others is a major source of suffering. Duality and separateness arises from *the gunas* and their propensity to suppress one another.

Pairs of opposites: Pairs of opposites are heat and cold, pleasure and pain, good and bad, and the like. Attraction and aversion to them subjects the mind to modifications and afflictions. By nature, we tend to seek pleasure and avoid pain. Disassociation from pleasure and association with pain leads to suffering. Disassociation from both pain and pleasure leads to sameness and equanimity. This is the ideal yoga aims to achieve.

Instability: The human mind is fickle by nature. An unstable mind cannot experience peace and equanimity. Instability of the mind arises from the activity of the senses and their involvement with the sense-objects. It is resolved when the mind is trained to stabilize in the thoughts of God and in sameness (*samatvam*).

Impermanence: The phenomenal world is impermanent and unstable. It results in the experiences of gain and loss, and attraction and aversion to things. When we cling to things that are impermanent and unstable, we suffer from the pain of loss and the expectation of gain.

Desire: When we perform desire-ridden actions, seeking their fruit, we suffer from their consequences. Desires arise from the activity of the senses. They lead to attachment. Desires are at the root of our suffering. They give rise to selfishness, greed and envy.

Egoism: The feeling that you are the cause of your actions and the source of your achievement, and the belief that you have to live for yourself and work for yourself, these arise from egoism. Your attachment to name and form leads to egoism and the desire to perpetuate yourself. Egoistic actions bind you to the world and subject you to the cycle of births and deaths.

Attachment: The activity of the senses leads to attachment. It is both positive and negative. One leads to attraction and the other to aversion. From attachment, arise desires. From desires, arise delusion, loss of intelligence and spiritual downfall.

Doership: God is the inhabitant of the entire universe. He is seated in everything. He is the real Doer and Enjoyer of things; but out of ignorance, we believe that we are the doers and we are responsible for our actions. When we assume doership, we suffer from the consequences of our actions.

Lack of intelligence: Without intelligence we cannot discern between truth and falsehood and that which leads to suffering and that which results in peace and happiness. When we do not have discernment, we do not know how to resolve our problems, navigate our lives and remain free from the afflictions of the phenomenal world.

Impurities of the mind and the body: The impurities of *rajas* and *tamas* prevent us from experiencing peace and stability within ourselves. These impurities bind us through ignorance and duality and lead to demonic qualities and moral downfall.

While outwardly the causes of our suffering are many, at the most basic level they arise from desire-ridden actions induced by the *gunas*. Human suffering is inevitable and unavoidable. The *Bhagavadgita* does not promise to end suffering, but only suggests the means to endure it and remain undisturbed by it by overcoming desires and duality and cultivating sameness.

The Purpose of Sorrow

Suffering serves a definite purpose in our lives. It prepares us well for the life upon earth and for the life hereafter in ways that eventually lead to our liberation. The knowledge and experience we gain out of suffering and the insights we gain in the process awaken us to a new reality about the world and people and to our own strengths and vulnerabilities. From that awareness and understanding, we become wiser and tolerant and work for our progress and transformation on the path of liberation and self-awakening. We turn to religion and spirituality mostly out of suffering only. Unless we have suffered enough, we do not realize the futility of worldliness and the need for renunciation. In suffering, we become introspective. We become wiser. We begin to look within. We learn to withdraw from the things that give us pain. When our hearts are heavy with the tears of sorrow, we become philosophical, even cynical about the world and the strange ways in which it holds our attentions and wields its influence. When we are in despair, we look for solutions to lighten our hearts and escape from the burdens of life. Sometimes, when we are not ready, it breaks our spirit and puts us on self-destructive paths; and sometimes, when we are ready for change, it builds our hopes and leads us towards our dreams. The Patient Lord does not grant us liberating and uplifting wisdom until we drink enough poison from the cup of life and open our eyes to the reality of the world and the need to escape from it. Sorrow is thus a divine opportunity that comes to us in the form of providence (*daivikam*) and a divine blessing (*prasadam*) to realize the delusion into which we have fallen and the need to recover from it.

It is wrong to assume that God always grants us our wishes or gives us whatever we pray. He shows His love and mercy in mysterious and most unexpected ways, sometimes doing exactly the opposite of what we seek. If we pray for happiness, He may give us pain and if we seek comfort, He may force us to deal with situations that we tend to avoid habitually. The purpose is to free us from the duality of attraction and aversion in which become caught. It is His way of saving us from our own ignorance and self-destructive tendencies. Our suffering mitigates greatly when we become equal to all the dualities in life and each suffering that we experiences in our lives we move towards that ideal goal.

Suffering may arise in our lives because of our own actions (*adhyatmikam*), the actions of Nature (*adhibhautikam*) or the actions of God or His manifestations (*adhidaivam*). In all these, the purpose is the same: to manifest our destinies according to the actions we perform and carve better persons out of us, by providing with opportunities to cultivate divine qualities, virtues, sameness, peace, balance and equanimity. We move towards this ideal disposition the hard way through suffering, learning from our mistakes, ignorance, indiscretion, delusion and imperfections. Sorrow wakes us up from our complacent and indulgent ways to open our eyes to the impermanent and uncertain world in which we are subject to Nature and its modifications. Thus, suffering is a seemingly negative and destructive but truly positive and constructive force, the precursor of enlightenment, in whose womb the soul prepares itself for its eventual liberation. By revealing the transience and meaninglessness of our existence and by bringing to light our own limitations and failures, it rather crudely and painfully nudges us towards our final destiny, which is liberation. It encourages us to with draw from the world and look within ourselves to find God, believe in Him, depend upon Him, surrender to Him and seek His help.

Suffering is thus a faithful messenger of truth. As an instrument of light, it subjects us to transformation, in rather unpleasant and frightening ways. It wakes us up from our illusions to remind us our essential nature and the true purpose of our lives. A teacher, it uses rather harsh methods to instruct us in the virtue of divine centered life and live virtuously and spiritually, so that we can transcend our ignorance and delusion. In the darkness of suffering and depths of sorrow only, we feel the need to change our lives and cleanse ourselves of the impurities that we accumulate in the course of our existence upon earth. Arjuna did not see the pleasant form of God. He saw His terrible aspect, Death (*Kala*) itself. He saw suffering in its most terrible and destructive aspect. In that symbolism is hidden the true meaning and purpose of suffering.

In our lives too, from time to time, God manifests Himself as suffering. We can learn from it and march towards freedom or ignore it to see His more gruesome forms. Unless one is burnt in the fire of sorrow and suffering, spiritual life is but a remote possibility, a distant dream, a mere intellectual debate or delight. The light of the Self cannot shine in the hearts of those who have not shed copious tears. Sincere prayers cannot come from the lips that have not quivered and cried for divine help. The world of God opens not to him whose heart is not drenched by the tears of his own suffering and cries of his own pain. Along the paths and grooves carved by the hands of sorrow travels the mortal man, by trials and tribulations, into an immortal world that is a negation of what he has experienced or understood before. In no other way can the human mind be shaken out of the stupor and the perversion into which it habitually descends due to the destructive influence of the impure *gunas*. Arjuna suffered and in the process became wiser. He sought divine help and God taught him valuable lessons about life and suffering in the form of the *Bhagavadgita*, which He Himself declared as the secret of all secrets. He revealed him His immortal celestial teachings, by knowing which one would attain freedom from suffering here and salvation hereafter.

Therefore, however distasteful it may be, sorrow is not to be despised but looked upon with respect, gratitude and sameness, for it descends from above with a definite purpose, hiding in its bosom the a hidden message, the seed of an awakening, or a line of spiritual instruction that can draw us close to the Universal Teacher. Sorrow is the poison that manifests as we start churning the ocean of mortal life to understand its mystery and transience and find the elixir that would make us immortal. Just as the great churning of the ocean of life led to the emergence of the elixir of life (*amritam*) the churning of the mind in the form of sorrow leads eventually to immortality only. However, unless we know how to deal with sorrow and respond to it with peace and equanimity, we cannot achieve this sacred and auspicious goal. Even the great gods and the mighty demons had to deal with the poison of suffering as they began churning the ocean of life in search of the elixir that would make them immortal. Lord *Siva* neutralized the poison by drinking it and holding it in his throat, without letting it either go up into his mind or go down into his heart. In both places, it would have caused great harm and destroyed the very balance of creation and the existence of life; but in His throat, it remained ineffective and harmless and helped the gods and the demons to proceed further with their quest for immortality. From this episode, we learn this lesson: you swallow pain, but do not let it destroy you mentally or physically. Do not speak about it vainly or worry about it. Just bear the pain with equanimity and let it go.

Suffering made the gods immortal and brought the worlds to order. In case of Arjuna, it opened His eyes to the profound truths. It earned him the grace of God and showed him the way to liberation. In its wake, he learned about the various yogas that would stabilize his mind and help him perform selfless actions in the service of God with equanimity. He learned the importance of performing his obligatory duties with detachment and sacrificial attitude to escape from their consequences. He learned the importance of virtue, purity and devotion to God in his life. The knowledge he gained out of his suffering restored his balance, cleared his delusion and freed him from sorrow. It led him on the path of enlightenment to witness the birth of a great philosophy that had the potential to wash away the sins of those who were willing to take a dip in it. Thus, the purpose of sorrow is to awaken us and prepare us for our liberation. It is a chiseling and refining mechanism used by God, the Supreme Sculptor, to improve our lives.

The Resolution of Sorrow

Since sorrow plays a vital role in our lives and comes in many forms, we need a suitable strategy to deal with it without being tormented by it. We have to find solutions that would not only resolve our suffering but also lead to our spiritual progress instead of our moral decay. As we have discussed before, sorrow serves a very vital spiritual purpose in our lives. It opens our eyes to our own imperfections and vulnerabilities. It is a teacher in disguise, which imparts valuable spiritual lessons the hard way so that we can resolve our problems and deal with our suffering with certain awareness, wisdom, maturity and intelligence. In the process of mitigating our suffering and dealing with adversity, we gain wisdom, patience and the resolve to break out of the mortal world and our own bodies in which we are held in bondage by Nature.

We cannot remove sorrow and suffering entirely from our lives. Suffering in the spiritual sense means suffering from both attraction and aversion to things. Even when you are happy, you are not free from suffering because your mind is filled with craving and desires. Even in happiness, it is subject to modifications arising from desires and expectations. This is the truth. Whatever we may do, suffering is inherent in our very existence and we can never be separate from it as long as we are subject to desires and the dualities of life. In this sense, living itself is suffering. Therefore, to believe that somehow we can cure our suffering magically, without addressing the basic problem, is pure delusion. We may resolve suffering through other means, but it would be temporary and it may even increase our suffering in the end. The Bhagavadgita suggests that we can resolve suffering permanently by acquiring knowledge and wisdom, and cultivating an attitude of sameness and equanimity. Until we reach that goal, we should learn to accept our suffering and bear with it, without being overly disturbed by it. We should not abandon life in the hope of mitigating our suffering because suffering arises not from actions but from our thinking and attitudes.

Truly speaking, the *Bhagavadgita* is a discourse on resolving human sorrow. It provides spiritual solutions that are plausible and practical to the problem of human sorrow, acknowledging at the same time that suffering is an inherent condition of earthly life arising from the modifications of Nature and the activities of the triple *gunas,* which cannot be resolved without addressing the basic problem, which is our propensity to desire. Therefore, it suggests a comprehensive approach to the problem encompassing the following.

1. **Identify yourself with your inner Self** rather than your mind and body. The Self is real. The mind and body wither and fall away. The name and form associated with them are temporary. If you think that you and others are mere mortals and identify yourself and them with names and forms, you will suffer from the dualities of union and separation that are inherent in all relationships. You are an immortal Self. If you are centered in it, you transcend your attachment to your mind and body and experience peace and stability. Therefore, always think that you are an immortal Self and live with that conviction.

2. **Know the causes of your attachment** and resolve them. Your attachments arise from your constant and repeated involvement with things and people. Attachment leads to habitual dependence upon things and to suffering caused by the duality and delusion of union and separation it creates. Desire and passions are at the root of your attachments. If you cultivate detachment and dispassion, you become equal to the pairs of opposites and experience peace and stability.

3. **Perform your actions without ownership and doership.** Ownership and doership arise out of egoism and the predominance of *rajas*. They are responsible for our striving and seeking and our bondage to earthly life. God is the true owner of

all things in the universe and He is the source of all actions. One should therefore renounce both these impediments to attain knowledge and liberation.

4. Offer your actions to God with surrender and devotion. When you offer your actions to God with surrender and devotion, He takes responsibility for your life and the consequences arising from them. God is the Sacrificer, the Sacrificed and the result of sacrifice. In the sacrifice of our lives, we can make God the true sacrificer, our actions the sacrificial material and the results arising from them the offering. This way, our actions do not bind us.

5. Acknowledge God as the Supreme Lord of the Universe and the source of all. When you see the presence of God everywhere, you will live with the sacred feeling that you are always in His Company and under His guidance. Therefore, develop the vision of unity, rather than division and find the presence of God in every aspect of creation.

6. Practice constant and continuous contemplation upon God. Whatever one thinks at the time of death, one becomes that. The *Bhagavadgita* assures that whoever contemplates upon God continuously acquires *sattva* and experiences peace, equanimity and sameness. What one remembers at the time of one's death is also important. Those who spend their time thinking of God only remember Him only at the time of their death and go to the world of immortals by the sunlit path.

7. Practice self-purification by increasing sattva. Predominance of *sattva* leads to purification of the mind and body. With the predominance of *sattva* and suppression of *rajas* and *tamas*, the practice of detachment, meditation, contemplation and self-absorption becomes easier. The mind becomes free from afflictions and experiences sameness towards the pairs of opposites.

8. Acquire right knowledge. With right knowledge comes right discrimination and the ability to distinguish the difference between reality and illusion, truth and false and real Self and false self. Right knowledge comes with self-study, practice of yoga, and the grace of God. With right knowledge, you realize that the Self is real, immortal and indestructible. You overcome delusion and see the world as a play of God.

Change and impermanence, attachment, desire, delusion, perceptual knowledge, duality, egoism, impurities of *rajas* and *tamas*, are some of the underlying causes of human suffering. Our suffering is a modification of Nature. It arises from the activity of the *gunas*, which are responsible for our desire-ridden actions and our attachment to material things. The knowledge of the *Bhagavadgita* helps us understand the causes and nature of our suffering. It teaches us how, with that knowledge, we may live in the world without being touched by its impurities. Suffering is a process of self-purification and inner awakening. Of this, there is no doubt. We can use suffering as an indicator to know how we are living and in what direction we are progressing. The cure to suffering is purity (*sattva*), obligatory duty (*dharma*), knowledge (*jnanam*), discernment (*buddhi*) and devotion (*bhakti*). The *Bhagavadgita* repeatedly returns to these subjects in the long discourse as the means to overcome duality and delusion and achieve liberation.

The Symbolism of Arjuna's Sorrow

Arjuna stands symbolically for the human personality that is part divine and part human, rooted in both knowledge and ignorance, subject to dualities and guided by gunas and desires. His predicament regarding the war and its consequences was essentially an expression of his ego that was firmly conditioned by tradition and authority and the temptations of worldly life. His pity was the pity of an ego bred on relative human values. His tears were the outpouring of limited human knowledge and untested egoistic beliefs. His depression was the depression of a mind propelled by its own prejudice and directed by its own fears. His grief was the grief of deluded being caught in the snares of worldly life pining for a permanent escape.

Sorrow and depression are the natural expressions of a mind that is overwhelmed with conflicting values and the realization that our actions may lead to death and destruction and bring misery upon others and ourselves. We stay within the confines of our comfort zones as long as our values and convictions are not challenged and our abilities are not to put to test. We open our eyes to the truths underlying our lives and actions only when we are confronted with our limitations and forced to perform unpleasant actions against our notions of right and wrong, which need not necessarily represent the eternal values enshrined in our scriptures or religions. In the middle of the battlefield, Arjuna was in the same situation. He had to deny a part of himself in order to resolve a serious moral conflict that confronted him, which arose because he decided to participate in a greatly destructive war.

Conflict and confusion are inherent in human life. In the oceanic depths of *samsara*, each being has to swim from conflict to conflict and confusion to confusion, until it finds the raft of wisdom by which it can safely swim towards the other shore. Arjuna was a great warrior, a man of learning; but he was not free from the confusion arising from his egoistic thinking, relative values and limited knowledge. His egoistic beliefs and values were seriously challenged by the needs of war and his duty as a warrior. Faced with the predicament of waging a war against his own relations, he had to rethink and relearn the truths about his duty and conduct. He needed new knowledge and awareness, which would absorb his conflicts without seriously disturbing the continuity of his life and actions. His consciousness needed the touch of divine knowledge so that it would attain peace and harmony. Spiritually he was ready for the dawn of light from above. It came to him in the form of Lord Krishna, his Friend, Philosopher, and the Supreme Self. Arjuna was an earthly being bound to his traditions and beliefs, with an ego that was caught in its own illusions. The words of Arjuna therefore echo the suffering and confusion we face in our lives and his conflict resembles the innumerable conflicts we experience everyday as we deal with our problems in which we have to compromise our values, beliefs, relationships and duties. We are not always wise in our actions. When we come under the sway of our emotions or when our reasoning is greatly impaired by fear and anxiety, we falter in our thinking and judgment. Nor can we claim authority over the forces of Nature with our limited knowledge. According to our scriptures, our knowledge is more qualified as ignorance rather than real knowledge. We are subject to many influences and susceptible to bias and perceptual errors. We cannot entirely rely upon our beliefs and conclusions because what we perceive and comprehend as experience is colored by our prejudices, faulty reasoning, selective memory and mental fatigue rather than truth and the reality of the world itself. Because of the impurities present in our consciousness, there are bound to be errors and mistakes in our awareness, which unfortunately we do not easily recognize and do not willingly rectify. This makes our effort of self-transformation a difficult, painful and arduous task.

The play of ego

The ego is responsible for all the activity arising from the desires that are induced by the *gunas*. It is responsible for our acts of self-promotion and self-preservation and thereby for our *karma*. It is a blind force, which is mostly mechanical, ignorant of the Self, deluded and predominantly selfish. As an instrument of Nature, it serves its designs and suffers from modifications. By nature, it is bound to the things of the world. This prevents us from seeing transcendental truths with the help of our intelligence and experiencing peace and stability within ourselves. By its actions and attachment, the ego keeps the embodied-self bound to the world and delays its liberation. It is not difficult to know what the ego stands for. We can identify it in our own consciousness and from our own behavior. Here are a few of its distinguishing features.

1. It is an impermanent and destructible self.
2. It is never liberated, because it is always part of Nature. It belongs to the earth and returns to it upon death.
3. It assumes ownership and doership on actions and thereby incurs *karma*, which results in rebirth and bondage for the embodied self.
4. It is induced by the *gunas*.
5. It can be purified and transformed through the practice of yoga.
6. It is a feeling of individuality and identity whereby we experience duality and diversity in our perceptions.
7. It is bound to the world through the activity of the senses.
8. It is part of the internal organ and subjects the mind to mental modifications (*vrittis*).

However, the self-correcting mechanism hidden in the Creation of God does not allow the ego to remain perpetually ignorant and earth bound. At some point in its long existence in the mortal world, each being has to wake up from its dream and see the truth that it has ignored thus far. It has to realize how its actions and desires bind the Self and how it may end the bondage of the Self. The ego, which remains for long as an enemy of the Self, has to become eventually its friend by offering its life and actions for its liberation. Having realized of the impermanence of the world and growing tired of its karmic suffering, it has to give up finally its identity and individuality and live selflessly, performing actions for the sake of the Self, without desiring their fruit. This is how, through purification and transformation, each being has to accomplish its own destruction and sacrifice itself at the feet of God to release the soul from bondage. If it is fortunate, human being comes under the influence of God and yields himself to positive and uplifting transformation. Knowing the difference between the true self and false self, and between knowledge and delusion, he achieves peace and sameness, resting his mind in the contemplation of God and His service. Even if he fails in one life, he takes his goal to the next since there is no loss in this kind of effort. Those who do not do so are dragged again into the phenomenal world and kept under the control of Nature where they have to go through the same hardships and remain bound to their own desires and attachments.

The True Meaning of Renunciation

According to the *Bhagavadgita*, *sanyasa* or renunciation is an attitude of selflessness and egolessness, marked by freedom from desires and absence of attachment in performing one's actions. True renunciation is renunciation of the fruit of one's actions, not the actions themselves. One should not give up one's obligatory duties and responsibilities, but desire for things and expectations arising from them. You practice true renunciation only when you become indifferent to your *gunas* and accept the pairs of opposites in your life with equanimity and sameness. For a seeker of liberation, renunciation of actions or his obligatory duties is not the goal, but renunciation of desires and attachment to actions (4.20) is. It is by renouncing the desire for the fruit of his actions a *karmayogi* becomes a true *sanyasi*.

Renouncing your favorite things mentally is much more difficult. You may wear the robes of an ascetic and give up attachments; but unless you are mentally free from the things of the world, your practice will remain incomplete and imperfect. You carry your mind in you and around you. In your wakeful state, it is an inseparable part of your consciousness. For ordinary people, it is the consciousness itself because they have not yet experienced the reality that exists beyond their minds and senses. Therefore, if you want to practice true renunciation, you have to free your mind from attachments. In true renunciation, inner conflicts and self-doubts do not exist. In your quest for liberation, you know where you stand and what you need to do. You would not practice renunciation even for the sake of liberation because doing something with a purpose or an end in your mind is against the spirit of true renunciation. In renunciation, you give up everything, including your thoughts and opinions and your desire to achieve liberation. The *Bhagavadgita* proclaims that a *karmayogi*, who neither hates nor desires, should be considered a true *sanyasi*, because it is by overcoming desires a person transcends the pair of opposites hidden in his passions and emotions (5.03). It also distinguishes the difference between renunciation and sacrifice (*tyagam*). Renunciation is giving up the desire in actions, where as sacrifice is giving up the fruit of all actions (18.04).

Lord Krishna says that one should not give up obligatory duties such as sacrificial rituals (*yajnas*), charity (*danam*) and austerity (*tapas*) because they are purifiers whose practice leads to the predominance of *sattva* (18.06). However, even they should be performed by renouncing attachment and desire for their fruit (18.06). Renunciation and action are interrelated. The yoga of renunciation and the yoga of action, both lead to liberation, when they are practiced in conjunction. Renunciation without performing desireless actions is futile. Hence, of the two, the yoga of action is said to be superior (5.02).

What you give up in your renunciation is also important. People practice renunciation according to their nature. Sattvic people renounce desires and attachments. Rajasic people renounce pain and fear. Tamasic people renounce action itself (18.07–09). In true renunciation, a yogi transcends all doubts, emotions and pairs of opposites. He is contended with whatever he gets by chance. Free from envy, he treats both success and failure equally (4.22). He is untouched by sin, just as the lotus-leaf by water. Mentally renouncing all actions and self-controlled, he lives in the body untouched by the consequences of his actions (5.13). Those who do not practice true renunciation suffer from the consequences of their actions. Pleasant, unpleasant and mixed, says Gita, are the results arising from their actions. God Himself practices renunciation in a sattvic manner. He performs actions even though He is complete and He has no desires.

Truly speaking, in terms of attitude and approach a *karmayogi* is not much different from a *sanyasi*. A *karmayogi* is a *sanyasi* in attitude and a *sanyasi* is a *karmayogi* in action. In both cases, action and renunciation are well integrated. A true *karmayogi* acts and lives with the attitude of a *sanyasi*, while a true *sanyasi* performs actions with the attitude of a true *karmayogi*. Both perform desireless actions, without any expectations and remain contented with whatever fruit that has been gained unsought. They are not troubled by either positive or negative gain. They are not elated when they unite with the sense objects or disengage from them. They react to pain and pleasures alike, knowing the fleeing nature of our existence and our bondage to the cycle of births and deaths. They are free from jealousy and such afflictions of the mind and remain inwardly detached from the noise and attractions of the worldly life. Though they participate in the affairs of the world, they control their senses and develop the ability to withdraw themselves from the sense objects at will. In this manner, a *karmayogi* lives like a *sanyasi* in thought and a *sanyasi* like a *karmayogi* in deed.

The *Bhagavadgita* provides a glimpse of how a true *sanyasi* lives and thinks. In the fifth chapter, we are informed, "Whether in seeing, hearing, touching, smelling, tasting, walking, sleeping or breathing, while performing actions a true *sanyasi* thinks that he is doing nothing at all. And when he is performing his bodily functions, he knows that only his senses are dealing with the sense objects." (5.8-9). Thus, a true *sanyasi* is but a *karmayogi* in daily life. A true *sanyasi* is God centered. His thoughts revolve around God and he thinks of God as he performs his actions. He performs his obligatory duties with detachment and offers them to God as sacrificial offerings. He is not concerned with the result as he acknowledges God as the real doer and himself as a mere instrument. Despite his lack of interest in ownership, he does not abandon his duties towards himself, his family and his society. Sattvic in nature, he is compassionate and unconditional in his relationship with others. He considers his life as an offering to God, surrendering himself to Him completely. The impurities of life do not touch him, because he is detached, in control of his mind and senses and free from egoism. Because he renounces doer-ship and acknowledges God as the real doer, he remains untouched by sin.

The *Bhagavadgita* declares renunciation as the highest form of spiritual discipline because peace follows renunciation immediately (12.12). The attitude of renunciation is well evident in the life and activities of Lord Krishna himself. Though he led a luxurious life, seemingly enjoying the privileges of royalty as the head of a clan, he was inwardly detached. He stood on the side of righteousness and destroyed demons and evil people, with a sense of duty rather than vindictiveness. In the epic *Mahabharata* while the various characters flit across the screen displaying tumultuous emotions, Lord Krishna remains calm and composed throughout. Truly, in Lord Krishna we find the perfect blend of a true *karmayogi* and *sanyasi*. You can bring into your life the spirit of renunciation practiced by Him by the following.

1. Performing obligatory duties
2. Knowing your essential nature
3. Identifying yourself with your inner Self
4. Acquiring knowledge and wisdom
5. Cultivating *sattva*
6. Practicing self-restraint and detachment
7. Offering your actions to God
8. Practicing devotion
9. Acknowledging God as the source of all
10. Cultivating intelligence

Symbolism in the Bhagavadgita

You may consider the *Bhagavadgita* a reference book on Hinduism. You do not have to read many scriptures to understand the tradition, which is considered eternal and divine. By reading the *Bhagavadgita* a few times with devotion and concentration, you will know the essential features of Hinduism better than most people who consider themselves Hindus. Lord Krishna was a great reformer. He incarnated upon earth to restore *dharma*, when it suffered a great decline due to the excesses of selfish kings, ignorance of worldly people and conflicting opinions of various scholars and ascetic schools. Lord Krishna revived the theistic elements of our tradition at a time when atheism and agnosticism were on the rise. He integrated diverse philosophies of the ancient wisdom and presented them together for the benefit of people in the form of the *Bhagavadgita*. You may consider the scripture a summary of the principles and practices of Hinduism, presented from a spiritual perspective for the liberation of those who are ready for it.

However, this scripture is not meant for religious propaganda. It is a book of duty, devotion and liberation. It is not meant to attract people from other faiths or confuse them with unfamiliar concepts. If you read the Gita, you know why this is important. In the Gita Lord Krishna Himself explicitly prohibits teaching the scripture to those who are not qualified for it. In other words, the *Bhagavadgita*, unlike the Bible, is not a missionary tool. Its knowledge is not for everyone. It is especially meant for those who are devotees of God, who have love and veneration for *Krishna* or *Vishnu* or *Isvara* and who are free from doubt and demonic nature. To follow it sincerely and benefit from it you must become pure like a clean mirror. To understand its percepts, your mind must be open and receptive to divine truths. You must have the discerning wisdom to know the right from wrong and reality from delusion. Liberation is not for everyone. If you are not naturally drawn to the subject of liberation, you should better focus on what you are good at and keep doing it dutifully until you get tired of it. This is the message of the *Bhagavadgita*. *Karmayoga* is the first step in our inner awakening because action, which is a form of dynamism (*caitainyam*), is the essential and inherent function of life. Your journey of liberation begins when you take your duties seriously and perform them selflessly. When your actions become offerings, your life takes a new turn. Your mind opens up and you begin to receive divine guidance, first imperceptibly, then clearly, and convincingly.

The antiquity of the scripture is uncertain. Whatever may be its true date, the philosophy contained in it is as old as the earliest of the *Upanishads*. We may consider it a compendium of the teachings of the *Vedas* and several schools of ancient philosophy that are now lost. While the teachings of Lord Krishna probably existed in a fragmented form in the Indian subcontinent since the later Vedic period, they might have been brought together as a scripture much later, probably after the death of the *Buddha*. Based upon the similarities in styles, according to some historians there are valid reasons to believe that the *Bhagavadgita* is a "genuine part" of the *Mahabharata*. As a scripture in its current form, it probably existed since 400 B.C.E. Its ascendance might be in response to the growing popularity of Buddhism and Jainism, at a time when the Mathura region, the birthplace of Lord Krishna, came under the influence of foreign rulers like *Sakas* and the *Kushanas*.

The *Bhagavadgita* is probably one of the most dissected, discussed and debated scriptures of Hinduism. In its message, it is more organized than the *Upanishads* and in comparison, it is easier to read and understand. Unlike the earliest *Upanishads*, such as the *Brihadaranyaka Upanishad*, it is more intent on the subject of liberation and self-transformation rather than the cryptic ritual symbolism and its associated terminology. Divided into 18 chapters of varying lengths, it contains 700 verses (according to some versions 699), which deal with various subjects such as the Self, the body and the senses, the field of Nature, Supreme Self, rebirth, *gunas* or qualities, liberation, devotion, surrender and so on.

The scripture is a purifier. Those who read its verses regularly find it very inspiring and enlightening. Some of the verses and phrases found in it make an excellent subject for contemplation and meditation, besides providing great insight into the nature of our lives and the means to liberation. If you read it every day, you are bound to feel the difference in your thinking and attitude. If you are in difficulties, you can use the book to find answers to your vexing problems. If you keep referring to it regularly, gradually you will gain peace and stability. You will not come to the *Bhagavadgita* and understand its percepts, unless you have done some good *karma* in the past and earned enough merit. As Lord Krishna said in the *Gita*, there is no loss in this effort. Even if you have put in some effort in the past, it will show up at the right time in your life and lead you in the right direction. It may not be appropriate to read the scripture with the expectation of some gain. However, if you begin reading it occasionally, you will gradually become aware of the importance of overcoming desires and performing actions for the sake of God rather than for yourself.

Do not be fooled by the apparent meaning of some verses or the archaic phrases you find in it whose meaning we have lost. It is just one aspect of it. People may interpret its verses in various ways, but what you understand from it is important because it reflects your own spiritual growth and inner transformation. I may tell you that the scripture is about monism or qualified monism, but you must arrive at it by your own convictions and feel it in your heart. The scripture offers you ample freedom to interpret its doctrine. Hence, scholars from every school of philosophy found in it enough evidence to justify their own arguments. To understand it clearly, you also need to know some important concepts of Hinduism, such as *karma*, Self, rebirth, yoga, Nature and so on. Some of the verses are also constructed like the *sutras*. You have to use your knowledge and imagination to fill in the blanks and understand their meaning.

Some of its verses are difficult to understand because the meaning and usage of certain words and phrases are either lost or changed overtime. You may also find that the chapter titles may not adequately represent the content presented by them. The scripture also contains some hidden symbolism. Even a seemingly inconsequential verse may contain some latent meaning, discernible only to a few. Conceived originally as a text within another text (the *Mahabharata*), it is presented as a conversation between Lord Krishna and Arjuna in the middle of the battlefield. While on the surface it may appear as a religious conversation, hidden within its verses you will find parallels between the main percepts of Hinduism and their symbolic representation. It is not clear whether it was intentional or coincidental, but the following striking examples of symbolism indicate that the scripture has a far deeper spiritual significance than what it presents superficially to the ordinary readers.

The title

Bhagavadgita means the song of the glorious Lord (*bhagavat*). It is derived from the Sanskrit word, *bhaga*, the equivalent of *"baga"* of Old Persian and *"bog"* of Slavic languages, meaning lord or god. The modern name *"Baghdad,"* meaning god-given is derived from Persian root word *"baga"* only. *Bhagavan*, another derivative word refers to Godhead endowed with six supreme qualities, namely strength, fame, wealth, knowledge, beauty and detachment. *Bhaga* is the name of one of the twelve solar deities (*Adityas*) of the Vedic pantheon. He is mentioned in the *Vedas* as the god of wealth and marriage. Known for his brilliance, he is mentioned in the *Rigveda* as the god who rewards people according to their merit. *Bhaga* also means wealth, prosperity, lordship, virtue, pleasure, enjoyment, beauty, dignity and distinction, which are usually the qualities, associated with God or someone in a position of great power and authority such as a divine king. Bhaga also means radiance or light used as an adjective in reference to fire or the sun.

Bhagavad means glorious, illustratious, powerful, divine, venerable and holy. *Bhagavadgita* is therefore a glorious song or a holy song. According to the *Vaishnava* tradition, the devotees of Krishna are of two types, simple devotees (*bhaktas*) and servants of devotees. The latter are known as the *bhāgavatas*, specially chosen or appointed by God to serve His devotees selflessly. The *Bhagavadgita* is not only a song about duty, devotion and liberation but also about how one may learn to serve the Lord by becoming a true *bhāgavata*, performing selfless actions in His service and offering their fruit to Him only. The *bhāgavatas* exemplify the principles of the yoga of knowledge (*jnana*), action (*karma*), devotion (*bhakti*) and renunciation (*sanyasa*). They perform actions with surrender, detachment and devotion without the expectation of reward or result. They simply obey the instructions of God with humility and submission. You may compare them to the *Bodhisattvas* of Buddhism, who delay their own liberation to render selfless service to the humankind out of pure compassion.

We may consider the *Bhagavadgita* a sacred song of God for the devotees and the servants of (the devotees of) God. It is not meant for everyone, but only for those who have faith, love and devotion to God and who are willing to give up everything and surrender to Him. In the scripture itself, Lord Krishna declares that of all the people, His devotees are dearest to him; however even among His devotees, He declares that none is dearer to Him than those who teach the Gita to His devotees. Thus, the Gita offers two choices to those who pursue its knowledge, to become a devotee (*bhakti*) or a servant (to the devotees) of God (*bhagavata*).

Kurukshetra

The dialogue between Arjuna and Lord Krishna took place in the battlefield of *Kurukshetra*, which is also known popularly as a holy land (*dharmakshetram*). It is holy because it is saturated with the blood of several great warriors (*yodhas*) and eminent souls (*mahatmas*) who fought and died in the performance of their duties. The location chosen for the occasion was not accidental. The *Bhagavadgita* was purposefully delivered in the middle of a battlefield and in a sacred place. Lord Krishna, being the Supreme Self and the Knower of past and future, would have chosen any other place to deliver the message. He would have anticipated the reaction of Arjuna and given him the counseling even before arriving at the battlefield; but he purposefully chose the battlefield to deliver a strong message about the nature of human life and our struggles against Nature's unrelenting forces. In the battlefield of life, we all are warriors. The Gita is appropriate and useful for everyone who wants to participate in this battle and become a divine warrior. Symbolically, *Kurukshetra* represents the field (*kshetra*), otherwise known as the body, the earth, Nature and world itself. These four aspects of our material existence have one thing in common: they are subject to the modification of the *gunas* and they keep the souls in bondage.

The body is a battlefield, in which the *gunas* wage a constant battle for their predominance, while the soul remains imprisoned. The conflict among the *gunas* manifests in us as a conflict between good and evil intentions and between pure and impure thoughts. The divine and demonic qualities arise in us because of them only. *Sattva* represents divinity and purity. *Rajas* and *tamas* represent egoism, darkness and delusion. The same conflict happens in the outside world also. Life is a hardship because we have to deal with many obstacles in our struggle for existence. If we are looking for liberation, we have to struggle even more. If we want to lead pure and austere lives, we have to overcome our evil tendencies. It is possible only if we deal with them with the firmness of a warrior, the wisdom of an enlightened yogi, the austerity of a *karmayogi* and the noble attitude of a person of renunciation. In the *Bhagavadgita*, Lord Krishna Himself described the body as the field (*kshetra*) and the Self as the Knower of the field (*kshetrajna*). If you are on the path of liberation, the first thing that you need to deal with is your attachment with your body and your dependence upon it for your identify and individuality. You have to support and promote good thoughts and intentions in you so that eventually you will overcome your own demons and become equal to all the modifications that arise in you. The battlefield was therefore appropriately selected for the discourse to remind us that in this great war of our lives, we have to fight our own battles both individually and collectively against our painful afflictions (*klesas*), evil tendencies and demonic qualities, with the help of God and the practice of yoga.

Krishna and Arjuna

Lord Krishna and Arjuna, the two principal characters of the *Bhagavadgita*, represent the two fundamental dualities of creation in the microcosm of a living being (*jiva*) and in the macrocosm of the Universal Being. In the macrocosm, Arjuna stands for the individual Self and Lord Krishna for the Supreme Self. In the microcosm, Arjuna stands for the ego-self and Lord Krishna for the inner Self or the eternal Self. Arjuna personifies egoism, worldliness, delusion, and ignorance, while Lord Krishna the immortal, and indestructible Self. The conversation between the two represents the reflection of the transcendental knowledge in the purified *citta* (consciousness) of an individual in a state of self-absorption. It is the reflection of the Knower of the Field in the field itself, whereby one overcomes delusion and becomes aware of the inner Self and the need for liberation. In a state of duality, Lord Krishna is the subject, Arjuna is the object and the *Gita* is the connecting link. Historically, Lord Krishna and Arjuna are referred to as the primeval being (*nara*) and the eternal Self (*Narayana*). They signify the relationship between man and God. Their relationship is not one-sided. It is one of mutual love and respect. When human beings love God and worship Him with devotion, God responds even more by showering His love and grace upon them. He provides them with knowledge, helps them in their liberation and gives them an exalted place in His Abode, higher than what He accords to the gods and the celestial beings in the creation.

The chariot and the Charioteer

You can see a similar theme hidden in the symbolism of the chariot. Before the discourse began, we learn that both Lord Krishna and Arjuna entered the battlefield in a chariot. Krishna was driving it, while Arjuna was sitting inside it as a passenger with his bow and arrows. This imagery has obvious implications. You can compare the chariot to the human body or the field. You, the eternal soul, enter the battlefield of life in a body, the chariot. The two wheels on which it runs represent the wheel of *dharma* and the wheel of *karma*. The spokes in the wheels represent the diversity, duality, divisions and the pairs of opposites inherent in our existence. Arjuna represents the embodied self (*jivatma*) and Lord Krishna the transcendental Self (*paramatma*). We may compare the horses to the sense organs and the reins to the limbs of yoga. The overall symbolism of the chariot and its occupants suggests that to win against adverse forces in the battlefield of life, you need to perform your duties, restraining your senses with the help of God, and allow Him to direct your life according to His Will. When you surrender to Him fully and unconditionally giving over to Him the reins of your life, He will take personal responsibility for you and your actions and guide you in the right direction towards liberation.

Sanjaya and Dhritarashtra

The *Bhagavadgita* begins with a question from *Dhritarashtra* and an answer from *Sanjaya*. Those who are familiar with the *Mahabharata* know that *Sanjaya* was appointed by *Dhritarashtra*, at the behest of *Vyasa*, to act as his official commentator and give him a firsthand account of the events in the battlefield with his clairvoyance. *Dhritarashtra*, as a blind king, personifies egoism, ignorance and delusion. *Sanjaya*, with his knowledge and supernatural abilities (*siddhis*) personifies discriminating intelligence (*buddhi*) or wisdom. Both aspects are part of the field (body) and this worldly (*apara*), in contrast to Lord Krishna and Arjuna, who represent the transcendental reality (*para*) as the individual Self and Supreme Self.

In terms of *gunas*, *Dhritarashtra* personifies the traits of *tamas*, Sanjaya *rajas* and Arjuna *sattva*, while Krishna embodies pure *sattva* (*suddha sattva*). *Dhritarashtra* lacked discrimination and thereby allowed his children to fall into evil ways and precipitate the war. From the question he posed to *Sanjaya*, it is clear that he was not at all interested in the dialogue between Arjuna and Lord Krishna. He just wanted to know what was happening in the battlefield and how his sons were preparing to fight. It was by chance that he happened to listen to the discourse; but from his reaction in the last chapter, we can discern that the entire teaching of the Gita had no impact upon Him, although he listened to it. In contrast, upon the completion of the discourse, *Sanjaya* was completely filled with rapturous joy.

In life, we get many opportunities to acquire knowledge that leads to our liberation; but if we are busy with our desires and attachments, we do not notice them. It was the same with *Dhritarashtra*. The discourse left no indelible influence upon him. He was fated to ignore it or not follow it because the *Kauravas* were already destined to die in the hands of their cousins as per the Divine Will.

Symbolism of the plot

The *Bhagavadgita* is a revelation. You find in it knowledge coming straight from God Himself. However, the scripture is not traditionally considered a revelatory scripture (*sruti*), a status, which is enjoyed only by the *Vedas*. This makes one wonder whether one should take this scripture seriously at all. If it is not an important scripture, one wonders why it has been held in such high esteem by the scholars of Hinduism on par with the *Upanishads* and the *Brahmasutras*. The answer is hidden in the scripture itself in the manner in which the narrative has been built and structured around the four important characters, namely Lord

Krishna, Arjuna, *Sanjaya* and *Dhritarashtra*. Although the scripture is a dialogue between Lord Krishna and Arjuna, it was heard by *Sanjaya* and conveyed to *Dhritarashtra*. Thus, technically the scripture qualifies as a sruti text because firstly, it came directly from God and secondly, it was composed after it was heard psychically by a few from the mouth of God. As a result, it became part of the human wisdom.

Symbolism of the participants

In the *Bhagavadgita*, the verses are attributed to four principal personalities, namely Lord Krishna, Arjuna, *Sanjaya*, and *Dhritarashtra*. Symbolically they represent the four states of consciousness, four levels of knowledge and four methods of validating truth and four methods in which knowledge is transmitted. *Dhritarashtra* represents the wakeful state (*vaisvanara*); *Sanjaya* represents the dream state (*taijasa*); Arjuna represents the deep sleep state (*prajna*); and Lord Krishna represents the transcendental state (*turiya*), which is described by the *Upanishads* as the state of Brahman.

There are four levels of knowledge, namely ignorance, lower knowledge, higher knowledge and transcendental knowledge. They are represented symbolically by *Dhritarashtra, Sanjaya*, Arjuna and Lord Krishna respectively. Ignorance is a state of delusion in which truth is not perceived at all. It is mental and spiritual darkness, in which one fails to discern right from wrong and truth from falsehood. Lower knowledge is the knowledge acquired by study, reason and observation. It is useful in the performance of obligatory duties and achieving worldly success, but not very useful in achieving liberation. Higher knowledge is the knowledge of the Self, which arises from inner purification and the practice of yoga. You can use it to practice yoga, cultivate virtue and develop discerning wisdom, but by itself, it does not give you a taste of the transcendental state. For that, you need to acquire transcendental knowledge, which comes in a state of concentrated self-absorption (*samyama*), after you perfect your practice of yoga and become an adept in it.

They also represent the four methods (*pramanas*) of ascertaining or validating truth, namely direct (*pratyaksa*), inference (*anumana*), comparison (*upamana*) and testimony (*sabda*). Not all traditions in Hinduism recognize these four. Some recognize only two or three. Of these, Lord Krishna represents the direct knowing because He is the Truth itself. Arjuna represents testimony (*sabda*) because he witnessed and heard the discourse directly from Lord Krishna, who is the source of all scriptures and revelations. Sanjaya represents inference (*anumana*), because he heard it indirectly from Lord Krishna through his psychic powers. Although he was not present at the battlefield personally, he inferred from the conversation that it happened between Lord Krishna and Arjuna. *Dhritarashtra* represents comparison, the fourth method of knowing truth, in which validation is done by comparing the knowledge one acquires with that, which one already has. *Dhritarashtra* was already prejudiced against Lord Krishna and Arjuna. Therefore, he did not pay much attention to the conversation that took place between them. He measured the teachings with his own beliefs and prejudices and ignored it.

Let us now turn our attention to the manner in which divine knowledge is transmitted to the human beings from heavenly heights. Divine knowledge flows to us in four distinct ways, direct, intuitive, indirect and memorial. In some instances, God appears before certain individuals and speaks to them directly. This is the direct method. In the *Bhagavadgita*, Arjuna received divine knowledge from Lord Krishna directly in this manner. In some cases, knowledge is transmitted through dreams and intuition. This is also a direct method, but you do not see God physically. Sanjaya received knowledge in this manner. History is replete with instances where men received divine messages through their psychic powers or in dream states. Many spiritual truths have been rendered into religious verses in this manner. Sanjaya was like the Vedic seers who composed the *Vedas* by hearing them in their minds. He received the entire *Gita* intuitively with his mind's eye. In the third method, knowledge comes to us indirectly through scriptures, spiritual masters and enlightened people. *Dhritarashtra* received knowledge in this manner. The method was appropriate for him because by nature he was ignorant and deluded. His blindness symbolically stands for his spiritual blindness. Most people in the world are drawn to spiritual subjects in this manner. The teaching of the *Bhagavadgita* was finally composed by *Vyasa* based upon his ability to remember what transpired in the battlefield on that particular day between Lord Krishna and Arjuna. This is intellectual knowledge or the memorial knowledge, which is reflected in the intelligence as knowledge and wisdom.

Lord Krishna represents transcendental knowledge, which does not require any transmission because it is free from the duality of subject and object and the process of knowing. It is an eternal knowledge, which can be neither learned nor acquired, and which can be known within oneself in a state of self-absorption. In the wakeful state, this knowledge can only be inferred but cannot be ascertained through intellectual analysis or empirical proof.

Lastly, we have to remember that the entire conversation took place in the middle of the battlefield, where a multitude of people, on both sides, stood with their respective weapons, ready to fight. They had no clue what happened between Lord Krishna Arjuna. They did not know why the two stood in the middle of the battlefield conversing. Their minds were seized with the thoughts of war. Their attention was focused upon winning against their enemies. They were busy preparing for the war. Symbolically the armies of *Pandavas* and *Kauravas* represent the humanity in general. A vast majority of people who live upon earth do not care for their liberation. They live in their egoistic and ignorant ways incurring *karma*. Even if great souls come and try to put sense into their minds, they simply ignore them and continue their mundane existence. They fail to realize that human birth is a precious gift and a great opportunity to escape from the cycle of births and deaths.

Symbolism of sorrow

The first chapter of the scripture is titled "Arjuna's yoga of sorrow." The whole discourse begins in response to Arjuna's sorrow, which symbolically stands for human suffering. Suffering opens our eyes to the truths of our existence and the needs for our liberation. Arjuna's suffering led him on a spiritual path in which he was given an opportunity to understand the causes of human suffering and find effective solutions for it without escaping from the harsh realities of life. We have discussed the significance of human sorrow and the symbolism of Arjuna's sorrow in another essay in this book. Therefore, discussion on this topic is not continued further here.

The Bhagavadgita in Daily Life

A scripture is useful only when you can relate it to your life and use its knowledge and wisdom to resolve your problems and deal with your suffering. The *Bhagavadgita* contains ageless practical wisdom, which you can use to expand your awareness, purify your consciousness and nurture compassion and devotion in your heart. The scripture is a manifestation (*vibhuti*) of Lord Krishna. By studying it sincerely, you enter into a conversation with Him and open your heart to His purifying influence. His message is clear about its purpose. It is meant for those who want to escape forever from the bonds of earthly life that is stifling and limiting in many ways. It tells you how to deal with the unpleasant aspects of your life, without ignoring your duty, and remain focused on your liberation following the essential principles of yoga that lead you towards it. The following suggestions are gleaned from the *Bhagavadgita*. They help those who want to bring the eternal wisdom of the *Bhagavadgita* into their daily lives.

Share your knowledge with others: Knowledge is central to our liberation. We are stuck here because of our ignorance and the belief that our perceptual knowledge is reliable. The *Bhagavadgita* cautions us against this. Lord Krishna says that we should not only know the truth ourselves but also help others know it to the extent possible. Teaching the knowledge of the Gita is in itself a source of liberation. He states clearly that those who teach the knowledge of the *Bhagavadgita* are the dearest to Him and thereby implies the importance He attaches to the act of teaching. The purpose of this teaching is not to proselytize but liberate ignorant people from the cycle of births and deaths. You should also do it without any expectation or reward. You do not have to be an expert on the scripture to teach it. You do not have to be a guru. Teach whatever you know from your study and understanding. Share your knowledge with your family members, especially children. Participate in discussions and gatherings (*satsangs*), where the scripture is discussed, and let others know what you know. You may even distribute copies of the scripture free. It is also important to teach it only to those who qualify and who are ready. The Gita is very clear about this. It says that you should not teach it to those who do not believe in God, who are disrespectful to Him and who are by nature violent and impure.

Delve deep into the scripture: The scripture reveals itself to the extent you probe into it. Your understanding of it grows as you progress on the path and increase *sattva* in your mind and body. You can delve deep into the knowledge of the *Bhagavadgita* by studying it regularly. With regular study, you become stabilized in the knowledge of the Self and contemplation of God. Your mind opens to the wisdom hidden in the universe. Therefore, let the scripture be your source of guidance and inspiration. Study it regularly. Read at least a few verses every day. Refer to it whenever you are in doubt. Learn from others the subtle nuances of the text. As you imbibe its knowledge, you will experience a great transformation in your thinking and attitude, which you may not even notice in the earlier stages. You begin to think about God more frequently and open your mind to higher knowledge. With regular study, you also earn the grace of God as vouched by Lord Krishna Himself in the scripture.

Know what others are saying about it. If you do not have time to study the scripture, you may improve your knowledge of the scripture by listening to others and attending to discourses and gatherings (*satsangs*), where knowledgeable people meet and discuss its wisdom and teachings. Nowadays you can also get audio video tapes on the subject and listen to them in your spare time. Listening provides you with a good opportunity to silence your mind and open yourself to the knowledge of the scripture letting go of your thoughts, opinions, ideas and judgment. You can make your act of hearing an act of surrender and a means to practice detachment and sacrifice, and cultivate *sattva*.

Virtue still matters in life. Virtue is the foundation of spiritual life. It is the foremost among human aims. It stems not from

Nature but from your knowledge and wisdom. Your humanity is part of it. It is what sets you apart from animals and other creatures. Without virtue, you cannot bring light and wisdom into your life. In recent times, the world has grown so complex that it is not possible anymore to draw a clear distinction between right and wrong. In these difficult times, we must aim to keep our heads clear and know the distinction between truth and falsehood to avoid falling into the trap of stretching the truth and rationalizing our actions for temporary gains. If you believe in God and afterlife, you must believe in the importance of virtue and the need for honesty and integrity in your thoughts and actions. The *Bhagavadgita* helps you realize the importance of moral purity and the need to live virtuously, serving God and Truth.

Be generous: One should not live selfishly for oneself alone or for one's own interests, relations and attachments. It is a self-destructive choice fraught with many dangers. However, most people do live selfishly, without showing any concern for others or their welfare. They do it even after they know that they live here temporarily and their actions bear fruit. One of the lessons we learn from the *Bhagavadgita* is we should live selflessly and do our duties not for ourselves but for others. There is a greater joy in transcending our selfishness and helping others. We do it effectively when we realize our oneness with God and the rest of the creation. We can serve God and His creation in many ways. As the name suggests, the scripture is meant for the guidance of the *Bhagavatas*, the true servants of God. They are dearer to God. You can become a *bhagavata* by performing selfless actions and help others in the service of God. When you serve others, you serve God. Helping others without expectations, you earn His grace and love.

Cultivate divine qualities: We can progress in whatever direction we want. With hard work and persistence, we can reach whatever goals we set for ourselves. Our minds manifest out dominant thoughts and desires. We have the ability to increase light or darkness in us. Therefore, we have to live responsibly, cultivating right thinking and attitude with the scripture as our guide. If you want to be closer to God, you must cultivate the qualities that are ascribed to Him. You must reflect godly qualities in your thoughts and actions so that the godliness hidden in you grows in strength and brings your transformation. If you are pure in your mind and heart, you will reflect the radiance of the Self through you. Therefore, in your thoughts and actions express the best and the highest in you and make your body a temple of God.

Seek the help of God: In living your life, you have many choices. What happens to you depends upon what you do with your free will and your freedom. You can either spend your whole life seeking and striving on your own or surrender to God and live your life as He decides it for you. You can either take the driver's seat on the highway of life or sit in the backseat and allow God to guide you as your charioteer. In all these, you have a choice. You can live for yourself or you can live for God, giving Him the ownership and doership of your actions and possessions. The best way to invite God into your life is to remember Him in whatever you do and attribute all your successes and failures to Him, assuming that He is working through you and using every opportunity in your life to let Him express through you and live in you. Although you have the freedom to exercise your free will, since your knowledge is limited, you may not always make right choices or choose wisely. You can deal with this problem by inviting God into your life and making Him your guide and benefactor. Through prayers and supplications, you can consult Him to resolve your problems and seek guidance.

See the sacred presence of God everywhere: The *Bhagavadgita* declares that God is the Creator of all worlds and beings. He is the Creator, Preserver and Destroyer. He manifests here variously and pervades the whole world. No one knows the true extent of His greatness or vastness. There is no end to His manifestations. Even all this represents but a little fragment of Him. One of the first steps to bring God into your life is to acknowledge Him as the source of all. Arjuna saw the universal form of God. We do see it every day; but we are too hardened in our minds to accept this whole creation around us as the universal form of God. However, if you are wise, you can use this knowledge to feel the sacred presence of God everywhere as if you are living inside a huge temple where every form is an aspect of Him. You can see His numerous manifestations and treat them with reverence and respect. As the scripture declares those who know the omnipresence of God worship Him with great devotion. The knowledge gives them an opportunity to stabilize their minds on the numerous forms of God and experience oneness with Him. Whether you find yourself or God in whatever you perceive, eventually both lead to freedom.

Know what sacrifice and renunciation means: The discourse of the *Bhagavadgita* begins in response to Arjuna's decision to renounce dutiful actions to avoid killing his own relations and follow a safer option by living like an ascetic and begging for alms. In life, we do not always get an opportunity to choose our actions. At times, we may have to perform both pleasant and unpleasant actions as the situations demand. The *Bhagavadgita* suggests that we should not run away from these situations and we should not renounce actions in the name of renunciation simply because they are emotionally taxing. True renunciation is renunciation of desires hidden in the action and true sacrifice is giving up the desire for the result. We can apply these two principles in our lives and perform our duties with detachment to deal with our suffering arising from unpleasant situations and work for our liberation. By applying these principles, we can live our lives peacefully without being crushed by the weight of our materialistic goals or our own desires and attachments.

Know the distinction between the body and the soul: The *Bhagavadgita* teaches you a very fundamental lesson about your own essential nature. It states very clearly that you are not your mind and body, but a divine soul who is caught in the web of Nature and bound to them by circumstances. You duty is to find a way out of this predicament and free yourself so that you can live eternally without bound to Nature or the cycle of births and deaths. Although most of us are aware of our spiritual nature, we do not acknowledge it or reflect it adequately in our thinking and attitude. Frankly, we do not consider ourselves divine souls. If this were not true, people would not be so preoccupied with their physical features or the class distinctions that set us apart. By studying the scripture and assimilating its knowledge, we can bring a paradigm shift in our awareness, accepting ourselves as divine souls and shifting our attention from physical to the mental and then to the spiritual.

See the role of God in every aspect of your life. If God is the source of all, it follows that He is also the source of our lives, actions and destinies. When we take pride in our achievements and feel depressed about our failures, we not only ignore the role of God but also fail to realize the significance of our actions and their consequences. In seeking things out of egoism and desires, we also allow our actions to shape our destinies and sow the seeds of our future lives. You must attribute to God both the positive and negative results arising from your actions, and accept them as the work of God and the manifestation of His inviolable will. You must surrender to the events that unfold in your life with equanimity accepting them as learning opportunities. Most importantly, you must open yourself to life and stop fighting with yourself for your failures and disappointments.

Focus on the effort not the result: We are mostly consumed by the expectations of what we want to accomplish rather than what actions we need to perform to meet our obligations. The Bhagavadgita says this is a flawed approach, which leads to suffering, fear, anxiety and disappointment. If you want peace, you must set aside your expectations and silence your desires. You can have goals, but your attention should be primarily on the effort or on doing the task rather than on its outcome. If you focus on the task, good results will follow automatically. Even if they do not, you will have the satisfaction that you have done whatever that was necessary. We have no control on what may happen or how our actions may turn out to be; but we can always control our actions and perform them diligently. The *Bhagavadgita* rightly advises us to perform our actions dutifully without desiring their outcome. When we focus on the results, we feel anxious. When we focus on the tasks, we become attentive and determined. When we focus on the techniques and the processes rather than on the results, our performance improves vastly. We also become confident and show greater willingness to undertake difficult and even unpleasant tasks for the sake of duty.

Be cheerful: Contended people are happier than those who take life seriously and demand too much from life. We enter this world with nothing. They we begin to accumulate things, relationships, thoughts, opinions and possessions. At some stage, life becomes burdensome. The weight of our own actions and their consequences begins to wear us out. We become serious about our actions, our identities and ourselves. We demand answers and solutions to problems we cannot resolve. We forget the journey as we focus upon our goals. We stop enjoying life and the opportunities we get to experience it fully. The *Bhagavadgita* advises us to lighten up and not to take our lives too seriously or selfishly. Instead of becoming attached to things, we should live like lotus plants in the waters of life unencumbered by its burdens. Renunciation does not means you have to live a life of depression. Actually, renunciation is supposed to unburden you and lighten you up so that you can live freely without worrying and feeling anxious about your life or your future. When you practice detachment, you become free from the bouts of depression and mood swings that are consequential to a life of desire-ridden actions.

Worship the Highest. Whom you worship has a bearing upon the quality of your life and experiences. You pursue what you worship and it eventually catches up with you and becomes part of you and your life. From the *Bhagavadgita* we learn that we should not worship material things, because it leads to attachment, delusion and bondage. Some people worship material things, such as name and fame, and fall down into lower worlds. Some people worship dark and evil beings ghosts, spirits and other beings of sunless worlds. Some worship divinities through sacrifices seeking their intervention and blessings. It is at least better than the other two types of worship mentioned before. However, better than all these is the worship of the Supreme Self. One may worship God in any form; but the best way to do it is to worship Him as the Highest Self. Alternatively, you may worship Him as your inner Self (*Isvara*). Both the approaches are recommended in our scriptures and both are beneficent.

Bibliography

Aurobindo, Sri. Essays on the Gita, Lotus Press (WI), 1995.

Aurobindo, Sri, Baran, Anil Roy. Bhagavad Gita and Its Message, Lotus Press, 1996

Aurobindo, Sri. The Secret of the Veda, Sri Aurobindo Ashram, Pondicherry, 1990. First published in a monthly review Arya 1914-20.

Aurobindo, Sri. The Upanishads, Sri Aurobindo Ashram, Pondicherry, 1972.

Besant, Annie and Das, Bhagavan. The Bhagavad-Gita, With Sanskrit Text, free translation into English, a word-for-word translation, and an Introduction on Sanskrit Grammar, Thesophical Publishing Society, 1905.

Besant, Annie Wood. The Bhagavad Gita Or the Lord's Song, Kessinger Publishing, 2005.

Bhawuk, Dharm P. S. Spirituality and Indian Psychology: Lessons from the Bhagavad-Gita, Springer, New York, 2011.

Byrd, Charles Michael. The Bhagavad-Gita in Black and White: From Mulatto Pride to Krishna Consciousness, Backintyme Publishing, 2007.

Chakravarti, Rajagopalachari. Bhagavad-Gita, Bharatiya Vidya Bhavan, 1967.

Chinmayananda, Swami. The Art of Man Making, 114 Short Talks on the Bhagwad Geeta, All India Chinmaya Yuva Kendra, 2000.

The Contemporary essays on the Bhagavad Gita (Siddharth Indian studies series), Siddharth Publications, 1995.

Dass, Ram. Paths to god: living the Bhagavad Gita, Harmony Books, 2004

Dayananda, Swami. Teaching Of The Bhagavadgita, Vision Books, Mar 1, 2005.

Easwaran, Eknath. The Bhagavad Gita, Read How You Want, 2010.

Edgerton, Franklin . The Bhagavadgita Gita, Motilal Banarsidass Publ., 1994.

Feuerstein , Georg. The Deeper Dimension of Yoga: Theory and Practice, Shambhala, 2003.

Giri, Satyeswarananda (Swami). Bhagavad Gita: Interpretation of Sriyukteswar, Sanskrit Classics, 1991.

Hawley, Jack. The Bhagavad Gita: A Walkthrough for Westerners, New World Library, 2001.

Judge, William Q. Bhagavad-Gita combined with Essays on the Gita, Theosophical Univ Pr., 1979.

Judge, William Quan. Bhagavad-Gita: Combined With His Essays On The Gita (Buddhist Tradition S.), New Age Books, 2002.

Kezwer, Glen P. The Essence of the Bhagavad Gita: Course Manual, CreateSpace, 2009.

Krishnananda, Swami. The philosophy of the Bhagavadgita, Divine Life Society, 2000.

Krishnaswami, O. R. The Bhagavad Gita: The Divine Message. Lightning Source, 2006.

Lasater, Judith Hanson. Living Your Yoga: Finding the Spiritual in Everyday Life, Rodmell Press, 1999.

Lipner, Julius. Fruits of Our Desiring: Enquiry Into the Ethics of the Bhagawad Gita, Bayeux Arts, Inc., 1996.

Lipner, Julius. The Bhagavadgītā for our times, Oxford University Press, 1997.

Mahajan, Yogi. Geeta Enlightened, Motilal Banarsidass Publishers (Pvt. Ltd), 2002.

Mahesh Yogi, Maharishi. Bhagavad-Gita, MIU Press, 1976.

Majumdar, Sachindra Kumar. The Bhagavad Gita: a scripture for the future, Asian Humanities Press, 1991

Malinar, Angelika. The Bhagavadgita: Doctrines and Contexts, Cambridge University Press, 2009.

Mathai, P.S. A Christian approach to the Bhagavadgita, Y.M.C.A. Pub. House, 1956.

Minor, Robert. Modern Indian interpreters of the Bhagavadgita, State University of New York Press, 1986.

Modi, Mohanlal Prataprai. The Bhagavadgita: a fresh approach, Modi, 1995.

Nicolas, Antonio de. Bhagavad Gita: The Ethics of Decision-Making, Ibis Press/Nicolas Hays, 2004.

Panda, N.C.Bhagavad Gita, Dk Printworld Private Limited, 2009.

Pani, Susmit Prasad and Satpathy, Geeta. Gandhi-Aurobindo and Radhakrishnan on Bhagavadgita, Kunal Books Publishers & Distributors, 2009.

Patton, Laurie L. The Bhagavad Gita, Penguin, 2008

Perrett, Roy W. Hindu ethics: a philosophical study, University of Hawaii Press, 1998.

Prabhupada, Swami Bhaktivedanta. Bhagavad-Gita As It Is, The Bhaktivedanta Book Trust, 1989.

Purohit, (Swami) and Burroughs, Kendra Crossen, Series Editor: Harvey, Andrew. Bhagavad Gita: annotated & explained, SkyLights Paths Publishing, 2001.

Radhakrishnan, Sarvepalli. Indian Philosophy, Vol. 1, Oxford University Press, 2000.

Ramacharaka, Yogi. The Bhagavad gita: or, The message of the master, Compiled and adapted from numerous old and new translations of the Original Sanskrit Text, The Yogi Publication Society, 1907

Ranade, Ramchandra Dattatraya. The Bhagavadgītā as a philosophy of God-realisation: being a clue through the labyrinth of modern interpretations, Bharatiya Vidya Bhavan, 1965.

Row, T. Subba. the Philosophy of the Bhagavad-Gita, Theosophical Publishing House, Adyar, Madras, India, 1921.

Sastri, A. Mahadeva. The Bhagavad-Gita, with the commentary of Sri Sankaracharya, G.T.A. Printing Works, Mysore, 1901.

Sharma, Arvind. New essays in the Bhagavadgītā: philosophical, methodological, and cultural approaches, Books & Books, 1987.

Sharma, Ishwar Chandra. Ethical philosophies of India, Harper & Row, 1970.

Sharma, Mahesh B. Bhagavad gita: a journey from the body to the soul, Authorhouse, 2005.

Sinha, Phulgenda. The Gita as it was: rediscovering the original Bhagavadgita, Open Court, 1987.

Telang, K.T. The Bhagavadgita, Atlantic Publishers and Distributors, 1990

Thomas, P.M. 20th century Indian interpretations of Bhagavadgita:

Tilak, Gandhi, and Aurobindo, Published for the Christian Institute for the Study of Religion and Society, Bangalore, by I.S.P.C.K., 1987.

Tirtha, Swami Sadashiva, Bhagavad Gita for modern times commentary by, Sat Yuga Press, 2007.

V, Jayaram. The Bhagavadgita Complete Translation, Pure Life Vision LLC, 2011.

Virajeshver, Science of Bhagavadgita: a study of ancient wisdom through modern science, Spiritual India Pub. House, 1977.

Vishaka and Prabhupāda, Bhaktivedanta. Bhagavad Gita: A Photographic Essay, Torchlight Publishing, 2010.

Yardi, M. R. The Bhagavadgītā, as a synthesis, Bhandarkar Oriental Research Institute, 1991.

Yogananda, Paramhansa. Spiritual relationships, Crystal Clarity Publishers, 2007.

Pure Life Vision Books

The Bhagavadgita
Complete Translation

- Most comprehensive work on the Bhagavadgita in recent times
- Complete text with word for word translation
- Detailed commentary without sectarian bias
- Original and inspiring
- Authoritative and scholarly
- No of pages 874
- Dimensions: 6.14 x 9.21
- ISBN: 978-1-935760-04-7

Discounts up to 50% are available on bulk purchases. **Order your copy from** http://www.PureLifeVision.com

Pure Life Vision Books

The **Bhagavadgita**
A Simple Translation

- Abridged version
- Complete text with word for word translation
- Ideal for recitation and reference
- Perfect Bound (paperback), Cover Matte
- Page count: 304.
- Dimensions: 6.14 x 9.21.
- ISBN: 978-1-935760-17-7.

Discounts up to 50% are available on bulk orders. For bulk orders, please contact the publishers at the following link http://www.PureLifeVision.com

Pure Life Vision Books

Discounts up to 50% are available on bulk orders. **Order your copies from** http://www.PureLifeVision.com

Pure Life Vision Books
Think Success – Combined Volume

- Combined volume
- Contains 44 mind-expanding articles
- Comprehensive information on self-help
- Motivational, inspiring and uplifting
- Improves your self-awareness and confidence
- Prepares you for success and achievement
- Guides you to excellence
- No of pages 492
- Dimensions: 6 x 9
- ISBN: 978-1-935760-03-0
- Book type: Bound Blue Cloth w/Jacket on Creme

Discounts up to 50% are available on bulk orders. **Order your copy from http://www.PureLifeVision.com**

www.ingramcontent.com/pod-product-compliance
Lightning Source LLC
Chambersburg PA
CBHW030310080526
44584CB00012B/514